HIDDEN RIVERS OF GOLD

First Published in 2026 by Echo Books

Echo Books is an imprint of Superscript Publishing Pty Ltd

ABN 76 644 812 395

PO Box 669, Woodend, Victoria, 3442

www.echobooks.com.au

ISBN 978-1-923441-36-1

HIDDEN RIVERS OF GOLD

The rise and ruin of Victoria's deep leads

Peter McCarthy

echo)))
BOOKS

Table of Contents

IMAGE ENHANCEMENT NOTICE

Some images in this book have been reconstructed from historical originals of varying quality using modern AI-assisted enhancement. These techniques – such as super-resolution, noise reduction, colour correction, and detail recovery – help clarify and stabilise images that were otherwise faded, damaged, or indistinct.

All enhanced images have been reviewed by the author to ensure they remain faithful to the original source material.

The historical images used as a basis for reconstruction are all more than one hundred years old and are free from copyright.

LIST OF PICTURES AND MAPS

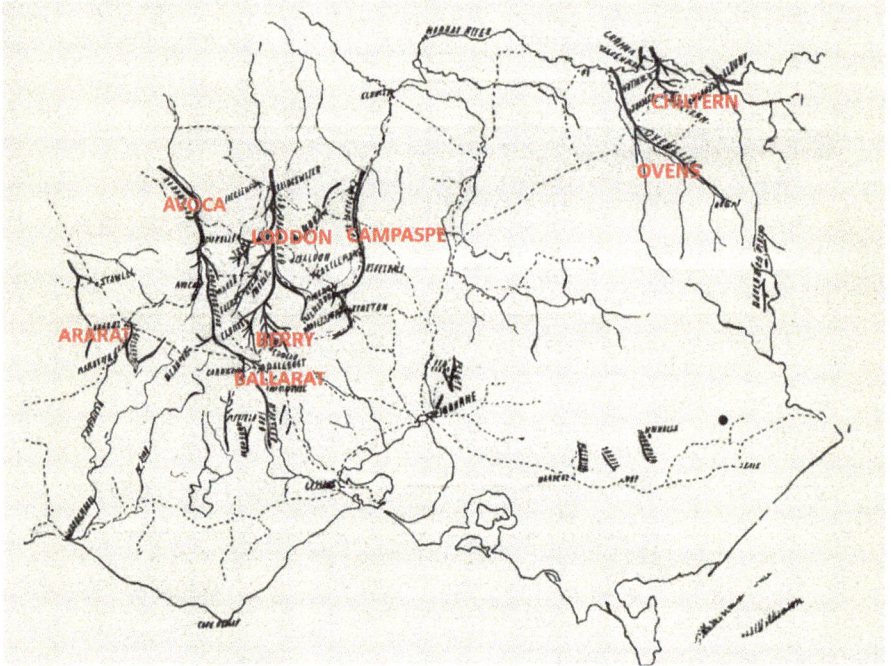

Figure 1 The principal deep lead fields of Victoria
after Wilkinson, 1905

Preface

THIS BOOK AROSE from my interest in the career of Herbert Hoover, a mining engineer who became the 31st President of the United States. In his autobiography Hoover described the mining operations at Moolort in Victoria, Australia as the greatest pumping operation in mining history. Moolort is just a half hour's drive from my home, so I visited the ruined sites of those mines and wanted to learn more. As I researched, I learned that Hoover was not an early principal character in the story but was later influential in encouraging investors to fund the huge pumping scheme and in making it happen.

In writing about the Moolort story it became apparent that I had to explain alluvial gold mining and particularly the methods used to follow the deep leads, which were buried riverbeds containing gold. I also had to present a sufficient history of alluvial gold mining to place the deep lead mines in their historical context. The story of John Phillips, an overlooked character who was the first person to try mining alluvial gold in Australia, seemed a fitting starting point.

As a young man in the 1970s I worked as a miner in many situations including timbering openings and sinking shafts, so I feel qualified to understand and hopefully able to explain the work that was done in the Victorian gold mines. I can also lay claim to being the last person in Victoria to build and commission a steam-powered stamp battery and a Cornish bob pump, at the Sovereign Hill outdoor museum more than 40 years ago. In my later career as a mining engineer, I was responsible for planning, reporting on and directing gold mines, so I have not ignored the corporate and financial aspects of the Moolort story.

I hope that the reader will be impressed, as I am, by the effort and ingenuity of the Victorian miners, engineers, managers and company promoters. The Moolort story is ultimately a story of failure, but they gave it a really good try!

Introduction

AFTER INITIAL ATTEMPTS to mine alluvial gold in South Australia in 1848, and the discovery of rich gold deposits and nuggets at Ballarat and Forest Creek in 1851, miners began following buried riverbeds deeper beneath the volcanic plains of central Victoria. Along the way, they developed new technologies and created jobs for thousands. While some mines struck great riches, encouraging speculation in new ventures, more often they spent years of effort and investors' money on mines that failed to deliver. Eventually, in the early 20th century at Moolort near Carisbrook, they encountered a vast sea of water that even the best engineers and geologists of the time could not overcome.

Gold and quartz originally formed together in deep underground veins, carried up and deposited by hot, high-pressure fluids from much deeper layers of the Earth. Over millions of years, erosion exposed and broke up the upper parts of these rich veins, leaving some gold on the surface or covered by a thin layer of soil. Some gold found its way into shallow streams, later buried under a few metres of sand and gravel. The diggers called these 'shallow leads' (pronounced *leeds*) because, when followed, they led to gold.[1]

Larger amounts of gold were carried along with boulders, sand, gravel, and clay into the beds of fast-flowing rivers and streams, later buried by erosion or volcanic flows up to a hundred metres deep or more, forming what the miners termed 'deep leads'. The deep leads were usually covered by a layer cake comprising multiple flows of basalt lava, with clay and gravel between, each from a different volcanic event stretching back hundreds of thousands of years.

More than 15,000 square kilometres of Victoria and South Australia are covered by volcanic lava flows and over 400 eruption points have been identified. The most recent eruption, at Mount Schank, occurred just 5,000 years ago and was witnessed by the Bunganditj people. Their creation story about the volcanic landscape was recorded by a local woman, Christina Smith, in 1880. Geologists believe that the volcanic province is still active and expect future eruptions in Victoria.[2]

The deep leads were saturated with water, with the surface of the water table often just a few metres below the ground. As the ancient rivers had no outlet, the water did not flow along them until miners attempted to pump out the water; then water could flow freely along the old stream to the pumps. As the gradient of the old riverbed was slight, it would flow equally from upstream or downstream.

The ancient riverbeds often contained boulders a metre or two in diameter, which the diggers had to work around. Usually, the gold had sunk to the bottom of the stream, so the material just above the bedrock, known as washdirt, was the richest. The washdirt ranged in thickness from just a few centimetres to a metre or two, and rarely to three or four metres. Sometimes there were two or more beds of washdirt separated by layers of clay. When this happened the upper clay layer was called a false bottom. Usually, the bedrock was soft, and gold had penetrated down into cracks, so the miners picked away deep underground to take out up to half a metre or so of the bedrock.

BALLARAT'S GEOLOGICAL HISTORY is distinctive; lava created a steep escarpment along the Yarrowee Creek's west side, burying the original land surface under 100 metres of basalt flows. This massive barrier lay above, and downstream of, gold-rich riverbeds and quartz reefs. Over millennia, erosion gradually filled the valley with a mixture of sand, gravel, and clay. As miners pursued the deep leads westward, they had to sink their shafts deeper, initially through the gravel and clay and then, once they reached the escarpment, through the basalt. A simple windlass and bucket were no longer adequate for the task.

The Ballarat deep leads were arguably the most historically important, followed by the Loddon group which included the Berry lead system near Creswick. In the northeast of Victoria there were Chiltern, Rutherglen, Harrietville and Buckland, while other areas included Bendigo, Langi Logan, Pitfield Plains, Stawell, Ararat, and a dozen or so other districts.[3]

The Loddon Deep Lead system had numerous tributaries, which included the rich Berry Leads and the Loddon and Moolort Leads. In ancient times the creeks around Creswick had joined a river that flowed northward parallel to today's Loddon River. Then volcanic vents poured out lava which smothered the deep gullies, filling the creeks and rivers, even covering the tops of hills, leaving a vast basalt plain. Buried deeply, along with the gold, were the charred and sometimes fossilised remains of native orchids, lilies and ferns, branches and giant tree trunks, and extinct animals including giant kangaroos, to be discovered by the marvelling deep lead miners.[4]

Technologies for shaft sinking, mine development, pumping and processing were developed by the deep lead miners over a 50-year period. Ultimately the largest shafts and pumps in Australia would be installed in the deep lead mines at Moolort, near Carisbrook. The Charlotte Plains and New Havilah mines were the first to have electric pumps powered by a dedicated generating station. Collectively, the pumps from six companies working on the Moolort field had a design capacity of 27 million gallons per day (1,419 l/s) from depths greater than 100 metres, though this was never achieved in practice. In his memoirs Herbert Hoover, later the 31st President of the United States, described the mining operations at Moolort as 'the greatest pumping operation in mining history'.[5]

A HOST OF FACTORS are required to develop a successful new mine. The geology must be understood, and the valuable material must be present in sufficient quantities and grade to make a case for investment. Costs must be managed. The market for the product must be reliable. Investment capital must be available for the opportunity. Environmental impacts must be acceptable. And so on. But one factor, above all, is required. There must be a person who champions the project, who encourages others when the inevitable delays and roadblocks appear and has the persistence to see it through. Without that person, even the best mineral deposit may remain undeveloped.

The story of each successful deep lead mine is associated with the story of a person (in the nineteenth century, invariably a man) who promoted the project and raised capital, often several times, until success was achieved.

Some were honest, some were scoundrels, and most were somewhere in between. There were many such men in Victoria, and it is possible to mention only a few in this book.

Toward the end of the deep lead mining era, two men championed the Moolort mines and made them happen, albeit eventually at great loss to investors. They were James Drysdale Brown and Abraham Kozminsky, two foreign-born Melbourne businessmen who saw the potential to repeat the earlier successes of the mines at Ballarat, Creswick and Allendale. For a time, investors in London, politicians in Melbourne and the Victorian community believed that fortunes would be made beneath the volcanic plains of Moolort.

CHAPTER 1

Enough Gold to Turn the Brain

SEVERAL YEARS BEFORE the gold rushes transformed Australia, a Cornishman named John Phillips made the first attempt to mine alluvial gold that was buried deep and not just lying on the surface. His efforts in South Australia in the late 1840s mark him as the earliest pioneer of deep lead mining – the laborious process of sinking shafts to reach buried ancient riverbeds. Just as importantly, Phillips was the first to attempt gold mining on a commercial basis at a time when colonial governments were hostile to the idea.[1]

Born into a tin mining family, Phillips became a prolific inventor and schoolteacher. In 1847, at the age of 38, he was hired to take a party of miners to South Australia and to manage a copper mine near Halletts Cove. Discovering that the venture was hopeless, Phillips reinvented himself as a mining surveyor in Adelaide, then as a prospector.

South Australia was experiencing a boom in copper mining, with the richness of the Kapunda and Burra Burra mines attracting immigrants and investment. But there was no provision in South Australian law for mining leases, so if minerals were discovered the land had to be purchased. The smallest section that could be purchased in the surveyed areas close to Adelaide was eighty acres (32 ha). Like all mining booms, the copper boom had its share of failures. Phillips decided to prospect for gold.

Armed with a shovel and the Cornish method of vanning – washing soil on a shovel to test for tin or gold – Phillips scoured the valleys of the Torrens, Onkaparinga, Para Wirra, and Barossa. He claimed success in many spots and even financed the sinking of a shaft about 8 m deep near Echunga in search of a buried streambed. The enterprise collapsed in comic fashion when a cow fell into the shaft; its furious owner, cattle dealer Henry Metcalf, chased Phillips and his two employees off the property.[2]

Behind the comedy lay a serious problem. By the late 1840s, South

Australia's best farmland was already settled. Landowners like John Barton Hack were transforming the Echunga district into English-style agricultural estates of wheat, vineyards, and dairy cattle. Prospectors such as Phillips were seen as trespassers rather than pioneers.

Phillips responded by trying to secure legitimacy. He prepared reports and maps and sent them to Sir Roderick Murchison, one of the world's foremost geologists, in London. Murchison presented the findings to the Geological Society and even urged Colonial Secretary Lord Grey to encourage development of South Australian goldfields. But on the ground, Phillips had no legal rights to work land or retain any gold he found.

He tried every avenue. He bid for riverfront land but was outpriced. He negotiated with a farmer named Warland, but the farmer's wife ended the discussion, saying 'she knew what mining was, and that she did not want to be let down in her bed at night into some hollow under her house'.[3] He petitioned Governor Sir Henry Young for a grant but was rejected. Still determined, he wrote letters across the empire – to Sir Charles Lemon MP in Cornwall, to mining engineer John Taylor in London, even to the Bishop of Adelaide – arguing that the goldfields contained 'enough gold to turn the brain of the wealthiest London citizen'.[4]

Phillips's persistence was also driven by personal stakes. He had left a wife and five young children in Cornwall, hoping to earn enough to bring them out. Instead, his ventures collapsed. He would not see any of his family again until 1870 – more than two decades later.

GOLD HAD BEEN on peoples' minds from the earliest days of settlement in Australia. And why not? This was a new country, unexplored, and occupied by people they considered primitive who had no knowledge of the monetary value of gold. Gold found in some of the Caribbean Islands, and in Mexico, Central and South America had made Spain the richest country in the world more than two hundred years before. And the Portuguese had called the north-western coast of Australia Costa – d'Ouro, the Gold Coast. Surely that meant something.[5]

As they began to move outward from Sydney the explorers, convicts and settlers kept an eye out for gold. Some found it and kept it quiet. In

1823, Assistant Surveyor James McBrien found gold at the Fish River near Bathurst, a location which much later became a minor goldfield. In 1839 the explorer Count Strzelecki found what he thought was payable gold in the Vale of Clwydd, near the modern town of Lithgow. The Governor of New South Wales, Sir George Gipps, told him:

> To keep the matter secret, for fear of the serious consequences which, considering the condition and population of the colony, were to be apprehended.[6]

In February 1841, the geologist and clergyman Reverend William Clarke discovered gold west of Hartley, but Governor Gipps told him to 'put it away or we shall have our throats cut'. Clarke later announced his discovery anyway and showed specimens to members of the New South Wales Legislature. There was a surge of prospecting in the bush, but the prospectors kept quiet about their finds. For some reason a shepherd named Macgregor decided to report that he had found gold in the Wellington district in 1843–44. Writing about this in 1861, Yorkshireman Simpson Davison (who had shared a ship's cabin with Edmond Hammond Hargraves) observed:

> I should think it not improbably represented a thousand separate instances of gold-finding between the years 1840 and 1850.[7]

In 1849, when Phillips' quest for gold was common knowledge, someone sent him a gold specimen obtained at Daisy Hill at the eastern end of the Pyrenees range, in what was to become the colony of Victoria. Phillips wrote to Charles La Trobe, Superintendent of the Port Phillip District of New South Wales as Victoria was then known, proposing that he work as a mine surveyor to prospect for gold.

But La Trobe had decided to suppress the discovery at Daisy Hill. The discoverer was a young shepherd, Thomas Chapman, who had sold gold to jewellers Charles Brentani and Alexandre Duchene. When he met with Duchene in February, La Trobe refused Duchene's request for a reward and a government appointment. Instead, La Trobe sent all available police to disperse the hundreds of gold seekers around Daisy Hill. Young Thomas Chapman fled to Sydney.[8]

It is no wonder La Trobe refused to engage John Phillips as a prospector. Like Governor Gipps in New South Wales a decade earlier, La Trobe was worried about the possible effects of a gold rush on a society with a large ex-convict population. His actions delayed the start of the big Victorian gold rush by two years, although gold prospecting and mining continued in secret. The legal position was that all gold belonged to the Crown; thus, anyone mining it without permission could be prosecuted. There was no arrangement for obtaining a permit or licence to dig for gold.

Rebuffed by La Trobe, Phillips accepted employment with a newly formed mining syndicate that had acquired rights to about 650 ha of prospective ground in South Australia. Among its employees was a younger man, Charles Adelberg, whose enthusiasm was not matched by experience. Phillips considered Adelberg to be untrained and ignorant and the two men soon clashed.

By January 1850 the South Australian Gold Company was ready to launch publicly. Its prospectus, buoyed by the glamour of California's success, declared that Phillips and Adelberg had already obtained specimens of unusually pure gold. The plan was ambitious: £25,000 in capital, raised through 5,000 shares at £5 apiece. But Adelaide investors proved cautious. The colony's agricultural prosperity and memories of past mining failures blunted enthusiasm. Within weeks of the float's announcement, deposits were withdrawn, and the offering collapsed.

The company was undeterred. Both Phillips and Adelberg led prospecting teams to Balhannah, in the Onkaparinga Valley, about 29 km southeast of Adelaide, on the traditional lands of the Peramangk and Kaurna peoples. Many of the recruits were Cornish alluvial tin miners, men well-versed in water and gravel. Phillips brimmed with confidence. Writing home, he boasted: 'The colony will soon be set in effervescence, and all eyes deflected from California'.[9]

The rivals adopted contrasting strategies. Adelberg dug trenches and pre-concentrated the washdirt, sending promising parcels – worth, he claimed, £40 per ton – back to Adelaide for treatment. Phillips, more methodical, had his men labour on a water race. When the rains came and the river rose, he expected to wash large volumes at once and produce a lot of gold. He showed visitors small samples, but Adelberg dazzled the company with regular shipments of gold.

Later, Phillips admitted the rivalry had been poisonous. His appointment, he wrote bitterly, was:

> offensive to a certain gentleman employed by the company, who would have laid claim to priority of discovery … whose policy it was to conceal everything possible from me, while he was dazzling the company with his reports.[10]

Success, Phillips insisted, would have required months of steady water flow – something his site never enjoyed.

By August 1850 his position was untenable, and the South Australian Gold Company dismissed him. Once more Phillips returned to Adelaide, reduced to taking work as an engineering consultant. Then in 1851 came the thunderclap: the Victorian gold discoveries, too rich and widespread to suppress. South Australia emptied of men almost overnight. Phillips joined the tide. In November, he auctioned nearly all his household and business possessions – surveying instruments, books, even his musical instruments – and set off for Victoria, where the great rush was beginning.

PHILLIPS TRIED HIS HAND at mining in Victoria but quickly discovered he was better suited to professional work than to wielding a pick. In 1852 he returned briefly to South Australia to prepare some plans for the Kapunda copper mine. Back in Victoria he turned to inventing mining machinery and taking short-term government contracts for geological surveys. In 1855 he mapped the geology of the rich Gravel Pits lead at Ballarat – a contract that underscored how crucial accurate prediction of deep lead courses would be to the success or failure of future mining.

By 1857 Phillips was lecturing in Ballarat on geology, gold exploration, gold washing, and quartz mining. Admission was one shilling, and sometimes only a handful of people attended. Still, he pressed on. His contour map of Ballarat geology – the first of its kind – was lithographed for publication, and he made sure that his papers to the Miners' Court, the deep lead miners, and the Philosophical Institute found their way into the press. Early in 1858 he lobbied for the newly created post of Chief Mining Surveyor and Engineer with the Mining Board, but his application failed. His paper on *The Goldfields of Ballarat, Victoria* was submitted to the Geological Society in London, where Sir Roderick Murchison provided a summary for publication in the *Proceedings*.

Phillips made no further contribution to deep lead mining and never managed to anchor himself in one occupation. His irascible nature, coupled with a restless mind, kept him moving. In mid-1861 he stood for election in Ballarat West. While his opponents were listened to with respect, Phillips was met with derisive laughter. Yet when the votes were counted, he came a surprising second, proof that some valued his vision. In 1865, during a debate in the Victorian Legislative Assembly, John Ramsay MLA argued that Phillips was the true discoverer of gold and should have been rewarded. Five years later, the *Ballarat Star* raised the question again, pointing out that Edward Hargraves had been awarded £15,000, William Esmond £1,000 and other sums – while John Phillips had received nothing. No reward ever came.[11]

At last, in 1871, Phillips found a secure position. He was appointed the first Resident Master of the new Ballarat School of Mines. The appointment allowed him, after two decades, to bring his wife Caroline and two of their daughters out from Cornwall. But even here his quarrelsome manner resurfaced. By 1873 he had fallen out with the school's Administrative Council and lost the post. He left for a job in New South Wales, leaving his family behind. Caroline died in Ballarat in 1875.

Phillips drifted again. In 1881 he returned to South Australia, where he became a schoolteacher at Palmer, near Tungkillo. After five years he went to live with a cousin at Kadina on the Yorke Peninsula. There, far from the mines he had once dreamed of opening, he died in 1889, aged 79 – penniless, ill, and buried in an unmarked grave.

Today Phillips is a forgotten figure, overshadowed by the rushes of 1851 and the wealth they unleashed. Yet he was the first to glimpse the possibilities of alluvial mining in Australia. His persistence, vision, and misfortune set the stage for the colossal undertakings that followed – a fitting, if tragic, prologue to the story of the deep leads.

What Phillips could only imagine, others would soon attempt on a vast scale: sinking shafts through basalt and clay, driving tunnels for miles beneath the plains, and harnessing steam engines to battle the floodwaters underground. The quest he began in obscurity would become one of the most ambitious, sometimes profitable but often costly chapters in Australia's mining history.

CHAPTER 2

Ballarat

THE WADAWURRUNG PEOPLE were the traditional owners of the land around Ballarat. They had lived undisturbed in the area near Melbourne, Geelong and the Bellarine Peninsula for at least 25,000 years, possibly much longer. The coastal explorer Matthew Flinders met several Wadawurrung people when he camped at Indented Head and climbed the You Yangs in May 1802. The Wadawurrung had occasional encounters with white people after 1802. Most famously, escaped convict William Buckley lived with them for 32 years from 1803. A tent town sprang up at Corio Bay, now Geelong, in 1835. Squatters rapidly moved out into Wadawurrung territory and conflict increased.

In August 1837, a party of explorers travelled overland to Mount Buninyong, a volcanic cone which stood in a rolling country of forest and swamp. Buninyong, a corruption of the Wadawurrung bunning-yowang, means a big hill like a knee. The explorers discovered excellent grazing land and returned as settlers the following year. One of them, Scotsman William Cross Yuille, took up a 10,000 acre (4,047 ha) run which included Ballarat. Balla-arat signified a camping or resting place. Yuille left in 1840 for New Zealand, where he fought in the Māori Wars. In later life, he returned to Victoria, becoming a noted sheep breeder, racehorse owner and billiard player.[1]

By 1841 a cluster of huts had appeared beside Mount Buninyong. These were permanent homes for sawyers and splitters who worked to clear the timber for sheep and cattle grazing. George Gab, George Coleman, and others were the pioneers in the Buninyong settlement. Gab's wife daringly rode astride, on a fine horse called Petrel, and both husband and wife were energetic people. Gab opened an accommodation house for travellers. Soon a general store and a blacksmith's shop appeared nearby. A doctor set up practice in 1844, and a clergyman arrived in 1847. The first school opened in 1848.

Buninyong had become a town. Bullockies and drovers could leave wives and children in town while they worked 'in the bush'. The people of the district looked forward to steady pastoral growth and prosperity. Still, there was ongoing conflict with the traditional owners of the land. Two Wadawurrung men were killed at Anderson and Miller's public house in Buninyong in November 1847. Several bullock drivers were drinking with the Aborigines when they got into a quarrel, leading to one of the bullock drivers being speared to death. A skirmish ensued, which ended in two of the Aborigines being killed. There do not seem to have been any legal consequences.[2]

THE CALIFORNIAN GOLD rush of 1849 had drawn many people away from the Australian colonies. To limit this, the New South Wales government offered a reward for the first person to find payable gold. Edmond Hammond Hargraves wrote to the Colonial Secretary in April 1851 to say that he had discovered gold and offered to show where it was found for a £500 reward. After this was refused, he revealed the location and a gold rush quickly followed. By June 1851 there were over 2,000 people digging around Bathurst. Hargraves was later paid a reward of £10,000 by the New South Wales Government, and the Victorian Government paid him £5,000. His claim was contested by associates who had shared in the discovery, but an enquiry in 1853 accepted that Hargraves was the first to discover the goldfield.

Not to be outdone, a committee chaired by the Mayor of Melbourne offered a reward for discovering payable gold within 200 miles (322 km) of Melbourne. James Esmond, an Irishman who had driven a mail coach between Buninyong and the Horsham area before going to California in 1849, was the first to report that he had found gold, at Clunes. He reported this on 1 July for a very good reason – this was the date that the Colony of Victoria was established, and the legal ambiguity was resolved, at least in the public mind. The British Act of Parliament separating Port Phillip District from New South Wales, and naming the new colony 'Victoria', had been signed by Queen Victoria in August 1850. Enabling legislation was passed by the New South Wales Legislative Council and took effect on 1 July 1851. Charles La Trobe became the new colony's first Lieutenant–Governor.[3]

Over the next few weeks and months, 'new' gold discoveries were reported across Victoria and the public interest increased. Thomas Hiscock, a blacksmith from Berkshire, England, spent some time searching around the Buninyong area, finally discovering a gold-bearing reef in August 1851 on a wooded slope south of a small creek. Hiscock broke up the ground with a crowbar and used an old milk dish in lieu of a proper gold pan. His find attracted many prospectors to the area, and many who had been heading north for Clunes decided instead to try their luck around Buninyong. After a couple of weeks, Hiscock returned to his anvil but, with people assuming he had made his fortune, was forced to advertise for months afterward that he was still in business as a blacksmith.[4]

The riches of Ballarat, on a 'flooded plain, and a dreary stringybark range' five miles north of Hiscock's find, were first revealed in late August 1851, to John Dunlop and his young mate James Regan. Other parties found the Ballarat gold simultaneously or very shortly thereafter, and a rush followed almost immediately.[5]

The first claims were laid out with a length of fifty feet (15 m) up the slope, and a frontage of ten feet (3 m) along the creek. Behind these claims was a right-of-way for huts or tents, and above them a second line of claims. It was thought that the ground would be worked out in a few months and so the uphill claims were second best, taken by late arrivals. The uphill parties were fortunate for the richest gold was found there, in a layer of blue clay about 1.5 m below the surface. The Cavanagh party washed 560 oz of gold from this clay in a few days, using only tin dishes, and returned triumphant to Geelong.[6]

Governor La Trobe reacted quickly to the news of the Ballarat gold find and on 20 September, only three weeks after the first gold was panned, Police Commissioner Doveton arrived to announce an exorbitant licence fee of thirty shillings a month and a limit of 8 ft (2.4 m) square to the size of a claim. Quarrels broke out between the previously peaceful diggers over their claim areas.[7]

One of the diggers, newspaper correspondent Alfred Clarke, was moved to write:

> ... if the truth be told the Government is the greatest gold digger after all, and
> the most lucky – for where they dig they find it in pockets and are saved the

expense of outfit or licence – work where they please, and sink a shaft in every man's purse – and, perhaps his heart, too.[8]

Still, by October there were 3,000 men on Ballarat. Money was scarce and many had to pay their licence fee in gold, for which they received £3 per oz. On nine out of ten claims they sank what they called shicers, or failures. This comes from the German word *scheissen*, which means the failed shafts were only good as pit toilets!

The Government then announced a doubling of the licence fee to £3 per month, which so aroused the diggers that the order was revoked. By December 1851 the limited surface deposits of Golden Point had been worked out, and when rich gold finds were reported from Forest Creek and Bendigo Creek, the Ballarat diggers rushed away to the new fields.

The deepest holes in the slope were only 3 m deep when, in early November 1851, a party on the flat by the creek found gold at 6 m. There was a sudden burst of enthusiasm for staking new claims in that area and sinking all the way to the bedrock. The deeper ground proved to be wet and difficult to sink through, and the diggers (who were not yet miners) found their enthusiasm waning quickly. They joined the drift away from Ballarat so that in March 1852 the Melbourne gold escort brought 12,055 ounces from Mount Alexander and only 129 ounces from Ballarat.[9]

The few diggers remaining at Ballarat continued following the gold deeper away from the hillside and tried to timber shafts through the wet alluvial wash and running sands. Yields were good if unspectacular until March, when David Ham's party bottomed in Canadian Gully, just south of what later became known as Sovereign Hill. They had discovered the first of the deep leads, the buried riverbeds rich in gold which were to create the legend of Ballarat. Ham's party took out £1,200 worth of gold before the cold autumn rains drove the diggers up the gullies to drier ground as the rising creek flooded the holes on the flat.

CHAPTER 3

The Rush Now is Immense

JACK EVANS, A MINER from Oldham in Lancashire, was lying on his stomach, digging in a narrow horizontal tunnel just 30 inches (76 cm) high and 3 feet (1 m) wide, at the bottom of a 66-foot (20 m) deep shaft in Canadian Gully, Ballarat, when his pick struck something unusual. It was early evening on 31 January 1853. Holding his candle close, he brushed away some of the mud to reveal what turned out to be the largest gold nugget ever discovered at that time. Trembling with excitement, he called out to his brother Dan, who was operating the windlass above. Dan told him to stay in the shaft and keep quiet while he went to get help. Dan walked to the camp, trying to appear nonchalant, and found their mate John Lees. He led Lees away from the cluster of tents to a quiet spot and explained the situation.

Returning to the shaft, they dropped an old sack down to Jack, who wrapped it around the nugget and sent it up in the bucket. Dan then slung the heavy sack over his shoulder and walked quietly through a crowd of diggers back to their tent, where he casually tossed it onto a dirt heap as if it were of no value.[1]

One of them went to fetch three policemen, who escorted the Evans brothers, carrying the nugget slung from the middle of a pole, on the long walk from Canadian Gully to the Commissioner's tent. The next morning, they washed the nugget and weighed it using potato scales. Shaped like a leg of mutton and about 18 inches (50 cm) long, it weighed just over 134 troy pounds, including quartz, with a gold content of 1,319 ounces.

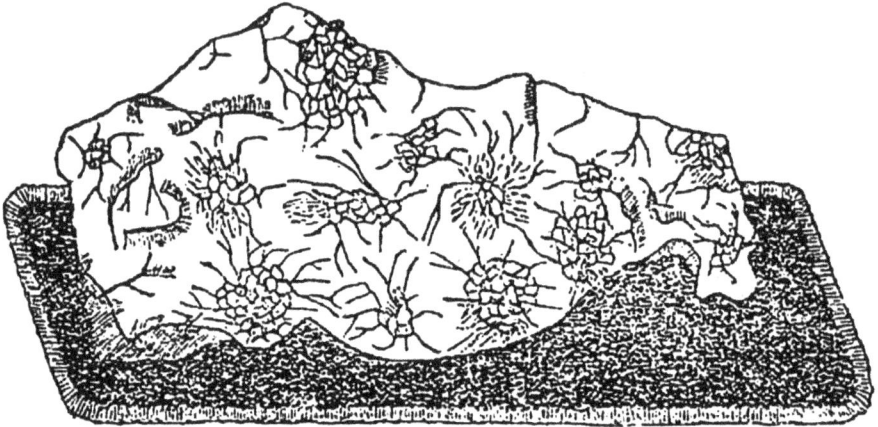

No I.—134 ilz. 8oz.

Figure 2 The Canadian Nugget
Geelong Advertiser and Intelligencer, 11 October 1853, p 6

The Evans brothers were both experienced coal miners, with 45-year-old Daniel being a skilled shaft sinker. Their expertise gave them an edge over other miners working in Canadian Gully – they knew how to support a deep shaft and could work safely in narrow, unstable ground. They also knew the importance of keeping their discovery very quiet.

THE DIGGERS IN CANADIAN Gully had begun sinking deeper shafts as they followed the gold-bearing washdirt down the gully. They used windlasses to bail out water and rock, using rawhide buckets and old nail cans. Most shafts were round or oval with no internal supports. To move up and down the shaft, miners would cut a series of toe-holes into one wall, climbing with their backs pressed against the opposite wall while holding onto a rope. Alternatively, they sometimes fashioned rough ladders from bush timber and in some cases, a miner would be hoisted up or down by his mate, standing with one foot in the bucket and holding onto the rope.

Initially, when miners drove horizontally into the wash from the bottom of the shaft, they left pillars of earth to support the roof. However, many, including the Evans brothers, realised that these pillars contained valuable gold. They began climbing down abandoned shafts to extract the gold from the pillars. Initially, they used a single prop with a flat piece of wood on top for support, but they soon started constructing frames with legs and caps for added stability. Pillar-robbing was dangerous, and many miners were buried when the roof collapsed.

In wet ground, the walls of a shaft also collapsed easily. Towards the end of 1852, a man named Beilby sank an 8 m shaft in wet alluvial soil, using cut saplings arranged in a box-shaped support. Others lined their shafts with bark and used saplings to construct frames. Over time, split bush timber began to replace saplings as the preferred material.

Since miners were focused on digging for gold rather than cutting and fetching timber, entrepreneurs stepped in to supply the needed materials. They began cutting and splitting timber, selling slabs to mining parties. A standard shaft size was eventually agreed upon: 4 feet long and 2 feet 10 inches wide (122 x 86 cm) inside the timber supports.[2]

The Evans brothers had started working at Canadian Gully in late 1852 as part of a four-man team with John Lees and William Poulton Green. During December, they worked abandoned shafts up to 50 feet (15 m) deep, tunnelling through the strata and removing support pillars, finding 132 oz of gold in just one week. Dan Evans then identified a promising spot in Canadian Gully where they began sinking two shafts, each (he said) precisely 37 inches in diameter – a measurement that reflects the Evans brothers' mining expertise. This was probably based on their experience with contracts to sink a minimum 3-foot (36 inch) diameter shaft in coal mines, using a measuring stick to ensure they satisfied the company's inspector. While Dan and his brother focused on sinking the first shaft, Green and Lees handled the hauling and carrying. The team worked tirelessly, reaching a depth of 15 m within a few days and extracting about 100 oz of gold before selling the claim for a substantial sum.[3]

The other shaft presented challenges as water began seeping in, so they brought in more timber, lined the shaft, and bailed out the water. Soon, they reached the clay layer rich in gold. They cut and split red gum planks from the bush to line the last 6 m of the shaft. At a depth of about 20 m they hit bedrock and began driving horizontally, finding small nuggets along the way. Then, they struck the jackpot – the Canadian Nugget.

The nugget was sent to Melbourne under armed escort, while the four lucky diggers travelled overland to Geelong and took a steamboat back to Melbourne. The nugget caused a sensation, attracting the attention of Lieutenant Governor La Trobe, the Bishop of Melbourne, government dignitaries, and merchants. Just ten days after its discovery, the owners packed the nugget with their other gold and left for England on the screw steamer *Sarah Sands*.[4]

Another group of four miners found two large nuggets nearby. William Gough, his 18-year-old son Tom, John Sully, and John Bristow discovered their first large nugget on 20 January and their second two days later. However, they kept their finds quiet for three weeks, which allowed news of the Canadian Nugget to reach Geelong first. The larger of the two nuggets they found, weighing 1,117 oz gross, was later mistakenly named the *Sarah Sands*, though it did not travel on that ship; the other unnamed nugget weighed 1,012 oz gross. Where the gross weight was reported, it included quartz and other contaminants.

On the morning the *Geelong Advertiser* reported the discovery of the Canadian Nugget, it caused a frenzy in the town, with more than sixty parties setting off for Ballarat before noon. Over the following week, newspapers across Australia picked up the story, spreading the news far and wide. A Melbourne paper observed:

> On horseback you can go to Geelong from Ballarat with ease in six hours. Before the news of the Nugget, they were coming up rapidly, but the rush now is immense.[5]

The *Geelong Advertiser* reported that:

> The monstrous nugget lately found in this district has created an amount of excitement not equalled even by the first discovery of glorious Golden Point, at Ballarat. Hundreds, yea thousands of diggers are crowding to the locality, and the diggings in the Ballarat district will again eclipse every other gold district in the colony.[6]

Another report stated:

> A complete rush took place from the neighbouring districts, and the rate of carriage went up £2 per ton instanter. The intelligence of these unparalleled

events created great excitement here, and they are expected to create still greater in the mother country.[7]

THE INFLUX OF NEW MINERS at Ballarat had to quickly learn how to safely sink deep shafts in the waterlogged alluvial ground, known as 'drift'. Initially, they attempted to drive timbers into the centre of the shaft to create a small well, which could be bailed out to lower the water level. Afterward, they would expand the shaft to its full size and line it with slabs down to the bottom of the well. Another method, called 'spiling,' involved driving boards down around the entire perimeter of the shaft. This technique created shafts with a double timber lining, with a foot of clay packed between the inner and outer layers to help keep out water. A group of blacksmiths working on the Red Streak Lead tried to use a caisson made of sheet iron to sink through the drift. However, the iron cylinders proved too weak to withstand the pressure.[8]

In 1853, William Kelly visited the goldfields of Ballarat and noted the severe deforestation in the surrounding areas due to the extensive amount of timber needed to support the mines and the careless use of wood in campfires. As timber became increasingly expensive, miners made it a practice to recover the timber from abandoned shafts in a process known as 'drawing slabs.' This operation was risky and often led to fatal accidents.[9]

In the area of Canadian Gully where large gold nuggets had been discovered, each 2.4 m square claim yielded about 420 oz of gold. Miners initially crafted wooden windlasses from local timber, lubricating the rubbing parts with mutton fat. Soon, windlasses with iron handles became available, making the task somewhat easier, though the work remained too strenuous for many diggers. Hoisting water was especially arduous; keeping a shaft open required constant effort from three or four men. Some groups had to manually bail water for six to eight months before reaching the gold-bearing washdirt. During the winter of 1853, cold and wet weather caused some shafts to collapse, and fences were erected to protect these hazardous openings until the ground dried out around Christmas.

With all the promising ground on the Canadian Lead already claimed, newcomers began sinking prospecting shafts elsewhere. In late 1853, workings moving down the Canadian Lead intersected with the Red Hill

Lead. The Red Hill Lead ran beneath the creek and the Plank Road, up to 40 m deep. For a time, this area became one of the primary sources of Ballarat's prosperity and fame, though the work was wet, slow, and challenging.

The Canadian Lead yielded impressive amounts of gold. The Blacksmiths' party extracted gold worth £24,000 from a small claim, averaging about one ounce of gold per bucket of dirt. Nearby miners tunnelled into this claim and stole some of the gold. Europeans subsequently worked the claim twice more with notable success. Eventually, Chinese miners took over the claim and discovered even more gold.[10]

At the junction with the Prince Regent Lead, the total yield of gold was approximately one ton, with miners earning between £1,000 and £2,000 each on average. They often sold their claims and left to enjoy their wealth before the claims were fully exploited, allowing others to benefit from the continued success. In September 1854, miners discovered a spectacular nugget, the Lady Hotham, weighing 1,118 oz at a depth of 41 m. From the same hole, more than 3,200 oz of additional nuggets were extracted, with a total value exceeding £13,000.[11]

The diggers discovered several tributaries feeding into the main Golden Point Lead, including the Bakery Hill, Old Gravels Pits, Specimen Gully, Eureka, Red Streak, One-eye, and many other leads. As they continued to follow the primary lead beneath the basalt, it intersected with additional leads such as the Nightingale, Malakoff, Milkmaid's, Redan, Miner's Right, and Woolshed Leads. These were part of a network of old streambeds rich in gold.[12]

At the head of the Red Hill lead was the famous Durham Hole. It was described as:

> THE MOST EXTRAORDINARY GOLDEN HOLE ON RECORD...
> the richest alluvial claim of gold ever heard of, not excepting any gold field known.[13]

Miners began working on the Durham Hole in early 1853, shortly after the discovery of the Canadian nugget. By 1857, when the *Ballarat Times* reported on it, three groups had worked the claim and sold it. The first group of eight men extracted 936 oz of gold; the second group of eight men extracted

2,304 oz, and the third group of twelve men extracted about 9,000 oz. By the end of 1856, a total of 12,240 oz had been recovered, valued at £48,961 (at £4 per ounce). In 1857 the *Ballarat Times* predicted that the final yield would exceed £50,000, a significant amount at a time when £100 was considered a good annual income. The Red Hill Lead continued to produce gold through 1854, with successful diggers extracting 3,000 oz of gold from some claims. There was even a report of 750 oz being taken from a single bucket.

After Jack Evans, Dan Evans, and their two companions returned home to England, they were granted an audience with Queen Victoria and Prince Albert, showcasing the Canadian nugget at several venues before selling it to the Bank of England for £5,532. John Lees married in 1854 and used his share of the proceeds to build the Ballarat Buildings on Nugget Street in Oldham. William Poulton Green also married and managed a hotel in Torquay. Meanwhile, Dan Evans exhibited a model of the nugget at the Lyceum exhibition in Manchester. The model, highlighted in rich gilt, depicted both the quartz and the gold visible in the original specimen.[14]

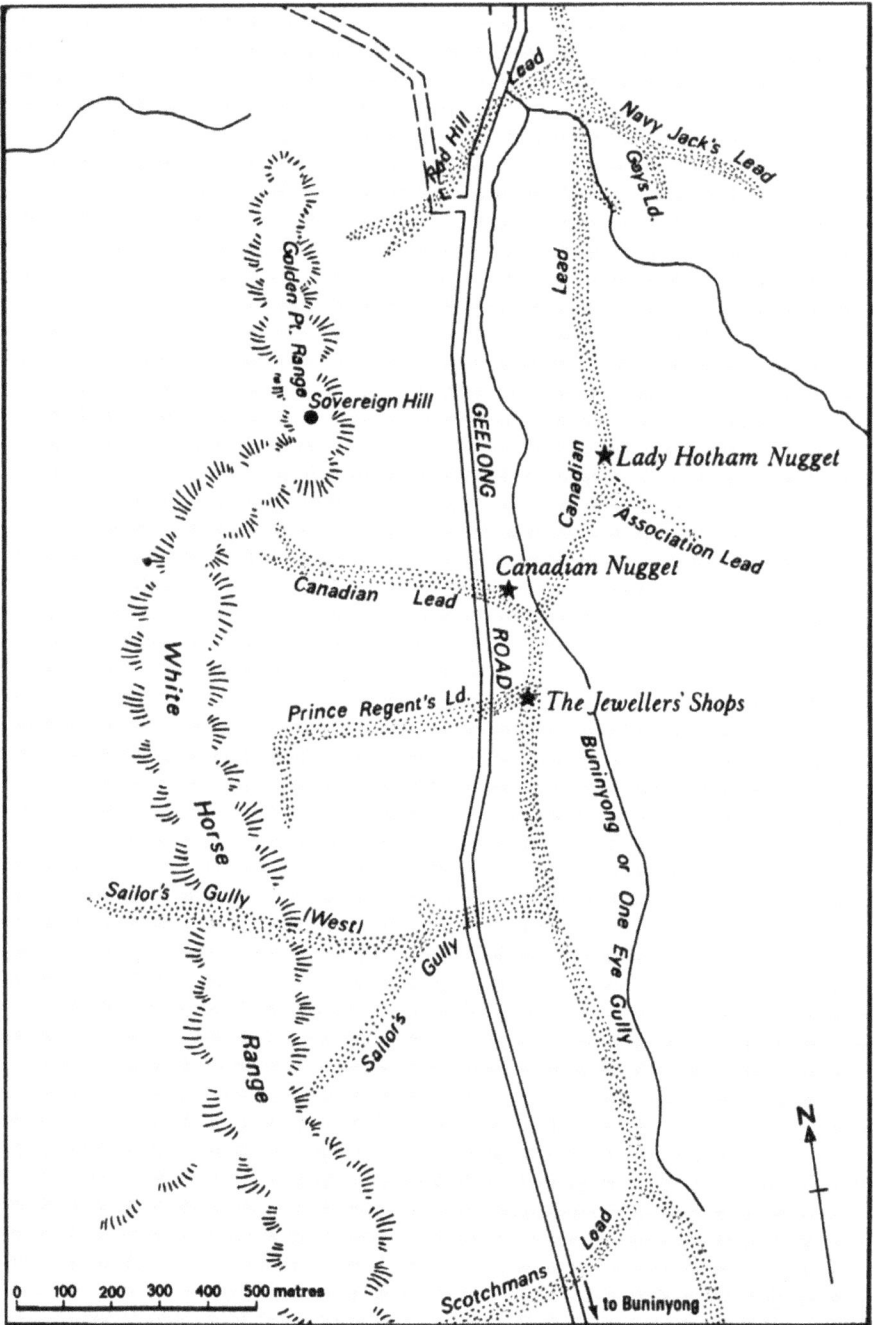

Figure 3 The Canadian Line
After RB Smyth, *The Goldfields and Mineral Districts of Victoria*, opp. p 164

Black Powder and Steam Engines

CORNISHMAN ROBERT MALACHY Serjeant was the son of a Royal Marines surgeon who died in Canada when Robert was just six years old. Serjeant started his career as a clerk in his uncle's attorney's office, focusing primarily on mining business. In 1848, he emigrated with his mother and two sisters to South Australia, where he found work in the copper mines before joining the gold rush to Victoria. Serjeant later claimed that he and his friend John Victor had been the first miners to sink a shaft through basalt, near Fryer's Creek, in 1853. Two years later, in Ballarat, he began dealing in shares and 'furnishing' equipment to mining parties. A furnisher became a 'sleeping' shareholder who held a share in the claim and its gold without being required to work as a miner.[1]

With their shafts flooding, the Ballarat miners needed steam engines. The first were a vertical engine used for winding and pumping by Dunstan's

Figure 4 Robert Malachy Serjeant
parliament.vic.gov.au/
members/robert-serjeant/

party on the Canadian lead, and one used by Major Talbot's party for pumping on the Gravel Pits lead. Many miners were afraid the engines would take away jobs and were against capitalism in principle. A group of men, intent on destroying the engine, marched to Talbot's claim. However, Major Talbot, armed with a gun, stood in front of the engine and threatened to shoot the first man who tried to damage it. After much angry shouting and fist-shaking, the protestors eventually withdrew. Yet, within a few months, steam engines on the field were regarded as essential.[2]

The first steam powered puddling machine was introduced by the mining engineer Peter Mathews on the Red Hill lead. Puddling machines, used to break up the clay and gravel and free the gold, were usually powered by a horse. The first steam engine to be directly imported from England to Ballarat was arranged by James Ivey in 1857, from Tangye Brothers of Birmingham. At that time, they were busy making lots of jacks for Isambard Kingdom Brunel, whose ship the Great Eastern was stuck in the Severn Estuary.

In June 1855, Robert Serjeant supplied slabs, ropes, and a windlass to Henry Davies, thus becoming a member of the first party to sink a shaft through basalt to reach the washdirt on the Gravel Pits lead. Meanwhile John Phillips, the Cornishman who had sunk a shaft for gold in South Australia, was surveying the geology of the Gravel Pits lead under a government contract. The ability to accurately predict the course of the deep lead and then to sink through basalt would prove crucial to the success of deep lead mining.[3]

To penetrate the basalt, shaft sinkers used a simple chisel-ended bar, repeatedly lifting and dropping it to bore out holes for black powder charges. They cleared the debris with makeshift iron spoons and kept the blacksmiths busy sharpening their drills. As the blasts echoed across the plateau, they sounded like the cannons thundering across the Crimean hills at that time during the siege of Sebastopol, lending the town its name. Similar echoes of conflict resounded in other parts of the goldfields, with places like Malakoff, Redan, Cathcart, and Inkerman reflecting names from battles fought in a distant land.

In October 1855, Bath's party began sinking a shaft through basalt at the corner of Lydiard and Sturt Streets. It took them eighteen months to reach a depth of 76 m, 30 m of which were through basalt. The mine was equipped with a ten-horsepower engine and a six-inch pump. The miners then drove horizontally about 200 m along the lead, ultimately extracting gold worth £17,000. However, by 1855, it had become clear that sinking shafts to find the deep leads was impractical. What was needed was a boring machine to determine the depth of the washdirt and identify the layers of sand, clay, or rock above it. Most importantly, they needed to locate the gutter – the original streambed. Boring machines, commonly used around the world for drilling water wells and exploring for minerals, would be the solution.[4]

THE ENGLISH BORING MACHINE used iron rods that were screwed together, with a blacksmith-made hard bit at the end. These rods could be rotated by men walking in a circle, and in harder ground, they could be lifted and dropped to pulverise stone. A common issue was the bit or a rod breaking inside the hole. Penetrating hard rock was challenging and the blacksmiths were kept busy sharpening the bits. In loose alluvial material, the hole was stabilised with an iron casing tube. Once in the alluvial material, an auger flight recovered a sample of the wash. The process began with a large diameter hole, which was gradually reduced until it reached a final diameter of 3 to 4 inches (8–10 cm). A boring machine was usually operated by manpower, though in later years, horses or steam engines were also used.[5]

A Chinese design featured a heavy bar six feet long and four inches in diameter, with a bit at the lower end and a cylinder to catch the cuttings. This bar could be lifted and dropped using a rope, which twisted as it was lifted, thereby rotating the bit. The entire assembly was then withdrawn to tip out the cuttings. An American improvement added a mechanism between the rope and the iron bar that indexed the rotation by a set amount with each stroke. To clear out the cuttings, the bit was pulled out, and a cleaning tube was lowered into the hole.[6]

In July 1854, a man named John McLay put down a bore at Clayton's Hill, and later that year, a party attempted to bore for the junction of the Eureka and the Red Hill leads. Engineer Jacob Brache claimed to have built a steam-powered machine capable of sinking 30 cm diameter hole 10 to 12 m deep in all but the hardest rock within a few hours. But people were sceptical, and their doubts were justified, as nothing more was ever heard of the machine.[7]

Miners on the Golden Point and Gravel Pits leads sought a boring contractor, asking for a guarantee that the work would be completed within a specified timeframe. In September 1856, a committee of miners from the Frenchman's and White Horse leads recommended that they purchase two sets of boring equipment, costing £150 per set, one for each lead. They believed this investment could save £100,000 in shaft sinking costs. At the White Horse lead, miners discussed the option of using contractors who had quoted 5 shillings and 6 pence per foot for their services.[8]

Figure 5 Raising the drill rods
after *Illustrated Australian News*, May 1894

The drill hole is at the rear of the picture, at the centre of the tripod. The
men in front are turning the windlass to raise the heavy string of rods from
the bottom of the hole, while the two men at the rear loosen the coupling.
The rope from the rods goes up to a sheave in the tripod, down the left leg
of the tripod to a second sheave at ground level, then across to the windlass.
The windlass only needs capacity for enough rope for the length of one
rod, because each is raised and then screwed on or off the string of rods.

IN THE END, the miners from the Frenchman's and White Horse leads
decided to hire Melbourne boring contractor John Seddon. Seddon, from
Lancashire, had been in the colony since 1848 and advertised his services for
boring water or coal, as well as assessing ground for mining, railway tunnels,
and bridges. He had bored for coal at Loutit Bay near Geelong and had
worked on water bores and other projects.[9]

The contract was expected to cost between £500 and £1,000. The funds
for mobilisation were sent to Melbourne, but Seddon failed to appear.
Eventually, he returned the money with a message stating that he had
submitted a tender for a government contract and would not be taking on
additional work at that time.[10]

In response, William Elder at Sebastopol arranged for a blacksmith to

Figure 6 Stripping off the sample
after *Illustrated Australian News*, May 1894

The drillers have withdrawn the auger tool from the bottom of the hole and
are stripping off the sample, ready to pan it off and check for particles of
gold. The single rod is attached to the rope held by the man on the left.

create a boring machine operated by two men, with rods raised by a windlass.
After Seddon's withdrawal, Elder was engaged at the White Horse lead. By
early March 1857, his hole had reached a depth of 21 m when the chisel-
point broke. Despite this setback, Elder managed to complete the hole.[11]

Within weeks, boring machines were in use on Frenchman's lead, the
Durham lead and Sebastopol, with several new machines enroute to Ballarat
by bullock dray. By August 1857, eleven boring machines were at work on
the Frenchman's, Miners' Right, Malakoff, Redan, and Golden Point leads.
A year later there were thirteen boring machines in Ballarat.[12]

Figure 7 Attaching a rod
after *Illustrated Australian News*, May 1894

The two men in the foreground on either side of the drill collar hold
spanners which are used to rotate the square rods and to couple and
uncouple the joints between the rods. The man on the right is holding
the next rod to be used, which is suspended from the rope. He is about to
swing it into position over the hole. The two men at the rear are holding
the weight of the rod. Because they are just lifting a single rod and not
the whole drill string, they do not need to use the windlass for this.

IN THE EARLY YEARS, mining equipment was imported from Britain,
arriving by ship and then transported by bullock dray. Most miners had
little capital, making it difficult to secure credit from merchants in Geelong
and Melbourne. When not engaged in sinking shafts and bailing water they
focused on tasks like cutting timber and firewood, hauling supplies, and

assembling machinery. They were resourceful and hard working.

Timber was a vital resource for deep lead mines, as every exposed metre of ground required support. The heavy ground often broke the timbers, which then needed replacement. To maximise working hours in larger mines, most timber was sent underground and stored during a 25-hour period starting on Saturday night at 11:00 PM, as mining operations were suspended on Sunday. For ordinary miners, Sunday was reserved for housekeeping, washing clothes, and attending church services.

The demand for steam engines led to the establishment of foundries and machine shops for their construction and maintenance. Ballarat quickly evolved into an industrial centre, with buildings constructed from brick and stone rather than canvas and saplings. Hotels replaced the grog shops, and schools and churches began to appear. In 1854, the city produced 700,000 oz of gold, with production reaching 920,351 oz in 1856. This was the high point in alluvial gold production, although the city's diverse industrial development was only just beginning.

The deep leads mines had now reached 100 m below the surface and were so saturated with water that in many shafts the pumps could not cope. Sinking a shaft through the basalt required a massive investment, and it could take up to three years before the first gold was recovered from a shaft that finally reached the gutter. Many shafts missed the gutter because, without extensive boring, the course of the leads could only be guessed. The Albion Company spent £12,000 and ended up extracting little more than water.

DESPITE THE CHALLENGES, the basalt plateau of Ballarat and Sebastopol buzzed with activity as numerous cooperative companies set up operations. Typically composed of 30 to 50 shareholders, mostly hardworking miners, these companies operated collaboratively. They were characterised by limited mining and engineering expertise, with many learning the business through trial and error.

The development of the frontage system of mining leases helped resolve disputes, although legal costs were always heavy. This system allowed the miners to secure a certain length of the lead if they were within a specific distance of a claim where the lead was known to exist. Unlike traditional mining leases, the plan of the lease on the ground would evolve as the course of the lead became known.

A horse-powered whim could be used for shaft sinking if water flow was minimal, but in more demanding situations and for hoisting large amounts of water and washdirt, a steam engine was essential. Consequently, rawhide buckets and iron kibbles were soon replaced by rectangular iron cages and bailing tanks running on timber guides set in the sides of a rectangular shaft. Mining became industrialised, with most miners working in cooperative parties and others working for them on contract or for wages.

The Old Gravel Pits Company, comprising seventy-two men, sank two shafts through the basalt and reached the reef wash at a depth of 128 m. The manager, Alexander Dewar, decided that the best method for mining this material was to use trucks and cages with water tanks underneath them. Installed in mid-1857, these were the first mine cages used in Victoria. The wash was processed in steam-driven puddling machines, which were round tanks with a central pivot. Rakes driven around the pivot agitated the wash, causing the gold to settle at the bottom. The steam-driven puddlers at the Old Gravel Pits mine operated effectively for nearly two years, handling an average of 300 trucks of dirt per day.

In January 1859, the New Constitution Company, which had sunk a 98 m shaft and driven 300 m along the bedrock, became the first to use horses for drawing trucks and to use flat iron sheets for turning the trucks. The trucks ran on wooden rails plated with iron. Ventilation was a problem which they addressed by constructing a brick furnace underground near the upcast airway. The rising hot air created a downdraft in the intake shaft.

At this time there were many companies like the Koh-i-noor, an amalgamation of five claims, which employed 230 men and operated with four steam engines totalling 130 horsepower. They used eight puddling machines,

Several factors contributed to the expansion of deep lead mining beyond the 1850s. These included the rapid development of regional engineering facilities and foundries, the enactment of laws that improved the certainty of mining titles, the introduction of legislation allowing Limited Liability companies, and the establishment of a local stock exchange.

With clearer titles, mine owners could secure capital through the stock exchange, obtain loans from banks, and procure machinery from skilled suppliers. Investors, in turn, were more confident purchasing shares, knowing that their potential loss in the event of a mining failure was limited to the value of their shares, thus protecting them from bankruptcy.

Figure 8 The St George United Mine, Ballarat
after *Dickers Mining Record*, 1867

THE BAND OF HOPE COMPANY was established by 120 men, mostly Cornish, who originally held 15 claims, each 54 m long, along the presumed course of the lead. After twelve months of exploration through boring, they began shaft sinking in March 1858. They quickly realised they needed a 12-inch pump to manage the water inflow.[13]

To reduce the flow, they lined the shaft with timber slabs and packed clay behind it. Despite these efforts, the lining burst two or three times and had to be rebuilt. Eventually, the water inflow proved too great for the 12-inch pump, and they bought a 15-inch pump. Since the larger pump wouldn't fit in the existing shaft, they had to enlarge it, starting from the top and replacing the timber and clay lining as they dug downward.

Sinking continued, but progress was very slow due to water flooding into the bottom of the shaft. The lining burst again and had to be rebuilt. In October 1862 they finally reached the bedrock at 80 m. They then sank an additional 24 m into the bedrock and drove horizontally 55 m until they reached the deep lead channel they were seeking.

As soon as they broke into the wash, sand and water rushed in, filling both the drive and the bottom 30 m of the shaft. Five years had now passed. Every attempt to remove the sand and water from the shaft bottom resulted in more flooding from the deep lead. Much time was lost repairing pumps damaged by sand. Eventually, they drove a new tunnel at a higher level and sunk a winze (internal shaft) onto the original drive. Through trial and error, they discovered that tightly packed stones could stop the flow.

Seven years had now passed. The pumps were rearranged, and the shaft was sunk an additional 16 m, reaching a total depth of 120 m, a little more than eight years after the project began. A new 52 m-long drive was developed, along with a 20 m rise (upward shaft) into the lead. However, sand and water once again rushed in, filling the workings.

A bigger pump was needed! They bought the largest pump available at the time, a 22½ inch, 90 horsepower Cornish beam pump relocated from a copper mine in South Australia. But while waiting for the new pump to arrive, they came up with an alternative plan. They abandoned the hard-won No 1 shaft and purchased the shaft of the nearby Golden Gate mine.[14]

This new shaft was enlarged, the new machinery was installed, and a long drive was developed from the Golden Gate shaft to connect with the Band of Hope lease. Finally, success! The washdirt was up to 2.1 m thick. The long drive was converted into a double tramway, with 12 horses pulling rakes of trucks. Gas lamps from the town supply illuminated the drive, and a steam-driven fan provided the first mechanical ventilation system in a large Ballarat mine.

They built an extensive puddling plant, and dividends began to flow as the mining rate increased to 600 tons of washdirt per day. The company later sunk additional shafts and became very profitable.

AS THE EXPENSE and difficulty of deep lead mining increased, Ballarat's gold production declined to a low of only 267,228 oz in 1860. Although a separate quartz mining industry would gradually develop, based on extracting gold from hard rock, Ballarat's fame remained rooted in alluvial deep lead mining. Hundreds of mining companies operated dozens of shafts at any time, with new shafts opening as others were worked out. As the gold came from buried riverbeds there was no deepening of the shafts, unless quartz reefs were fortuitously found in the streambed.

The mines faced challenges with foul air caused by the breathing of men and horses, decaying timbers, rotting vegetation, and oxidising minerals in the alluvial wash. Wind sails made of calico, like those used on ships, were effective for ventilating shallow shafts. Hand-operated fanners, sometimes connected to the windlass and later driven by steam power, were also used. Some mines included an air stack or chimney over an air shaft, which connected to one of the compartments of the main shaft, to improve ventilation.

As the mines expanded, ventilation became increasingly challenging. Typically, mines relied on a single shaft, with airflow dependent on air-tight partitions (brattices) that separated the shaft compartments. However, these partitions were often poorly constructed and ineffective.

Air circulation was generally induced by the movement of cages or cascading water in the shaft, with air flowing down one compartment and up another. Some mines used underground furnaces to create an upward airflow, drawing fresh air through other compartments. In 1866, the Ballarat Tunnel Company began using compressed air to power an engine underground. It was claimed that the exhaust air from this engine helped ventilate the entire mine.

Ventilation conditions in the 1860s were challenging, and the working environment – wet, cold, dark, and smelly – was extremely trying. By the 1870s, some mines began running compressed air pipes throughout their workings to improve airflow. The introduction of the Roots Blower, after 1880 marked a significant advancement in ventilation. This engine-driven device blew air through ducting down the shaft and along the levels, greatly enhancing the working conditions in the mines.[15]

By the mid-1860s, deep lead mining techniques on the Ballarat field were virtually fully developed. The miners sank their shafts into the higher

Figure 9 Mining at the Buninyong Company 1863
From a lithographic print by H Deutsch, author's collection

bedrock away from the main gutter, where water was less problematic, and then drove tunnels called reef drives to reach positions directly under the gutter. To drain the water, miners then bored holes from the drives up into the wash, which was then accessed via rises (called jump-ups), which were shafts driven upward from the reef drive.

Hand-pushed trucks, loaded with washdirt by shovel, were pushed on temporary rails and then lowered to the drive below in a balance shaft. This had two cages joined by a rope passing over a pulley, with a friction brake. The weight of the loaded truck raised a cage and empty truck, or timber and supplies, on the other end of the rope.

The trucks were assembled into rakes of six or more and pushed by hand or pulled by horses to the main shaft. Getting the horses down the shaft required careful trussing and slinging under the cage. Bringing them back up was even more difficult, especially if the horses gained weight underground. To address this, stables were cut above the main drives to keep the horses safe in an air pocket in case of flooding. Sumps were also cut under the main drives to manage water.

Figure 10 Underground stables at the Buninyong Company 1863
From a lithographic print by H Deutsch, author's collection

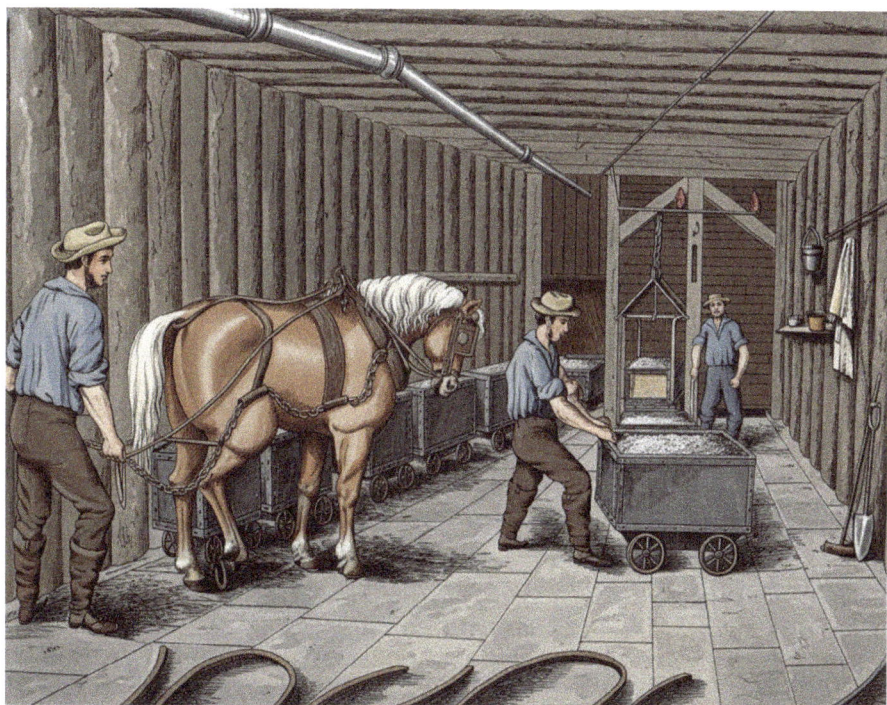

Figure 11 The plat at the United Extended Band of Hope Mine
Dickers Mining Record, 29 October 1867

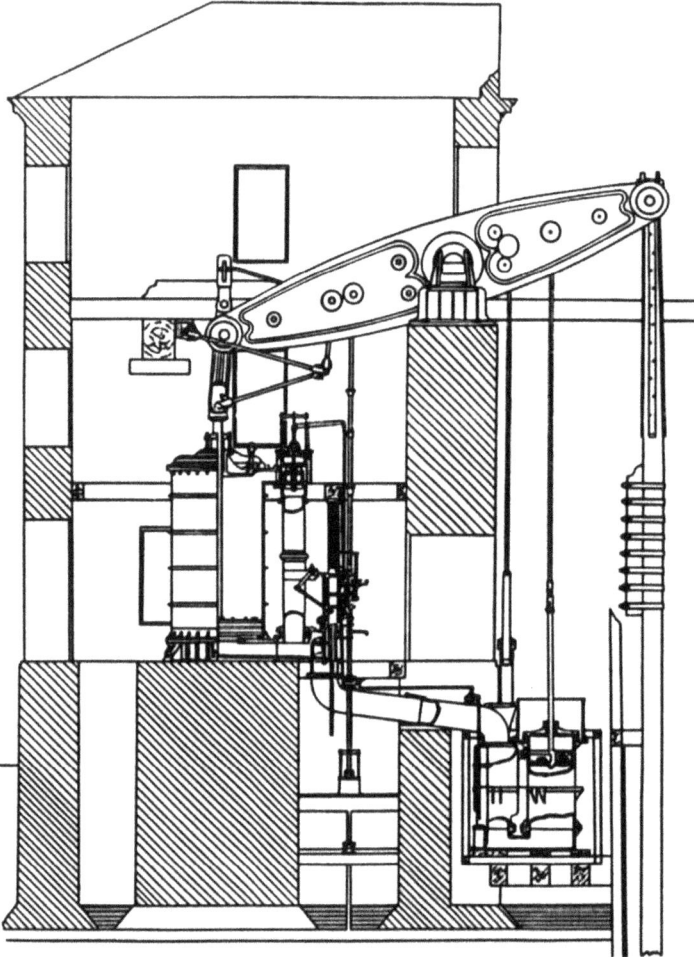

Figure 12 The Cornish pumping engine of the Berry No1 Mine
Mines Department Annual Report, 1884

The early miners sinking vertical shafts faced significant challenges, as the shafts often deviated sideways due to varying geological conditions. Traveling down these shafts, especially when the cage struggled past tight points, was colloquially referred to as 'going around the Cape' or 'rounding the Horn.' Remarkably, in these tight and convoluted shafts – so narrow that sometimes the flanges of pump columns had to be trimmed in places to allow the cage to pass – up to 1,000 trucks per day could be hauled to the surface.

When water inflow exceeded the capacity of kibbles or bailing tanks, 12-to-14-inch diameter Cornish pumps were installed. These pumps were operated via cranks by a conventional steam engine. For dealing with larger volumes of water, some mines used a Cornish beam engine. This setup required a substantial brick or stone building at the edge of the shaft. The beam bearings rested on the wall of the engine house, necessitating a heavily constructed shaft side wall, often three feet thick or more. Inside the engine house, the engine cylinder was mounted vertically, and the piston rod connected to the beam. From the outdoor end of the beam, a string of timber pump rods extended down the shaft to operate the pump.

The Buninyong Gold Mining Company installed an 18-horsepower engine and boilers underground. The engine hauled trucks along the drive and up an incline using a continuous rope, while also operating a pump. The Great Northwest Company's claim featured a 40-inch Cornish engine housed in a substantial brick engine building. The beam for this engine, imported from England, was made of wrought iron. Over time, many Cornish engines were installed across central Victoria. Robert Serjeant installed a massive 60-inch Cornish beam engine at the Band and Albion No 9 shaft.

Robert Serjeant also introduced the first cast iron puddling machine and iron sluice to Ballarat. From around 1865, these puddling machines were mounted above ground in a timber structure adjacent to the head frame, so the waste could be dumped directly onto the ground below. The rakes in these machines were also made of iron. The material from the puddlers was removed by shovel and then sluiced.

Like most of the mining leaders in this story, Serjeant had political aspirations and served as a Member of Victorian Parliament between 1859 and 1861. He then managed the Chryseis, Isis and Garibaldi mines on the Durham lead downstream from Ballarat. He battled with high water inflows and observed that the water was flowing horizontally to the Chryseis shaft from beneath the Sebastopol plateau. This led him, years later, to propose a 10.5 km long drainage tunnel be developed, along the lines of the *Great County Adit* in Cornwall. This would be funded jointly by the mining companies and government, but despite a decade of debate, it did not proceed.

In 1868, Serjeant became involved with the successful Band of Hope company as a director of the St Andrew company, which merged with it. The merger process was contentious, with the original St Andrew board opposing it. Supporters of the merger forced an election, bringing Serjeant to power. When the old board refused to acknowledge the new one, Serjeant and his associates broke into the office at night to remove company seals and cheque books. Subsequent legal action and appeals favoured Serjeant, who then helped organise a further merger with the Albion company. In December 1868, at the age of 40, Serjeant was elected manager of the merged Band and Albion Company, earning a salary of £10 per week, which was four times a miner's wage.

In 1870, Robert Serjeant was appointed as a foundation Councillor of the new Ballarat School of Mines. The Council's first staff appointment was the Cornish gold-discoverer John Phillips as the Resident Master of the school. Serjeant, a prominent Freemason, also served as a Justice of the Peace and was involved with the Art Gallery, the Old Colonists Association, and the hospital. He made sure the Band and Albion Company contributed generously to public institutions.

Serjeant transformed the Band and Albion mine from deep lead mining to quartz mining after discovering rich reefs beneath the old riverbeds. The company extracted more than £600,000 worth of gold from quartz mining, with £250,000 paid out as dividends. In 1898 Serjeant retired when the Band and Albion merged with the Sir Henry Loch United Company. The Band and Albion became the largest and most successful mine in Ballarat, and Serjeant's diligence and prudence as manager continued to be recognised long after his death in 1902 at the age of 74.

CHAPTER 5

265 Tonnes of Gold

DEEP LEAD MINING quickly expanded beyond Ballarat to other fields. In northeast Victoria, deep leads like the Lancashire lead near Chiltern were discovered and mined as early as 1858. As the Ballarat deep leads were gradually worked out in the 1870s, new fields were opened at Creswick and Amherst. By the early 1880s, mining activities extended to the north of Creswick, in the Berry Lead system near Allendale. The late 1880s saw further expansion with mines like the Chalks group being developed near Carisbrook and Majorca. The 1890s marked the peak of mining operations in the Maryborough and Timor areas, while deep leads in the Ararat region, such as Cathcart and Langi Logan, were also being mined during this time.

The unique challenges of mining deep leads in Victoria had resulted in the development of specialised technology and skills. While mining and pumping machinery from other countries could be adapted, mining and to some extent processing methods were unique. Consequently, deep lead mining in Victoria evolved into a largely self-sufficient industry, with much of the equipment being designed and produced within the state.

Once the value and location of the leads were estimated using results from government and private drill bores, the mining company would engage drilling contractors to determine the best locations for the shafts. These shafts needed to be sunk into solid ground on the flanks of the lead, a safe distance from the deep lead gutter, to avoid problems with water or unstable drift. The shafts were designed to be sunk 10 to 12 m below the deepest part of the old stream as shown by boring, but sometimes the stream was deeper than expected, which could then make the shaft useless for gold production because water would not flow back to the shaft pumps. Before electric pumps became available, no high-capacity pumps existed that could work away from the shaft.

From the shaft the miners tunnelled horizontally, passing under the main channel of the deep lead, in 'levels' typically measuring 1.5 m wide and 2.1 m high that were called reef drives. From these drives the miners drilled bores upward and installed pipes and valves every 5 to 7 m along the old riverbed to drain water in a controlled manner. The big pumps in the shaft were activated once the water flow was sufficient.

Once the channel was adequately drained, a 'rise' or 'jump up' was excavated from the reef drive until it reached the height of the wash in the riverbed. Instead of being positioned directly under the wash, the rise was typically placed into one of the banks of the old stream, but close to it. Once the rise reached the appropriate height, a drive was put in from the top until wash was encountered in the face of the drive.

The drive was then carefully extended through the wash, and as soon as possible, cross drives were developed to divide the area into blocks, like the grid of streets in a town. Once the wash was sufficiently drained, it was mined block by block and brought to the surface in large quantities for processing. Typically, mining was done using the retreat system, which involved allowing the roof to collapse after the wash was extracted.[1]

The volume of material mined was measured not by weight, but by fathoms. A fathom of alluvial ground was equal to 36 square feet, or about 3.3 square metres. When reporting the yield of gold per fathom, the depth of the wash was not considered. This same reporting method is used even today in flat-dipping reef mines in South Africa, where the gold yield is measured in grams per Centare.

THE WASHDIRT or auriferous gravel was brought up by the cages in box trucks to a platform called the brace, located up to 20 m above the ground in the timber headframe. Each truck was then pushed along a tramway into a 'kick-up' or 'tippler,' a device that revolved on an axle, allowing the braceman to tip the dirt into one of the puddling machines. Once enough trucks had been emptied to fill the puddling machine, water was added through valves from an elevated tank, and the dirt was agitated by revolving iron harrows until all the clay dissolved. The entire treatment process from the time the washdirt left the truck was powered by the puddling engine, which drove the harrows or agitators.

Once puddling was complete, labourers used long-handled forks to remove the larger stones. This process, known as 'stoning the machine,' was followed by dumping all the fine gravel left behind through a door at the bottom of the puddler onto a sluice platform about 2.4 m below. The gravel was then shovelled into sluice boxes by the assistant sluicemen, and water was turned on. The sluicemen kept the gravel in motion using a six-prong fork, allowing the gold to sink to the bottom. The gold was caught in the head of the box and in the ripples fitted along the sluice box, which extended 3 to 5 m below the point where the dirt was shovelled in.

If there was any fine gold, blanket strakes were added at the end of the sluice boxes. These blankets were removed once a week and washed to recover the fine gold. This method of processing typically recovered about 98% of the gold contained in the washdirt, resulting in clean gold of high purity. In 1895, this gold fetched a price of £4 2s 6d per ounce, or more.

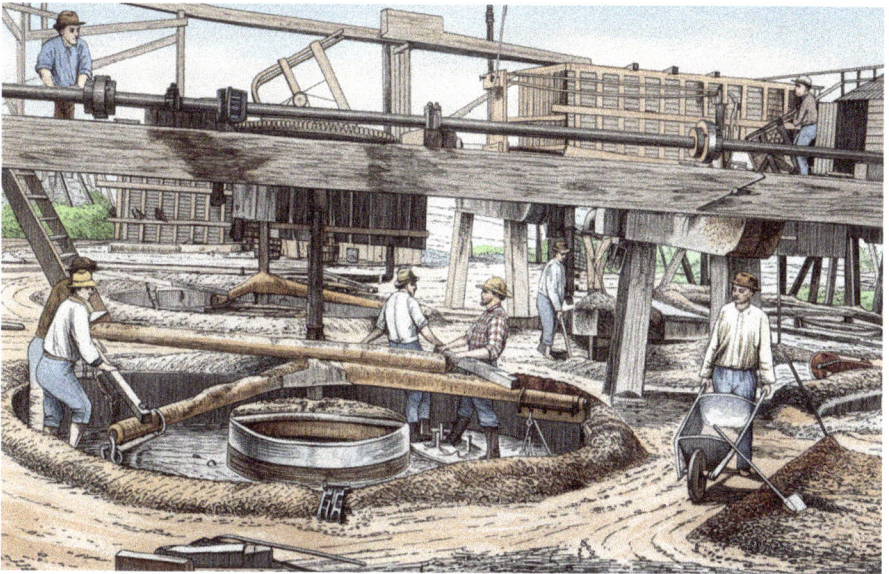

Figure 13 Raking up puddling machines, Ballarat Freehold Mine
after *Dickers Mining Record*, 1867

Mines were usually designed so that the underground levels graded upward from the shaft, at a slope of 1% or slightly more. This design allowed loaded trucks to be pushed downhill to the shaft, while the empty trucks were pushed slightly uphill. Any water entering the mine would flow beside or beneath the rails, back to the shaft, and then down into the shaft sump.

There were two main types of steam-driven pumps. In very wet mines, the old-fashioned but reliable Cornish beam pump was used. This pump featured a large vertical steam cylinder housed in a substantial stone or brick building. It operated a horizontal beam that pivoted at the top of the masonry wall, driving strong rods that hung down the shaft and powered the pumps at the bottom. The rods, fittings, and pumps at the shaft bottom were collectively known as Cornish pitwork.

By the 1890s, most mines had switched to using conventional horizontal steam engines. These engines drove a crank through a reduction gear, which, in turn, operated the Cornish pitwork via a series of rods. To balance the weight of the heavy pump rods hanging in the shaft, a 'balance bob' pivoted like a child's see-saw in a 'bob pit' at the edge of the shaft. Weights were added in a balance box to fine-tune the load on the engine.

With either type of pump, a 'surface frame' or collar made of heavy timber was installed at the top of the shaft to a depth of about 5 m, often supported by brick or stone masonry. Additionally, a strong frame of square logs, resting on bearers at each end, was installed every 12 to 15 m down the shaft. This framework supported the weight of the rising main and provided guides for the pump rods. Every 60 to 100 m down the shaft, a chamber was excavated to install a balance bob, like the one at the shaft collar, which helped to further offset some of the weight of the pump rods.[2]

The pump at the shaft bottom operated with a plunger, which displaced the water, and flap valves that prevented the water from flowing back into the sump. A simple single-cylinder pump was used during shaft sinking, but a more complex and heavier pump was installed for permanent operations. The pump was driven by the weight of the pump rods; the steam engine lifted the rods and then allowed them to fall, pushing the water up the rising main. This permanent pump was housed in a sizable pump chamber, with dimensions tailored to accommodate the pump and its associated fittings.

SHAFTS WERE TYPICALLY rectangular in cross-section. Although a square shape had theoretical advantages, it would require very thick cross-bracing to withstand ground pressure. A rectangular shaft, on the other hand, could handle side loading more effectively with sturdy *centre* timbers. The outer perimeter of the shaft was closely timbered with sawn slabs.

Shafts were divided into several compartments, including those for pumps, cages, ladderways, and ventilation. These compartments were separated by *batten* boards, which were sealed wherever possible to prevent ventilation leakage. In strong rock, the pump compartment might be framed with heavier timbers called *buntons* rather than lined with boards. Other compartments were lined to prevent loose rocks from falling onto the cages and ladderways.

A shaft compartment that was 6 feet (1.8 m) wide could accommodate a cage holding two trucks end-to-end on its deck. These trucks could transport either rock or water.

The overall size of the shaft and the number of compartments were determined by the number and size of the pumps. Each pump required a set of pump rods and a rising main. For example, the main shaft of the Spring Hill and Central Leads Company at Smeaton Plains measured 16 feet by 7 feet (4.9 by 2.1 m) *in the clear*, while the nearby Berry No 1 shaft had five compartments and measured 18 feet by 9 feet (5.5 by 2.7 m). Two of the smaller compartments in the Berry No 1 shaft were used to lower mine timber with a winch and brake, allowing the cages to be used for other tasks.

Shaft sinking in hard, strong rock was a well-established technique practiced for thousands of years, including in ancient China and the Roman empire. However, the challenge in deep lead mines was sinking shafts through layers of wet and unconsolidated clay, sand, and water-worn rocks, interspersed with hard bands of basalt. Each layer could vary from 1 m to 15 m in thickness, and the water within could be under significant pressure. For example, about 22 km north of Ballarat, an exploration drill penetrated basalt into drift, where the hydrostatic pressure was so great that it ejected water and sand to a height said to be 140 m above the drill rig. In the 19th century, no borehole pump was available that could remove enough water to make a significant impact before the shaft was sunk.

In soft ground when water pressure was moderate, shafts were sunk by first driving piles around the perimeter and then installing shaft timbers inside. Additional piles were driven when the shaft bottom reached about halfway down the previous set. If conditions permitted, a *drift box* made of boiler plate could be driven down using heavy weights or screw or hydraulic jacks, with other horizontal jacks supporting the box. Timber sets were then suspended from the ones above until the drift box had descended to a lower level.

The concept of the drift box evolved into what was known as a *telescope* or *traveling shaft*. This method involved starting a large cross-section shaft by driving an iron box down into the drift until side pressure jammed it in place. A smaller box was then placed inside, and the process continued. The success of this method depended on reaching the bottom of the drift before the available space became too small for the next box. If the side pressure caused the box to collapse or twist, recovery was impossible, and the shaft had to be abandoned. To help maintain the integrity of the box, water was often allowed to rise in the shaft while spoil was removed from inside the box using a bucket scoop.

In rare instances, experienced divers were brought in from the coast when the drift boxes became jammed. The shaft would be allowed to fill with water to counteract the outside pressure while men in diving suits worked to remove sand and make repairs. However, this approach was generally unsuccessful.

A further development of the *traveling shaft* concept involved using a heavy circular or elliptical *caisson*, like those used in building bridge pylons. For instance, a circular *caisson* was employed to sink the North Homebush shaft at Avoca after other methods had failed. When the Berry Consols shaft was inundated at a depth of 134 m, an elliptical *caisson*, measuring about 5 m by 2.1 m internally, was constructed. The idea was that the weight of the caisson would drive it downward as the drift was removed, but this attempt failed, and the shaft was abandoned.

Another technique borrowed from civil engineering was the use of a pressurised *caisson*, accessed through an airlock. This method was used by the Madame Berry company when their second main shaft at Allendale was inundated at a similar depth to the Berry Consols. A chamber approximately 6 m long by 4 m wide was excavated and lined with concrete in the clay beneath the basalt at a depth of 122 m. Three iron cylinders were used for sinking: one for the pumping compartment with a 6-foot (1.8 m) inside diameter, and two for the hauling compartments with a 1.4 m inside diameter. Two 18-ton girders spanned the chamber, from which a hydraulic ram could apply a force of about 600 tons to each cylinder. Each pressurised cylinder had an airlock at the top. Two men worked four-hour shifts inside each cylinder, passing dirt up through the airlock. The three columns of cylinders were sunk about 30 m to bedrock using the airlocks. Below this point, the shaft was continued in the usual way with three rectangular timbered compartments.

A similar approach involving airlocks was later used by Berry Consols after their previous attempts had failed. They employed two 2.4 m diameter cylinders to cover the area of the original shaft timbers, allowing the four compartments to be continued once bedrock was reached.

At the Ascot Deep Leads mine, an ammonia refrigeration plant was installed with the goal of freezing the wet ground by pumping calcium chloride through a ring of holes around the perimeter of the shaft. However, this method failed because the water did not fully freeze and continued to flow into the shaft.[3]

WHY DID PEOPLE continued to invest in mining despite its difficulties and the high rate of failed ventures? The answer lies in the fact that some ventures were incredibly successful – hope and the potential for immense rewards drove their persistence. Gold yields varied significantly; for example, the Berry Lead system averaged over 0.75 oz per square metre of floor area, while the Chiltern-Rutherglen area and many other regions produced around 0.225 oz per square metre.[4]

The richest lead system by far was the Berry lead. By 1904 it had produced £5.5 million worth of gold, with £1.6 million coming from a square mile (2.6 sq km) around the Madame Berry claim. Next was the Majorca lead, with £2.3 million from the Chalks No 1 and Chalks No 3 mines.

It is estimated that approximately 265 tonnes of gold were extracted from Victoria's deep lead mines, representing about 11.5% of all the gold mined in the state up to 1974. The remainder came from shallow alluvials and quartz mines.[5]

CHAPTER 6

We Had to Feel for the Water

AS THE MINERS SANK their shafts, they encountered water-saturated rock, usually within 10 to 20 m below the surface. The deeper they went, the more water flooded in. Upon reaching the deep leads, they found a vast reservoir of water filling the gaps between the grains of sand and gravel. While this water no longer flowed along the ancient riverbeds, it moved toward their shafts as they drained the wash and pumped it out.

All deep lead mines faced the constant risk of inrush. Flooding could occur from the saturated material in the deep leads, from breaking into old workings, or even from surface floods. Many such instances, often fatal, occurred. To illustrate the reality faced by the miners during an inrush, the following story, drawn from newspaper reports, is told in some detail.[1]

THE GREAT NORTHERN Junction Company operated a deep lead mine just north of Ballarat. The shaft was in a low-lying area though, under normal circumstances, the water would drain away quickly. Nearby residents, some of whom had lived in the area for over twenty years, could not recall any flooding in the immediate vicinity.

One Saturday morning in October 1869, however, a severe storm inundated the area. The water reached the mouth of the shaft, initially trickling down. Workers hurriedly nailed planks around the shaft to try and contain it, but the water soon carved a channel through the bob-pit – an excavation connected to the shaft collar that housed the balance-bob for the mine pump. The flow into the shaft intensified, sweeping loose timber and debris along with it.

The 58 men on the day shift had started work as usual at 8 am. Around 10 am, Andrew Robertson, the mining manager, was underground when an alarmed James Cooper, the platman, rushed to report a torrent of water pouring into the shaft. The platman was the person responsible for loading and unloading the cages and signalling to the engine driver.

Robertson immediately made his way toward the shaft, wading through water that was rising rapidly. By the time he reached the plat, the water was already up to his knees. He ordered all the men to get to the surface as quickly as possible. The shift captain, James Anderson, shouted, "Hurry up for your lives, or you'll all be drowned!" – and the men did not hesitate. As they reached the plat, Robertson swiftly pushed them into the cage and gave the signal to the engine driver to hoist them to safety.

There was confusion which grew into panic. Robertson shouted, "Keep orderly!" though his voice was barely audible over the roar of the water. Many of the 58 men on shift had been working on the lower level, and each cycle of the four-man cage took several minutes. As impatience grew, tragedy inevitably struck.

In the dim light and chaos, as men jostled for a spot in the cage, Thomas Mountjoy was caught as the cage was hoisted before he was fully inside. He was crushed between the cage and a timber cap-piece at the top of the shaft chamber, suffering severe back injuries. The cage was signalled back down, and Mountjoy was carefully removed. Robertson remained at the shaft until the last man was safely evacuated.

Meanwhile, Anderson carried the injured Mountjoy through the rising water along a drive and waited at the jump-up, a point where they could ascend to a higher level using a balance-cage. By the time Robertson joined them, the water had risen to their chests. To make matters worse, the strong air current created by the falling water in the shaft blew out their only candle, leaving them in darkness.

After ensuring that Mountjoy and Anderson were safely up the rise, Robertson returned to the main shaft, swimming through the water in complete darkness. He called out for William Smith, who had been working alone on the lower level, but received no reply. Unable to feel the cage in the shaft, Robertson made his way back to the jump-up and was hoisted to the higher level.

Navigating in the dark, Robertson made his way to the shaft plat on the upper level. He found a box of candles, but when he lit one and approached the shaft, the strong wind caused by falling water extinguished it. He tried again, but with no better success. Hearing voices, he realised that several miners were still waiting there. He reached his arm into the shaft to check whether the cage was passing and, feeling the cage arrive, called out for the men to get in. They did so, and the cage made several trips – sometimes with five men, sometimes one, and occasionally with no one on board. The signalling system had stopped working, so the winder driver on the surface relied on his own judgment, keeping the cage moving up and down with reasonable pauses at the bottom to allow men to board.

For the final trip, Robertson instructed Anderson to get into the cage and urged a few other men to join him. However, the intensity of the falling water had increased to the point where the remaining miners were too afraid to enter the shaft, as it would have felt like being pulled up through a waterfall. They believed that the flow of water couldn't last much longer and thought it would be safer to stay put.

Robertson went to the pump compartment and placed his hand in, hoping to assess whether a man could keep his head above water if the water continued to rise and flood the upper level. However, the force of the falling water was so strong that he couldn't hold his hand in the shaft.

In the total darkness, Robertson called out to the men he believed were nearby, asking if they had any objections to him going up the shaft to try and stop the water inflow. He occasionally heard noises through the roar of the water, sounds that made him think some men were still there. After calling out, he thought he heard someone answer, but the noise was too overwhelming for him to make out any words.

Shortly after, the cage descended again, and Robertson called out for the men to get in, as he had done each time. However, none of them did. With no time to waste, Robertson jumped into the cage himself, and it began to ascend. On the way up, he lost his hat and reached the surface nearly suffocated by the force of the water. Once at the surface, Robertson asked to borrow a hat, intending to descend again. However, the men around him held him back, preventing him from risking his life further.

Meanwhile, a dam of sandbags was being constructed around the bob-pit to control the water. Unfortunately, the bags had to be gathered from farmers and others in the area, and with the ground around the claim already flooded, the process was agonisingly slow.

While the efforts continued at the surface, the cage kept running, and two other men, Crane and Chapman, made it to the top. Crane reported that he had seen Thomas Mountjoy lying on some dry laths of timber at the upper level, covered with a coat. Mountjoy, appearing gravely injured, had asked for a drink of water, which was given to him. He told Crane that he knew he was dying.

Chapman, the other late arrival, recounted how he had narrowly avoided suffocation by covering his face with his hat during the ascent. Both men described a harrowing scene below, where many of the remaining miners had lost hope. "Cries, prayers, and entreaties were heard throughout the blackness of the dark chamber, above the splash and din of the falling water," they reported, painting a grim picture of the despair below.

A roll-call was held and the missing men were identified as Thomas Gilmour, married, with four children; Robert Organ, married, with either six or seven children; William Smith, a 'Swede', married with two adult children; Thomas Mountjoy, married, with two children; Frederick Disney, Frank Bennetts, John McDonald and three *lads*; Thomas Attewell, Thomas Smith and John Osborne. Lads were employed from the age of fourteen years as truckers and general assistants to the miners.

Several men who had ascended the shaft before Robertson were bleeding from their noses and ears due to the force of the water. Those who had come up in groups of five were severely bruised because parts of their bodies had protruded from the cage and struck against the shaft timbers. Some survivors were dragged from the cage in a semi-conscious state, and most were too weak to contribute further to the surface work.

A few clung to the suspension chain of the cage with such a 'death-like grip' that their fingers had to be pried apart, while others immediately turned to the brandy bottle for relief. Fortunately, men from the nearby Rose Hill mine arrived to help, working tirelessly to dam up the shaft.

It was estimated that the water had risen by 30 m in the shaft, reaching about 10 m above the upper level. The upper level sloped upward away from the shaft, providing a slender hope that the men there might have enough air to survive, although most at the claim remained pessimistic. Unfortunately, no hope was held for William Smith, who was trapped on the lower level, 30 m below the water's surface.

As soon as Robertson reached the surface, the 12-inch pump was set in motion, and two bailing tanks were activated using the winding engine. The pumping engine, with a 5-foot (1.5 m) stroke, was operated at an increased rate of 15 strokes per minute.

Nothing more could be done until the water level was lowered to the top drive. By mid-afternoon, the entire area surrounding the claim was flooded to a depth of up to 1.2 m, forcing reporters and officials to swim their horses to reach the site. At the shaft, someone descended on a bailing tank every four hours to check the water level.

Pumping continued throughout Monday, and by early evening, the upper level became accessible. By 9 pm, a rescue team had advanced 12 m along the top drive, but the air quality was so poor that a candle could not stay lit. To improve ventilation, the Western Fire Brigade's pumping engine was brought to the mine in the early hours. Despite four sections of hose bursting, the engine's strong jet of water gradually cleared the bad air.

However, the candles extinguished due to bad air after they had advanced 30 m along the level, and the men pressed on section by section in the darkness. Unfortunately, they discovered that the drive had collapsed 60 m from the shaft where it passed through an alluvial drift. The leading men convened to discuss their options and resolved to continue working despite the darkness and poor air quality. Meanwhile, many on the surface, weary from the long hours of waiting, chose to go home. Most of the large crowd of friends and family, however, opted to stay at the mine, with many lying close together to sleep briefly in the warmth of the boiler house.

Between noon and 1 pm on Tuesday, the rescuers and the trapped men came within communicating distance. The men below heard their rescuers working nearby and used their hands to burrow into the wet, sandy material that separated them from the outside world. The trapped party responded to shouts of "Come on down here" from the rescuers.

The rescuers made a hole, and young Thomas Smith was the first to appear. The other trapped men quickly crawled through the opening and were hurried to the shaft by their rescuers. At 1:05 pm on Tuesday afternoon,

Thomas Smith emerged blinking into the sunlight, the first of the trapped men to be rescued.

One by one, Frederick Disney, Frank Bennetts, Thomas Attewell, Thomas Selman, John Osborne, and Robert Organ emerged at the surface. The rescued men were taken to the boiler house for warmth and refreshment, surrounded by pressing crowds eager to congratulate them on their safety and learn about their harrowing experiences.

Thomas Mountjoy had only survived for an hour after the others reached their refuge. He hardly spoke after his accident, though he did say "Oh, my poor wife and children, they will suffer greatly for me." After some time, he pleaded, "I can't breathe; give me air." Mountjoy passed away quietly.

After Saturday afternoon, there was no light because the atmosphere could not support a flame. Smith explained, "We lit matches and marked with a stick on a bucket to see how high the water was. When we couldn't burn any more lights, we had to feel for the water with our hands."

They suffered greatly from thirst. While drinking surface floodwater might have been acceptable in an emergency, it would have been dangerously contaminated once it flowed into the mine. At that time, underground mines lacked toilets, and the men used any nearby corner or mined-out area while avoiding the current stopes and travelling ways. Crouched on the air pipes for nearly three days, they had nowhere else to relieve themselves but into the water below.

"As soon as the water was lowered in the shaft it ran back along the drives and carried laths and candle boxes and things with it. When they got on the hose pipes, I suppose it was, the fresh air came in as free and nice as that", Selman said; "I felt at once that I was on the surface, safe."

Mountjoy's body was brought to the surface, but two men – John McDonald and William Smith – remained in the mine. There was some hope for the fifty-three-year-old Smith, as he had last been seen on the lower level at the junction of two drives. If he had managed to navigate the 210 m along the level to the No 3 rise and then climb 12 m up it, he might have found refuge in an air pocket.

Smith was familiar with the workings of the mine, but when asked about his chances, the experienced miners shook their heads, suggesting he would hardly be able to wade through the water for such a great distance in time to escape up the jump-up. For McDonald, no hope was held. He had been with the rescued group on Saturday morning, but they heard a loud splash and did not see him again. He was presumed to have fallen down a jump-up into the water and drowned.

By ten o'clock the following morning (Wednesday), the water level was 1.5 m below the cap piece. It was thought that a tall man could keep his head above water while walking the level to the west in search of Smith. The mining manager, Andrew Robertson, set out with two shift captains and another miner, with the water up to their shoulders. The pumps and bailing tanks were temporarily halted to prevent waves each time a tank entered the water.

There were two drives in the western workings leading from the lower chamber. The search party was divided into two groups, with one going along each drive until they met again at a junction. At this point, one man was sent back to the shaft to keep the bailing going while the other three continued their search. However, at 76 m, their candle went out.

Robertson noticed that a joint in one of the air pipes was loose. He pulled it apart and called down the pipe for Smith and McDonald. There was no response, so he called again, this time louder. A faint reply came back, mentioning the name "Smith." The rescuers hurried to the No 3 jump-up and found Smith near it in the drive. He was standing but appeared exhausted, and he was "much affected" upon realising he was saved. Supported by two men, he was carried to the plat and rested above the water level on some stacked timber.

Smith emerged on the surface to "a loud and enthusiastic round of applause," but he was in no condition to enjoy it. He complained of severe pain in his leg to Dr. Bullen, who wrapped him in blankets, placed him beside the fire, and provided him with "a little stimulant." Shortly after, Smith was taken home in a photographer's buggy.

Meanwhile, the miner who had left the search party was waiting at the shaft for their return when he probed the water at the bottom of the shaft and discovered McDonald's body. He pulled the body out, and after Smith had been rescued, McDonald's body was wrapped in canvas and sent to the surface, then taken to the Junction Hotel. The hotel flags, which had been hoisted in celebration of Smith's rescue, were dutifully lowered to half-mast in mourning for McDonald.

The mine was back in production one week after the inrush, with gold production hardly affected. Within days, Bardwell photographers in Ballarat were selling postcard sized group photograph of the survivors, with the proceeds totalling £25 going to Mrs Mountjoy. She also received £100 from the accident fund and various donations.[2]

Figure 14 Survivors of the Great Northern Junction Inrush
from a postcard which was made as a composite image in 1869

THE DEADLIEST INRUSH occurred at the New Australasian No 2 mine in Creswick in December 1882. It was triggered by a breakthrough into old, flooded workings, a result of poor record-keeping. The new mine manager, William Nicholas, believed the old mine was 100 m away, relying on incorrect plans that showed the shaft in the wrong location.

The miners' ordeal mirrored the previous story, but in this case, 27 men were trapped, and only 5 survived. Working the night shift, the miners descended 76 m down the shaft and then travelled 600 m horizontally to reach the working face. At 5:30 am, the wall of the reef drive gave way under the pressure of water that had built up from the Australasia No 1 Mine.

In the minutes that followed, some miners managed to reach safety, but 27 workers remained trapped. Over the next hour, the trapped men made at least two attempts to escape from the air pockets where they had sought refuge. With no way out, they climbed into jump ups.

For nearly three days, the mine's three engine drivers ran the pumps at over ten times their normal speed, desperately trying to lower the water and rescue the trapped miners. A special train was dispatched from Melbourne, carrying diving equipment borrowed from the warship Her Majesty's Victorian Ship (HMVS) *Cerberus*, and experienced divers to assist in the rescue effort.

After the accident, word spread quickly through Creswick, and people rushed to the mine to await news. After three days of effort, rescuers finally reached the trapped miners. Sadly, 22 men had perished, but 5 survived. In their final moments, the trapped men wrote farewell notes to their loved ones on billy cans. Some of these cans, still bearing the messages, have been preserved. One, now displayed at the Creswick Museum, reads, 'We are all happy'.

The 22 men who perished left behind 18 widows and 75 dependent children. For the funeral, more than 15,000 people lined the road from the mine to the cemetery. The funeral procession included over 4,000 people – so large that as the first mourners reached the cemetery gates, the last were still leaving the mine. Every mine in the district shut down, and the entire town closed to allow everyone to attend the funeral.

Even Australia's worst mining disaster at the time couldn't halt the search for gold. Just two weeks after the tragedy, miners were back at work, cleaning up drives, and soon the mine resumed production. In the half-year leading up to April 1883, just four months after the tragedy, 7,224 oz of gold were produced, with a total of £203,578 worth of gold extracted by the mine up to that point. Annual production over the next three years ranged from 12,000 to 14,000 oz. Dividends, after accounting for compensation and lawsuits related to the disaster, varied from £3,500 to £9,250 every six months.

Numerous reports have been written about the disaster, including a booklet produced by the Creswick Museum titled *Diary of Disaster*.[3]

AN INRUSH OF WATER often carried large quantities of drift – sand and gravel – into the workings, blocking the pumps and filling the drives. Recovering from a serious inrush was often difficult, impractical, or uneconomical. The experience of the West Loughlin Company on the Australasian lead illustrates this challenge.

In 1887, the company installed a complete plant, including a steam winder, large pumps, a poppet head, and two boilers. By 1888, they were developing towards the gutter through seven watertight doors but were repeatedly flooded. To manage the situation, miners filled the level with firewood to keep it open and filter the sand before it reached the pump.

Operations were suspended until November 1890 when capital raising allowed pumping to resume. They repaired the levels, drove and rose into the gutter, and installed puddling machines in anticipation. Despite these efforts, development work was continually hampered by flooding and was ultimately halted in March 1893. A further attempt was made in early 1895, but it failed. No additional work was conducted, and no gold production was ever reported.

Another example is the Lord Harry Company at Kingston. After completing six diamond drill bores, the directors decided to sink a 175 m shaft on a hillside. The lead was encountered in early 1883 but was extremely wet, causing the level to flood. After pumping out the water, it was discovered that the level was filled with sand. Extra drives and rises were added to improve drainage.

In 1884, the pumps were replaced with heavier units, and pumping continued until October, but work was suspended with the water still 36 m above the level. Pumping resumed a year later but ceased after six weeks. It was not until July 1886 that pumping was restarted, but the water was not fully cleared until the end of 1887. The mine then operated for nearly four years but never paid a dividend. It closed at the end of 1891, and the plant was sold off. The shareholders had invested £116,000 to recover gold worth only £48,000.[4]

BY THE MID-1890S, techniques aimed at managing inrushes had been developed. These included heavy iron watertight doors, like those found later in submarines, and sand-locks which had hinged floodgates at either side of the watertight door to prevent sand and mud flowing through the drains into the main portion of the mine. Miners had to pass through the doors to reach their workplace, while truckers had to push their trucks back and forth through them.

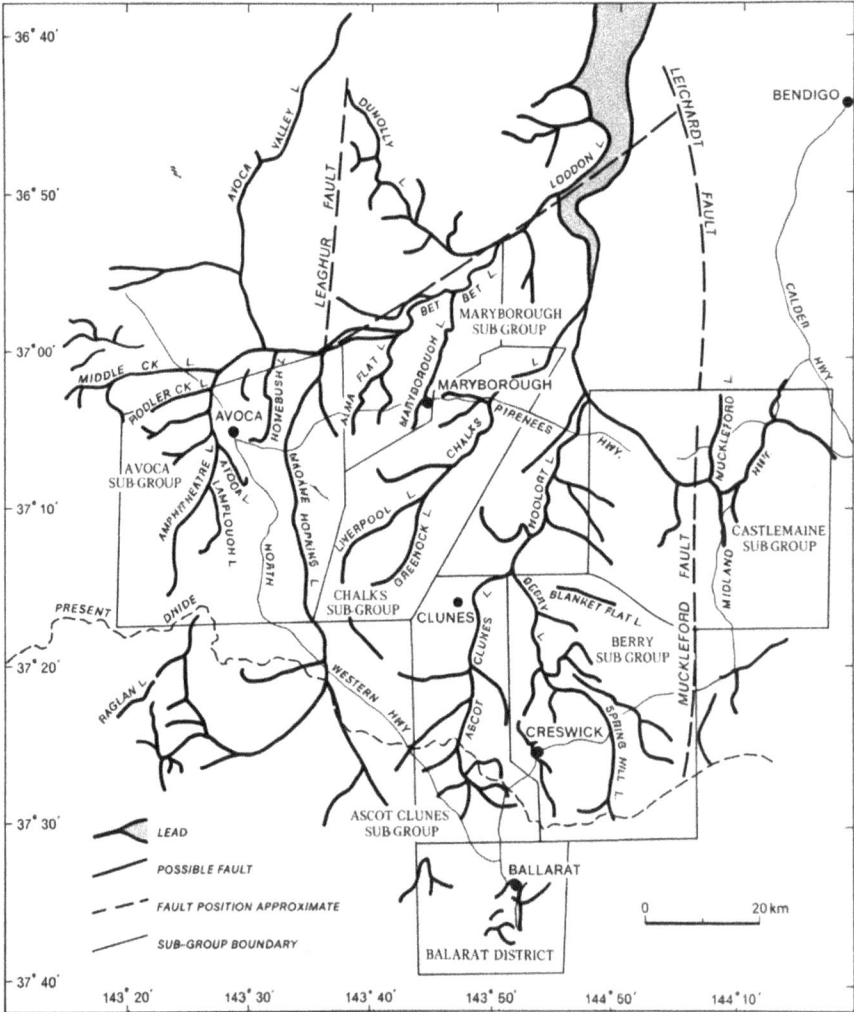

Figure 15 The Loddon Deep Leads
Canavan, 1988

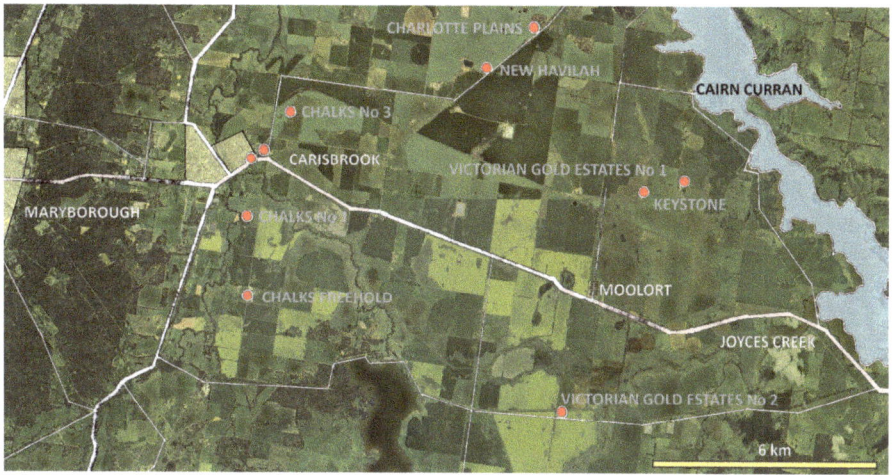

Figure 16 Location of shafts around Moolort

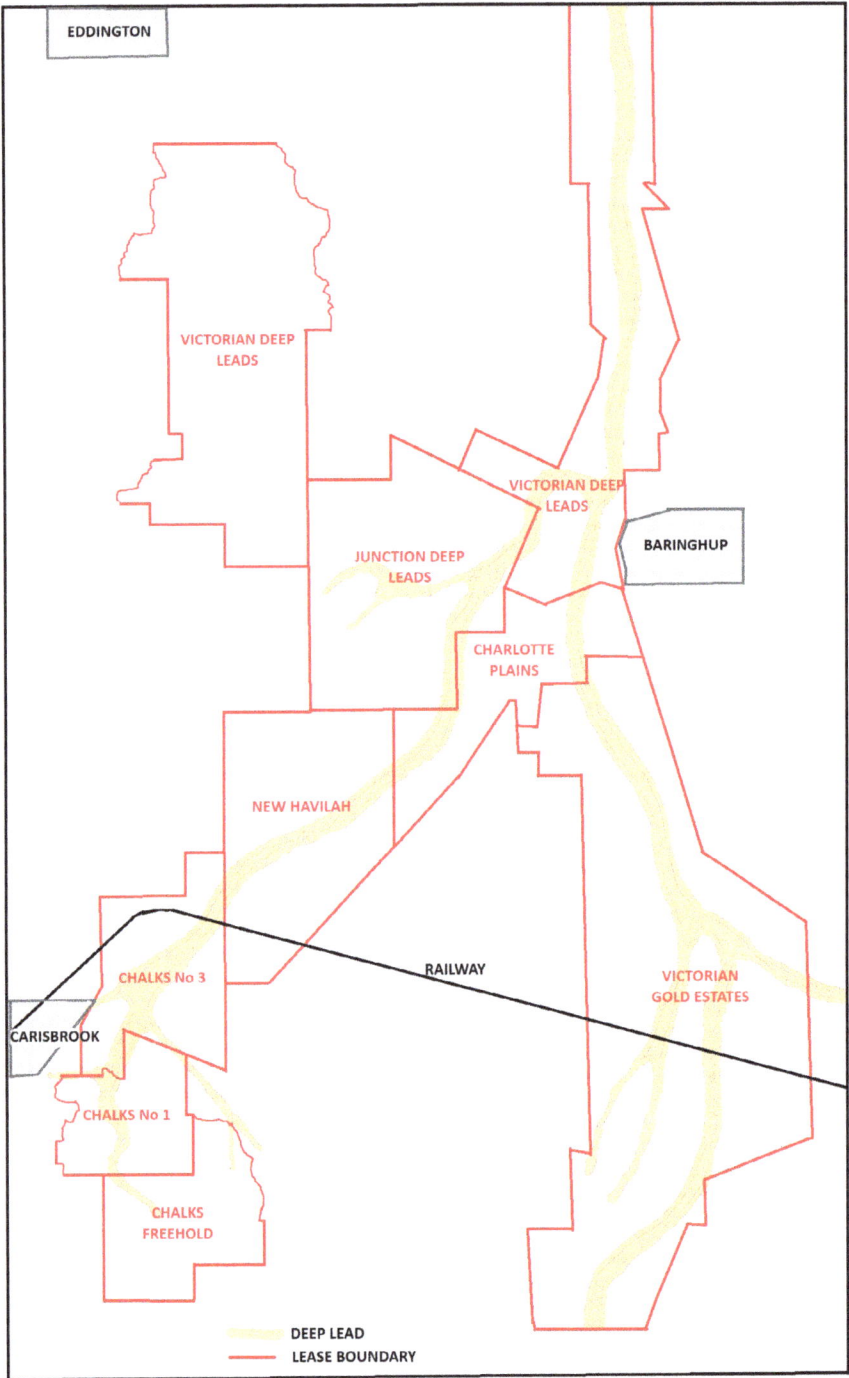

EDDINGTON

VICTORIAN DEEP
LEADS

VICTORIAN DEEP
LEADS

BARINGHUP

JUNCTION DEEP
LEADS

CHARLOTTE
PLAINS

NEW HAVILAH

RAILWAY

CHALKS No 3

VICTORIAN
GOLD ESTATES

CARISBROOK

CHALKS No 1

CHALKS
FREEHOLD

DEEP LEAD
LEASE BOUNDARY

Figure 17 Location of leases around Moolort
After *Engineering and Mining Journal* September 29, 1904, p. 510.

The Pioneer Mine

THERE WAS A DEEP lead system near the town of Majorca, south-east of Maryborough, where an early investor was Lowe Kong Meng, a leader of the Melbourne Chinese community. As deep lead mining followed the Majorca lead north from the Kong Meng mines the Majorca lead became known as the Carisbrook lead.[1]

After 1886 new mines were established on the Charlotte Plains near Carisbrook. These included Chalk's Freehold, Chalk's No 1, and Chalk's Junction. Further north, along the anticipated course of the lead, the Chalk's No 3 company held the ground but chose to wait and observe the results of the other companies before deciding to bore or sink a shaft. No work had been done beyond that point, though it was apparent that the rich Carisbrook lead might run in that direction, and the New Havilah company held a lease north of the No 3.

The Charlotte Plains, originally a large sheep station on the Loddon River, was named in 1837 by pioneer Donald Simson after his wife. It was located on an extensive basaltic plain northeast of the later gold-mining town of Maryborough, which was established in 1854. The volcanic soil of Charlotte Plains was reasonably good for pasture, but the surface was generally too rocky for cultivation. The area practiced mixed farming, including sheep grazing, dairying, horse breeding, and some cropping in paddocks cleared of stones. The farms featured well-fenced paddocks, solid houses, and outbuildings.

Mining on the Charlotte Plains was initiated by John George Paull, who was born in Cornwall and had arrived in Australia as a child. By 1887, aged 41, he was established in Maldon as a draper and was a leading figure in the town; a mining investor, chairman of the successful South German Mining Company, and a prominent member of the Methodist church.[2]

John Paull was the leader of a group of Maldon businessmen who formed a syndicate to search for a northward extension of the Carisbrook lead by boring. They secured a 290 ha lease north of the New Havilah and 6 km north of Chalks No 3. Their six bores proved successful, leading them to establish the Charlotte Plains Pioneer Mining Company in May 1888 with an authorised capital of £40,000. The authorised capital was the amount the company could legally raise from its shareholders; it did not mean that the amount had been raised or was available to the company.[3]

One of the early Pioneer company shareholders was Melbourne investor James Drysdale Brown. Drysdale Brown was born in 1850 in Yorkshire, where his father worked as a bank accountant. The family moved to France, where he was educated in Le Havre and at a Paris academy, before the family moved to Victoria in 1862. Drysdale Brown grew up in the mountain gold-mining town of Woods Point, but despite his Australian upbringing, he maintained the demeanour of a highly educated Englishman with a refined French manner. Early in his career, he felt that the name 'Jim Brown' was too ordinary and chose to be known as J. Drysdale Brown.[4]

Figure 18 James Drysdale Brown
www.parliament.vic.gov.au/
members/james-brown/

At sixteen, Drysdale Brown began working as a clerk for the Hobsons Bay Railway Company, where he stayed for seven years. He later worked as an accountant with the Bank of Victoria in Inglewood and St Arnaud, in the familiar surroundings of small gold-mining communities. By 1877, he had become a branch manager at the Colonial Bank and became involved in the building boom that became known as Marvellous Melbourne. By 1886, while still managing a Colonial Bank branch in Carlton, he was also developing six properties on Bell Street, Coburg.

The affordability of funds on the London market had enticed Australian borrowers, both public and private, to invest heavily in projects such as railways, residential housing, and office buildings. By 1888, land values in parts of central Melbourne reached levels comparable to those in London. The city saw the emergence of grand office buildings up to twelve stories high; many built for thriving building societies, land banks, and mortgage companies. In just a decade, Melbourne's population had doubled to 500,000, making it larger than most European capitals.

By 1887, a dozen women telephonists were handling 8,000 calls daily for wealthy business subscribers. The first cable tram debuted in 1885, and by 1890 the city would have 65 kilometres of tram tracks. The area of metropolitan Melbourne was now greater than that of London.

After purchasing a large block of shares following the 1888 flotation of the Pioneer company, 38-year-old Drysdale Brown contracted typhoid fever, which left him with lingering effects. On his doctor's advice, he spent over a year traveling around New Zealand and Samoa. After returning to Melbourne, he decided to study law in England. He was called to the bar in London and, after returning in 1894, was admitted as a barrister in Melbourne just after the peak of a serious financial crisis.

Meanwhile, the Pioneer company had made significant progress. They erected machinery, sunk a shaft just over 100 m deep, drove 366 m from the shaft to a point beneath the gutter, and began boring upward to drain the water. The tunnelling process proved slow, difficult, and costly. In November 1892, an inrush of water, sand, and gravel filled the drives and shaft. The only viable solution was to sink a new shaft, but the company had exhausted its funds. Its only remaining assets were the mining lease and the surface machinery.[5]

Raising money became increasingly difficult in the 1890s, leading to what became known as the *Panic of 1893* in the USA, and a banking crisis in Australia. It began with the near failure of Barings Bank in 1890, a failed wheat crop in the USA, and a spreading global economic depression. As Melbourne land prices began to fall, financial turmoil ensued as British investors pulled out of their Australian investments.[6]

Despite these challenges, John Paull, and many of the original investors remained loyal to the company. The directors attempted to raise additional funds but found it impossible. But Drysdale Brown had valuable connections from his time in London, when he had walked the streets for 16 km every day for four years and mixed with his fellow law students, lawyers and their families.

With only £28 left in the company's bank account, the directors enlisted John Walker, a London agent, to raise £250,000 to establish a new company. Although Walker made little progress initially, he expressed hope that recent discoveries in Western Australia might attract London investors to Australian properties when they returned from their holidays in October 1894. But no progress was made, and in May 1895 the shareholders gave the directors permission to sell the mine on the best terms they could get.[7]

Drysdale Brown had two further London contacts who he hoped could help to sell the property into a new London flotation. Frederick Dutton, a 40-year-old South Australian who had become a London solicitor and was a director of the Broken Hill Proprietary Company (BHP), had a network which included several wealthy individuals who were associated with BHP. Dutton's father had been the South Australian premier and the original discoverer of the copper deposit at Kapunda. Dutton may have introduced John Orlebar, who had left Warrnambool in 1874, was now a member of the London Stock Exchange and was planning to float Victorian properties.[8]

The buyers demanded that the proposed royalty payment to landowners be reduced to 3% and those negotiations took some time, after which the sale contract was signed on 31 August 1895. The Charlotte Plains Proprietary Gold Mines Limited had an authorised capital of £150,000 in £1 shares. The existing Pioneer Company, as vendor, was to receive 50,000 shares, while £40,000 would be provided for working capital. Drysdale Brown, John Paull, and most of the original Maldon shareholders would now hold a significant stake in the new company through their interests in the Pioneer Company.[9]

After the new company was registered in September 1895 the London market began to recover. A prospectus was prepared for a float, but the market was soon disrupted by a crash in South African stocks and political uncertainty, which were exacerbated by the Jameson Raid into the Transvaal in early January 1896. As a result, the London mining market was paralysed for several months. The new owners would not commit their personal funds to the project in this environment. Now the company could not meet its labour requirements, and without funding, no work could be done on the lease. The Pioneer Company shareholders were aware that the lease was vulnerable to claim jumpers but were powerless to act.[10]

DURING THIS PERIOD, many areas were being tested by government bores using diamond-tipped drills. Diamond drilling was costly and often beyond the reach of individual prospectors or small mining companies. Accurate information from these bores was crucial for selecting leases and positioning mine shafts effectively. Access for boring was made difficult by some farmers, who could block mining activities by applying for mining leases themselves and then failing to develop them. Aware of this tactic, the Victorian government, eager to support the mining industry, rarely granted leases to obstructive applicants.[11]

In July 1895, the annual report of the retiring Secretary for Mines, Alfred Howitt, was released. Howitt, the son of author William Howitt, had been educated as an engineer before arriving in Australia in 1852 to join the gold rush. A skilled bushman, he led the Victorian relief party in 1861 that rescued John King from Cooper's Creek and recovered the bodies of Burke and Wills. His report addressed the financial depression in Victoria and the migration of capital and labour to Western Australia, and it examined the prospects for revival in various Victorian goldfields. He wrote:

> Although I see little probability of the discovery of any extensive surface alluvial fields, there are still remaining to us really immense tracts where alluvial gold exists in 'deep leads.' On the northern side of the divide, and to the westward of the meridian of Melbourne, there has been proved by diamond drill borings an aggregate length, estimated by the Government Geologist, of 10 miles of leads, following well defined auriferous belts, and where some of the drill bores proved the existence of gold.[12]

Howitt mentioned that he had prepared a proposal for Mr. Foster, the Minister for Mines, which aimed to support large-scale mine development through an annual subsidy. This subsidy would be repaid over several years from the gold produced. The plan included withholding leases from neighbouring areas to prevent 'royalty sharks' from acquiring them. Additionally, other mines on the lead would be required to either work their leases, share the cost of pumping, or surrender them.[13]

Howitt's successor as Secretary was James Travis, a Canadian-born experienced miner. At the request of Minister Foster, Travis compiled and sent a large volume of information on unworked mines to the Agent General in London to attract investors. This information package included an extensive report by Reginald Murray, the Government geologist, on the deep leads of Victoria. Travis wrote

> Mr Murray thinks that a large proportion are likely to prove payable, but the work will require heavy capital owing chiefly to the water difficulty.[14]

Murray's report detailed the various deep lead systems, highlighting the most significant ones. He noted that bores near Moolort on the Charlotte Plains had identified a large and well-defined trunk lead and mentioned that the Charlotte Plains Pioneer mine had found gold before being flooded.[15]

Reginald Augustus Frederick Murray had emigrated with his family to Victoria at the age of nine. He qualified as a mining surveyor and joined the Geological Survey, working mainly in the goldfields. From 1873 he worked on reconnaissance surveys in eastern Victoria and became Government geologist in 1881. He was sensitive about his speech impediment and once wanted to fight a fellow stutterer who he thought was mocking him, until the publican bought them both a drink.[16]

In October 1895, the *Argus* published an article titled *'The Creswick Gold Mines – A Deep Alluvial Lead.'* The article described the Creswick goldfield as the richest alluvial deep goldfield in the world and provided a history and status of several mines, including the Madame Berry, Berry Consols, Madame Berry West, Berry No 1, Berry Consols Extended, and the Spring Hill and Central Leads. Prospecting was ongoing in the north drive of the Madame Berry, while the Spring Hill and Central Leads were in the shaft-sinking phase. The other mines were actively producing gold.[17]

Four of the companies were under the legal management of Alexander Peacock, a Member of the Legislative Assembly of Victoria (MLA). Born in Creswick, 33-year-old Peacock had represented the seat of Clunes and Allendale since 1889. Deeply involved in the local gold mining scene, he had served as a director for several gold mining companies and operated his own legal mining manager's business in Creswick, handling some of Victoria's wealthiest gold-mining operations, including the Berry group. Peacock had also been a member of a Royal Commission on gold mining from 1889 to 1891. His affable and approachable demeanour made him popular among local electors, who valued the employment and business opportunities his activities generated.

Several investor groups in London reviewed the data at the Victorian Agent General's office. The Honourable Duncan Gillies, the Agent General, recommended that Reginald Murray write a supplementary report on the deep lead systems. Murray complied, also preparing plans that covered the area from Creswick to Moolort, including existing leases and the locations of bores. He described the Main Trunk Lead, which extended slightly east of north from Bucknall's Estate, between the Moolort outcrop and the Loddon River, crossing the ground already applied for by one Abraham Kozminsky and extending into the Charlotte Plains Pioneer Company's area, where he noted that work was suspended despite gold having been found.[18]

Murray observed that the depth required to reach the lead was *decreasing* to the north, despite the buried riverbeds flowing in that direction. This was because the topographic surface sloped downward toward the Murray River more steeply than the deep lead. He also noted that little gold had been detected in diamond drilling, as gold particles were often washed out of the sampling tubes by the water used to flush the hole. He pointed out that the area was well-serviced by roads and railways.

CHAPTER 8

Abraham Kozminsky

WHILE DRYSDALE BROWN was struggling to finance the Pioneer Company, another Melbourne businessman, Abraham Kozminsky, was considering opportunities in deep lead mining. Despite recent setbacks, Kozminsky remained well-off and sought a substantial new project that could yield significant returns.

Kozminsky, a handsome man with a dark beard, was well-respected along Collins Street and within the local Jewish community. Though his hair was starting to recede, he remained energetic and determined.

Figure 19 Abraham Kozminsky after *British Australasian*, 11 May 1899, p12

Despite difficulties with his Tasmanian silver mining company and failed efforts in Western Australia, he remained confident in the mining sector. Kozminsky was keen to identify a major mining project which could be financed in London, where he believed substantial investment was available. With significant English capital flowing into the boom at Coolgardie and Kalgoorlie, he thought some of it could be redirected towards a mining project in Victoria.

Abraham Kozminsky was born Avraham Ben Kozminsky to Russian Jewish parents in Krotoszyn, in the province of Posen, in 1853. A Polish province, Posen had been annexed by the Prussians in 1815. The Jews of Posen were maltreated, because they had tended to support the Prussians in the failed Polish uprising of 1848, so life was not ideal for the Kozminsky boys. Abraham's older brothers Simon and Marks emigrated to Victoria in

the early 1860s and went into business as country storekeepers. Abraham joined them, aged fourteen, in 1867 and the Kozminsky brothers operated stores in Deniliquin, Nhill, Wycheproof, and Kaniva.[1]

Abraham Kozminsky managed the Wycheproof store until his marriage in 1882. He then moved to Melbourne, where he transitioned into land development and finance, becoming actively involved in the Jewish community. His timing was fortuitous; the Melbourne land boom started in 1883, credit was readily available, and the Kozminsky brothers thrived.

Marks Kozminsky emerged as a prominent figure in Nhill, where he became a leading citizen, developer, storekeeper, and hotel owner. Meanwhile, Simon's pawnbroking business on Collins Street evolved into one of Melbourne's leading jewellers.

At 35, Abraham Kozminsky was actively developing land, and he had become a director and shareholder in several finance and stockbroking companies. He formed a partnership with accountant Andrew Lyell, establishing offices in Sydney and London. However, the partnership was short-lived, dissolving within a year when Lyell became insolvent, leaving Kozminsky as an unsecured creditor. Following this, several of Kozminsky's other investments also failed.[2]

Michael Cannon, a historian writing of the Land Boomers more than seventy years later, wrote:

> In its period of generosity, the Commercial Bank heavily financed such leading speculators as Thomas Bent, Edward Latham, J.A. Kitchen, Abraham Kozminsky and many others.[3]

Kozminsky decided to shift his investments into the mining industry, drawn by the silver boom on the West Coast of Tasmania. A new railway was being constructed through the Big Henty to Zeehan, fuelling optimism. This was only a few years after the successful Broken Hill boom, which had been financed from Melbourne, and Kozminsky saw potential in this new opportunity. BHP had been securing favourable prices for its silver by compelling banks to tender for their product. Great expectations were placed on West Coast field, where high-grade silver had been discovered in outcrops.[4]

Kozminsky travelled to the West Coast and secured three leases at Mount Dundas, where a significant formation of galena (lead sulphide) had been uncovered. The conditions were challenging; prospectors had to forge their own paths through dense, sodden scrub and navigate steep slopes. The main access route into Mount Dundas was too steep for horses, so all supplies had to be carried by hand. [5]

Kozminsky established the Mount Dundas Proprietary Silver Mining Company, floating the leases with a capital of £100,000. To attract investors, Kozminsky appointed three prominent and wealthy figures as directors of the Mount Dundas Proprietary Silver Mining Company.[6]

Henry Gore was a civil engineer and former Shire Engineer for the Creswick district, a shareholder and director in many Victorian gold mines. Joseph Clarke had inherited extensive estates in Tasmania, South Australia, and New Zealand. Clarke had a large home in Toorak and served as a director for both the Hobson's United Railway Co. and the Mount Lyell Mining Company in Tasmania. Benjamin Josman Fink was the owner of furniture and music stores, who had merged his small Joint Stock Bank of Ballarat with the City of Melbourne Bank, creating the colony's largest gold buyer. His Mercantile Finance Company Limited was a major player in the land boom. Fink also owned several notable properties, including Fink's Buildings at the corner of Flinders and Elizabeth Streets, the original Cole's Book Arcade, Gresham Buildings, The Block Arcade, and Georges Limited.

The new company, commonly referred to as Kozminsky's Mount Dundas Company, held the largest claim on the field. It quickly accessed three lodes through tunnels and a 30 m shaft. However, it soon faced litigation from professional claim jumpers, who sought to exploit any flaws in the pegging process. Kozminsky defended the company's interests, and the Supreme Court dismissed the claim jumpers' case with costs.[7]

Despite the court victory, progress on the Mount Dundas project slowed as autumn weather set in, which hindered the delivery of supplies due to poor road conditions. The share price continued to fall, and by July 1892, it had run out of funds and work was suspended.

The financial situation in Melbourne was deteriorating. In September 1892, Benjamin Fink held a meeting with his creditors. His estate yielded only a halfpenny in the pound, and Fink fled Melbourne for London with his family, having transferred some large assets into his wife's name before leaving. Joseph Clarke also suffered significant financial losses in the crash and would die two years later. Henry Gore, having avoided excessive debt, continued as a director for several mining companies. However, in September 1892, he lost his seat in the Legislative Assembly.

Work at Mount Dundas remained suspended until 1894, when the company was reorganised as the New Kozminsky Silver Mining Company, No Liability. However, this new venture also failed. Despite these setbacks, Abraham Kozminsky remained determined.[8]

In March 1894, he secured a contract with the Victorian Railway Department for exclusive advertising rights in their printed timetables, which were distributed across Australia. This was expected to be the Australian equivalent of the English Bradshaw's Guide. His Railway Guide ran intermittently for four years, but it would end in what one newspaper described as 'the Kozminsky Railway Guide Scandal', when Kozminsky was paid £1,500 by the Railway Department to cancel the contract.[9]

Kozminsky travelled to Perth in 1894 to market the railway guide and to look for mining opportunities for a syndicate of his Melbourne business associates. Gold discoveries in Western Australia had begun as early as 1885, but the real rush started in September 1892 when Bayley and Ford announced a major find at Coolgardie. Just nine months later, Paddy Hannan and Tom Flanagan made an even more significant discovery at Mount Charlotte, which would become the Kalgoorlie field. Kozminsky visited Coolgardie and then travelled to several new fields, seeking leases to purchase.[10]

While in Coolgardie, Kozminsky coincidentally saw a leading article in a local paper about claim jumping, a topic familiar to him from his experience at Mount Dundas. Western Australian mining laws required continuous labour employment on a lease, necessitating that anyone attempting to float a company in the eastern states or London leave sufficient funds locally to meet these labour requirements until major funds were secured. These laws favoured local small miners over external investors.[11]

Kozminsky acquired two blocks at the Ninety-mile, north of Coolgardie. As anticipated, his leases faced challenges from claim jumpers, but they were ultimately granted to him in early June. He travelled by coach to Albany and then by sea to Adelaide to arrange the floatation of his new company, returning to Perth in July. Back in Kalgoorlie, he purchased two leases at Broad Arrow and another lease south of the Croesus mine. By early October he returned east, satisfied with his acquisitions and prepared to float the new company.[12]

Kozminsky's concerns about claim jumpers proved justified. He was compelled to forfeit the leases at Broad Arrow, and loss of the properties he had acquired near the Croesus lode was a major disappointment. Kozminsky later remarked that they were jumped while he was away seeking fresh capital, despite having left sufficient funds to meet the labour covenant.[13]

At the end of 1894, Kozminsky sat in his study, reviewing various businesses and opportunities. The new Victorian government under Premier Turner appeared to be struggling to improve the colony's economy. Local manufacturing industries remained in a prolonged depression despite high import tariffs. Agriculture did not appeal to him: the wheat crop had been poor due to hot weather, and wool prices were low. Although the prospects of shipping frozen mutton to London were intriguing, it would require several years and significant investment to develop the trade. Fruit growing and other rural ventures did not offer the scale he desired.

Mining investment was largely focused on Western Australia, leading to a shortage of capital and mining labour in Victoria. However, Kozminsky, along with others, shared the view that Western Australia was 'a vast wilderness of drought, desolation, and disappointment.' Still, in 1894 Victoria had produced nearly 740,000 ounces of gold compared to only 200,000 ounces in Western Australia. Despite its challenges, and although Drysdale Brown had so far been unable to finance the Pioneer mine, Victorian mining still seemed to be the most promising business opportunity.[14]

Reflecting on his experiences in Tasmania and Western Australia, Kozminsky decided to focus on the Victorian goldfields. He hoped to find large, promising properties that could support a London flotation. To secure these large leases, he would need government guarantees ensuring their security until sufficient funds were raised. His Melbourne associates would join him as partners in this ambitious venture.

The major mining centres in Victoria were Ballarat and Bendigo, now both primarily known for hard-rock quartz mining. The deep lead mines in Ballarat were mostly depleted and closed. Both cities had well-established stock exchanges, and their mining shares were traded in Melbourne and beyond. Identifying overlooked opportunities in these well-trodden areas required a shrewd operator.

In Bendigo, production was declining, having fallen from 213,000 oz in 1893 to just 172,000 oz in 1894. This was a significant drop from its peak production of nearly 610,000 oz in 1856. Although thirty-six mines in Bendigo were still paying dividends, most yielded only £2,000-£3,000 or less. Major mines like Johnson's Reef and Garden Gully were well-traded and did not present viable opportunities for new investors.[15]

At Ballarat, the Sebastopol deep lead mines had either closed or been converted to quartz mining, and they were struggling with increasing water inflows. Investors worldwide were growing impatient, waiting for the South Star mine to cease making calls for additional funds and begin paying dividends. In Ballarat East, several mines, including the Last Chance, New Normanby, and North Woah Hawp were producing steady but modest dividends. However, none of these mines generated much excitement among investors.[16]

One mine that caught Kozminsky's attention was the Hepburn Estate on the Berry lead. After a lengthy period of development and several setbacks, the mine had successfully reached the gutter and was proving to be payable. Despite £90,600 in calls, the mine had paid £108,868 in wages, produced gold worth £125,087, and had recently issued its first dividend. The richest deposits were found at the northern end of the lease, near the Lady Hepburn company's ground. The Hepburn Estate had secured the right to work an additional mile to the north.[17]

Located at the northern edge of the Berry Lead system, just north of the village of Allendale, the Hepburn Estate's success suggested that the deep lead could continue further north. This potential for extension into reasonably obtainable ground intrigued Kozminsky, who saw an opportunity to float a large venture based on these promising prospects.

A visit to the Creswick district could provide valuable insights for

Kozminsky's plans. He might have hoped to discuss opportunities with Isaac Bentwitch, a fellow Polish-born mining investor who had run a tobacconist and jeweller's shop in Creswick. However, Bentwitch had passed away the previous year.

Another potential contact was William Walton Bell, who was born in Allendale, Northumberland, and arrived in Victoria in 1857. He worked as a deep lead miner in Ballarat and was a pioneer of Creswick, even naming the town of Allendale. Known as 'Baron' Bell during the peak of the Spring Hill goldfield, he was recognised as an enterprising individual with a knack for innovative ideas. Bell was reputed to have made and spent several fortunes through his mining investments.

Alexander Peacock MLA was an obvious contact. Kozminsky, aware of the risks posed by claim jumpers, was determined to secure his leases discreetly before making his plans public. Peacock was now serving as

Figure 20 Alexander Peacock, 1898
Official album of the Australasian
Federal Convention, Melbourne, 1898

the Minister of Public Instruction (which meant Education) but had the right mining credentials and connections within government. Kozminsky saw him as the key to obtaining the necessary leases for his venture. The two would be business partners for the next 25 years.

AT THE BEGINNING OF 1895 a group of potential investors, described as 'representatives of the leading London financial institutions', visited Victoria to evaluate the prospects of reopening the deep leads on a large scale. They asked whether the known rich deep leads might continue downstream and why the mines had previously shut down. They were told that many mines had been flooded, with pumps unable to manage the inflow as the workings expanded. In other areas, the gold-bearing wash had spread across such a large area that, although gold was present in the gravel, the average grade was too low to cover the costs. Additionally, numerous companies had failed due to boundary disputes and costly lawsuits.[18]

The London visitors discovered that the Victorian economy was in a severe depression, with no local funds available and no interest in speculative or any other kind of investment. However, they were excited by the story of the thirteen Ballarat deep lead companies which had previously paid out £1,878,900 in dividends from a total paid-up capital of only £145,000.

James Jones, writing to *The Argus*, argued that the government should encourage large investments in deep lead projects by offering special leases at nominal rents and providing favourable labour conditions. Jones, who was the manager of a company developing a deep lead mine at Moondarra, south of the Baw Baw range, believed that the government could do more to support the industry.[19]

The first outcome of the London investors' visit was the purchase in late February of a large lease at Moyston, near Ararat, by the West Australian Development Corporation. This property, located on the Moyston wet lead, had been actively promoted by local interests. The company promised to deploy 'the latest and most perfect machinery' to develop the mine.[20]

The West Australian Development Corporation, which had been established in London three months earlier, described its scope as activities including farming, grazing, planting, mining, coal and iron production, quarrying, and brickmaking. The Coolgardie Miner newspaper, miffed that the Western Australian name was being used to promote Victorian mining, observed that

> The 'corporation' is going to do all this with a capital of £10,000. Jacks of all trades, probably masters of none.[21]

The company lasted less than six months before undergoing a financial reconstruction and it ultimately failed in early 1898, with no work ever conducted at Moyston. However, the announcement of the deal in early 1895 further motivated both Drysdale Brown and Abraham Kozminsky to look toward London.

MID-1895 WAS a challenging time for Abraham Kozminsky. First, his brother Marks passed away suddenly at Nhill from accidental mushroom poisoning. Then, in June, his brother Simon filed for insolvency. Despite his own financial challenges, Abraham helped support his extended family, becoming further financially involved in the jewellery business.[22]

Deep leads were being worked across Victoria, including at Stawell, Malmsbury, Rutherglen, and Omeo, as well as in the traditional mining areas of Ballarat and Creswick. Good results in any of these mines could trigger a rush of claim staking nearby, but Kozminsky had bigger ambitions.

The two major opportunities appeared to be the northern extensions of the Majorca/Carisbrook Lead west of Moolort, or the Berry Lead north of Allendale. Drysdale Brown's Charlotte Plains Pioneer Company already controlled the Carisbrook ground, leaving only the Berry Lead as a potential focus for Kozminsky. However, government bores had not shown promising results just north of the Berry and Hepburn lines, and there was a 32 km gap before bores indicated a gold-bearing lead near Moolort. Although there was no concrete evidence that the Moolort lead was an extension of the rich Berry Lead, the idea was intriguing and likely to appeal to investors.

Victorian Gold Estate Corporation

REGINALD MURRAY'S REFERENCE to Kozminsky's lease application in his 1895 report was premature, as Kozminsky was trying to keep a low profile while negotiating the terms. Key concerns included labour and expenditure requirements, given that sinking the shaft and dewatering the lead would take several years. It wasn't until the end of the year that the applications were formalised. In late December, Kozminsky published two Notices of Application for mining leases at Moolort.

The name *Moolort*, (more correctly pronounced Moolart) is derived from the word moola which means bracken in the local Dja Dja Wurrung language. As an Aboriginal placename Moolort refers to Long Swamp, south of today's Pyrenees Highway. A similar word Mooller refers to the redgum tree.[1]

The applications, for 15-year leases, detailed all the names and occupiers of the affected land. One lease application covered 1,485 ha, and the other 2,300 ha, unprecedented large areas in Victoria. Each lease was expected to require £50,000 in expenditure, with work scheduled to begin as soon as the leases were granted. Under 'General Remarks' in the application Kozminsky added:

> Being deep ground and with enormous quantities of water to contend with, will require very powerful machinery and large capital to develop.[2]

Meanwhile, Kozminsky was working to float his leases on the London market once they were issued. Communication with London via telegraph took about seven hours, effectively an overnight process in either direction, through the network of telegraph operators across Australia, Asia, and Europe. While Ballarat and Bendigo had been linked by telegraph with Melbourne since 1856, primarily for stock market news and transactions, the London connection was relatively recent. With Kozminsky's previous London agent

Robert Walpole having returned to Melbourne, Kozminsky decided to travel to London himself.

He left Melbourne on the RMS *Australia* for a five-week voyage, arriving in late February 1896. He discussed his mission with Lord Henry Loch, who boarded the ship at Gibraltar. Loch had been Governor of Victoria from 1884 to 1889 and had visited the Madame Berry mine. Lord Loch, now a director of the London and Globe Finance Company, with significant interests in Western Australian gold projects, invited Kozminsky to present his case to the London and Globe board.[3]

The London and Globe Finance Company was run by James Whitaker Wright. Following Lord Loch's introduction, Kozminsky had several meetings with him. Wright was a heavy man with a large head, small eyes, a receding forehead and chin, and a bulky neck that swelled over his collar. He disliked being photographed and despised references, saying 'I judge a man by his face, I don't care tuppence what other people say about him.' On that basis he must have warmed to Kozminsky, or at least to the proposition that Kozminsky set before him.[4]

Figure 21 Whitaker Wright
A sketch from *The Sphere* that was circulated by police in 1903.

Wright had made and lost a fortune in the USA before starting to rebuild his wealth in England. Although some in the establishment viewed him with suspicion, his skill in raising money and manipulating markets allowed most to set aside their reservations. Now based in Surrey, Wright had swiftly capitalised on the Western Australian gold boom, securing options on leases in the Coolgardie district and forming the West Australian Exploring and Finance Corporation in September 1894. Despite his questionable reputation, that public offering was quickly taken up.

Whitaker Wright was born in Stafford in 1846. Before emigrating with his family to Toronto, Canada in 1870, he had worked as a printer and Methodist preacher. After moving to the USA, he found work as an assayer and began trading in mining claims and shares. Though he started with very little, he managed to build a stake of around $2,000.

After his marriage in 1878, Wright became a company promoter, launching dubious silver-mining companies in Leadville, Colorado, and Lake Valley, New Mexico. His first venture, alongside two equally impoverished associates, involved purchasing three claims which they then floated as the Denver City Consolidated Mining Company in New York and Philadelphia, taking a large vendor payment. The company only found low-grade ore, never paid a dividend, and closed its mine in 1882. Despite this failure, Wright spun off another equally worthless venture, the Lee Basin Company, walking away with enough money to fund other projects and purchase a four-story house in Philadelphia.[5]

In 1881 Wright, acting on behalf of a syndicate of investors, purchased several adjacent claims in New Mexico. These claims were floated as the Sierra Plata, Sierra Apache, Sierra Madre, and Sierra Grande companies, collectively known as the Lake Valley mines. Although the mines initially yielded high-grade ore, providing temporary profits, the rich patches were quickly exhausted. Wright sold his shares while prices were still high, and the mines never became profitable afterward.

In early 1887, Wright made a quick trade in the Crown Point Gold Mine at Grass Valley in Nevada County, California. Another significant venture was the Gunnison mine in Colorado. He began buying stock, eventually acquiring a controlling interest. Wright then spun off three companies – the Gunnison Mine Company, the Gunnison Coal Company, and the Gunnison Land Company. Each of these new companies was capitalised at two to five million dollars, more than triple the original Gunnison company's capitalisation. This technique of property inflation was one Wright would later perfect in England.

Wright became a millionaire at the age of 36, purchasing a luxurious summer home in Long Branch, New Jersey, and owning several expensive yachts. However, his fortunes took a downturn in 1889 when the Gunnison companies collapsed, forcing him to flee to England with his wife and three children, leaving behind significant debts.

In September 1894, Wright launched the heavily promoted West Australian Exploring and Finance Company Limited. The company was capitalised at £200,000 in £1 shares, with an initial offering of 150,000 shares. The London-based consulting firm Bewick, Moreing and Co, later to feature in the story of the Moolort mines, was appointed as the company's consulting engineer.[6]

The prospectus highlighted 'the marvellous developments in the recently discovered goldfields of Western Australia' and outlined the company's plans to acquire options or purchase mining leases, trade in properties, raise finance for development, and establish offices in the goldfields. Wright had already secured options on several properties in the Murchison and Coolgardie fields, which would be floated as separate companies, with shareholders in the West Australian Exploring and Finance Company receiving preference in subscribing to them.

As a reward for his efforts, Wright was to receive 5,000 fully paid shares and the right to subscribe for an additional 45,000 shares at par. This arrangement seemed reasonable and further encouraged investors. The float was oversubscribed, prompting Wright to hire German engineer Charles Kaufmann, based in Western Australia, to visit locations and report on opportunities.

Four London-based companies then agreed to collaborate: Wright's West Australian Exploring and Finance Company Limited, the West Australian Goldfields Limited, the London and Western Australian Exploration Company Limited (a subsidiary of Bewick Moreing), and the West Australian Pioneer Syndicate Limited. They believed cooperation would yield better results than competition, and each planned to float a new company for every mine or group of mines to be acquired or developed.[7]

As the boom in West Australian shares continued, Wright launched a second company, the London and Globe Finance Corporation, in April 1895. A key aspect of Wright's strategy was to attract prominent figures, pillars of society, to serve as his directors. The original company's board included, alongside Wright himself; Frederick Thompson, Esquire as Chairman; The Right Honourable Lord Edward Pelham-Clinton (Master of the Queen's Household, Deputy Governor of Windsor Castle, and younger brother of the Duke of Newcastle); Lieutenant General The Honourable Somerset J. Gough-Calthorpe (a close friend of Queen Victoria); and Allen H.P. Stoneham, Esquire.

Frederick Thompson was an established mining company chairman, and Stoneham managed West Australian Goldfields Limited. When Thompson died shortly afterward, Wright replaced him as chairman of both companies with Sir William Robinson, who had just retired as the Governor of Western Australia. He also added Lord Henry Loch, former Governor of Victoria, to both boards, and Lieutenant-Colonel E.C. Cradock Hartopp to the London and Globe board. There were later allegations that payments ranging from £5,000 to £10,000 had been made to some sitting directors to induce others to join.[8]

Wright continued acquiring several Western Australian properties and floated subsidiaries throughout 1895, capitalising on the booming market in Western Australian stocks. In October, he was shown the data from the Victorian Agent General's office and soon obtained a copy of Reginald Murray's supplementary report on the deep leads, which identified Kozminsky as a key applicant for large leases. When Wright met the dapper Kozminsky he agreed to float yet another subsidiary company.

Whitaker Wright was at the height of his financial career when Kozminsky met him. Shares in Western Australian gold mines were still booming in London, and Wright's reputation and wealth seemed to have fully recovered from his troubled period in the USA. In 1896 he bought two large tracts of land near Hazlemere, paying £150,000 for the Lea Park estate, which included the nineteenth-century manor house, and a further £100,000 for the adjacent South Park Farm estate. Together these had an area of about 3,650 ha. He began transforming these properties into a single estate, creating three lakes and undertaking extensive landscaping over the existing farmland. He hired architects and trade specialists to extend and improve the house and grounds at a cost of £400,000. The features included a domed observatory and a glass-roofed underwater billiard room. The money required for the deep lead project may have seemed to Wright like mere petty cash compared to these lavish personal expenditures.[9]

IT WAS AN EXCITING TIME for Kozminsky to be in London. Asphalt roads, electric lighting, and telephone lines were rapidly spreading across the city, and moving pictures from M. Lumière's cinematograph were on display. The city was linked by more than 32 km of pneumatic message tubes, operating through exchanges, allowing small items, cash, or documents to be sent between businesses, with originals or receipts returned within minutes. The city of Melbourne had been another pioneer of this system, as well as the new hydraulic elevators that were allowing buildings to rise well beyond the previous five-story limit.

The International Exhibition of Motors showcased vehicles powered by internal combustion, steam, and electricity. A company was being floated to introduce electric buses, which had been trialled since 1890, onto London's streets. Another company was displaying Count de Dion's self-acting motor tricycle, which had an air-cooled petrol motor.[10]

In April, the half-yearly reports for the Madame Berry and Berry Consols companies arrived in London. Since its inception, the Madame Berry had paid out £848,700 in dividends, distributed regularly every four weeks over the past fifteen years. Additionally, £128,342 had been paid in royalties to the landowner, while the company had called up only £15,976 in capital. The Berry Consols had produced gold valued at £600,000 but required only £76,000 in capital. These impressive figures greatly supported Kozminsky in his negotiations with Wright.[11]

Kozminsky hadn't forgotten his Tasmanian project. In June, he cabled geologist Reginald Murray, requesting a report on the property at Dundas. After a brief visit to Tasmania, Murray seemed optimistic about its prospects, though progress remained slow.[12]

The leases at Moolort had still not been granted. At a hearing by the Mining Warden, Mr. Anderson, in June, Kozminsky was represented by Henry Goldberg under a power of attorney. The applications covered more than 3,650 ha in the parishes of Rodborough, Moolort, and Baringhup. Negotiations with the landowners were ongoing. The Warden inquired if there was any evidence to justify granting such a large area.

William Luplau, a mining agent and investor, testified that the ground would be costly to work due to the substantial amount of water that would need to be managed. He suggested that it would not be worthwhile to take up the lease unless a very large area were granted, as Kozminsky would not be able to raise sufficient capital otherwise. The Warden, however, was not convinced. He mentioned that he might not feel justified in recommending the Minister grant such a large area but indicated that if arrangements could be made with all the landowners, the application might proceed.[13]

Luplau, an ideal witness for Kozminsky, was born in Denmark in 1832. He started his career as a sailor but left his ship with a group of crewmates to seek his fortune on the goldfields, first at Bendigo and then at Ballarat. Luplau became immensely popular within the digger community and was narrowly defeated by Peter Lalor for a seat in parliament. He later transitioned to being a sharebroker, share trader, and commission agent. By 1894, his knowledge of mining was described as 'second to none in the colony.' Luplau had opened an office in Collins Street, Melbourne, but spent much of his time in Ballarat.[14]

At the end of June 1896, the Victorian Minister for Mines, Travis, issued his 100-page annual report. He wrote that the Government had provided financial support in the form of a loan to the Langi Logan Company, which was sinking a shaft on the Main Trunk Lead south of Ararat, highlighting this as an example of the state working with capitalists to develop the deep leads. The Minister's support would also be crucial for Kozminsky's project. Despite this, there was significant public concern about the granting of such a large lease to a single operator, even after the evidence heard at the Mining Warden's hearing.[15]

In July the Minister announced his intention to grant the leases, although finalisation was still months away. The Secretary for Mines had recommended that four leases be granted, each with a working capital of £20,000 to be provided in bank deposits. The two interested companies were Whitaker Wright's West Australian Exploring and Finance Corporation Limited and the London and Globe Finance Corporation Limited.[16]

With the financing arranged, Kozminsky travelled home on the RMS *Oceana*, arriving in Melbourne at the end of August. By then, the Victorian Gold Estate Corporation, a new subsidiary within Whitaker Wright's empire, had been registered in London. The company's authorised capital was £350,000 in £1 shares, with a working capital of £100,000 allocated for development.[17]

As usual Wright had assembled an imposing board. The chairman was Francis Greville, 5th Earl of Warwick. Other directors included Leonard Fawell Esquire, a director of the London and Lancashire Fire Insurance Company; George Leveson-Gower Esquire, former M.P. and Comptroller of the Royal Household; W. Henry Pelham-Clinton Esquire, representing the London and Globe Finance Corporation; and Tyndale White J.P., Director of Lake View Consols Limited, which was developing a Kalgoorlie mine.

A Victorian advisory board was also announced, ostensibly to enable quick on-the-spot decisions, but primarily to lend credibility for investors. Members of the Victorian advisory board were Sir William Zeal, President of the Legislative Council of Victoria, and director of the National Bank of Australasia, the Australian Mutual Provident Society, and the Metropolitan Gas Company; John Wallace, MLC (Victoria), consulting engineer and geologist, and Duncan McBryde, Chairman of BHP and former MLC for the North-Western Province of Victoria.[18]

The Victorian advisory board appears never to have met after the company was floated. When asked about the new company, Sir William Zeal explained that he had been invited by cable to join the advisory board and to nominate two additional members. While he had done so, he was not aware of the company's specific objectives. He believed its purpose was to attract capital for mining in general, rather than focusing on a specific project.

Confusion regarding the company's objectives persisted, as the Acting Secretary for Mines stated that he understood the company was meant to work the Berry leads in the Smeaton district. Later reports clarified that the focus was on the area near Moolort.[19]

Once the company was floated, Joseph English, Abraham Kozminsky, and Alexander Peacock were appointed as its colonial directors. Henry Gore, who lived at Kingston near Ballarat, was appointed as the consulting engineer and mining superintendent. Gore was the recent President of the Mine Owners' Association of Victoria, Chairman of the Ballarat Prospecting Board, and a former MLC for Wellington Province, Ballarat. He had been in London since April, unsuccessfully attempting to float three Victorian gold projects, and had returned to Melbourne in December.[20]

Joseph English had arrived in Ballarat in 1858, at the age of 30, as an experienced blacksmith and ironworker from Durham, a coal-mining town. Initially trying his luck at Creswick, he later took a job as a blacksmith at the Long Tunnel mine in Walhalla. One day, noticing a change in the rock and clay on the picks and tools he was sharpening, he predicted that the tunnel was about to strike a reef. Acting on this insight, he hired a messenger to telegraph an order to

Figure 22 Henry Gore
www.parliament.vic.gov.au/
members/henry-gore/

buy shares in Melbourne, where they were then very cheap. Shortly after, the share price soared, and Joseph English profited significantly from his shrewd observation.

English then moved to Woods Point, where he continued to make money and was quite well-off by the time he returned to Creswick. He invested in many claims along the rich Berry Lead and was chairman of the New Australasian company during the 1882 flooding disaster but remained financially successful. He also chaired other companies, including Dyke's Freehold, Madame Berry, and Hepburn Consols. English saw substantial returns from his shareholdings in the Madame Berry and Long Tunnel mines, and later from West Australian ventures.

Reginald Murray, who had submitted his resignation as Government Geologist, was appointed consulting engineer on a five-year contract at £2,000 a year.[21]

Ignoring the 32 km gap between the Moolort leases and the northernmost Berry mine, the prospectus described the property as

> ... a continuation extending from 7 to 9 miles in length by from 1½ to
> 2½ miles in width of the well-known auriferous Deep Lead belt known as
> the Berry Leads from which gold to the value of over four millions sterling

is stated by the above experts to have been won from the Berry group and adjacent mines.[22]

Reports by Reginald Murray and Henry Gore were quoted extensively, providing a detailed description of the area and adjacent leads, which were expected to be found at a depth of 82 to 91 m based on the boring results. The lease terms included a nominal rental of sixpence per acre per year, with no royalty payable, for 15 years, with the option for renewal thereafter.

The vendor consideration for the leases was £250,000, payable as £25,000 in cash and the balance as shares in the new company. Using the composite price index published by the UK Office for National Statistics, this vendor consideration equates to nearly £42 million in 2024 UK pounds, a tidy reward for obtaining leases on which no work had been done. The value of the vendor shares would be even higher if they could be sold at a premium after the float.

The £125,000 cash to be raised from the new share issue would provide £100,000 for working capital, which included £3,000 in compensation to landowners, and the remaining £25,000 would be paid the vendor of the property. The vendor was named in the prospectus as Mr. Abraham Kozminsky, which was misleading, as the vendor was really Whitaker Wright and his two companies and associates, based on a deal already done with Kozminsky. The purchase consideration included 225,000 £1 shares, which represented the entire balance of the authorised capital.

Kozminsky's name was used to lend legitimacy to the transaction, but how much did he really receive? The Melbourne Punch reported that Kozminsky had 'cleared a cool ten thousand' from the float. Journalist and Irish Parliamentary Party MP Michael Davitt, who had toured Australia and New Zealand for seven months in 1895, noted that the new company was absurdly overcapitalised, and would need to pay dividends on shares worth £350,000 while capital of only £100,000 would be available to earn those dividends, with a significant sum also required to pay for the advisory board.[23]

Henry Gore gave an extensive interview to the British Australasian just before leaving London. In the interview, he recounted his early career in mining and the development of the Berry mines. He encouraged investment in Victorian mines and spoke very positively about the prospects of the new company, as one would expect given his role.[24]

In early January 1897, shares in both the London and Globe Finance Corporation and the West Australian Exploring and Finance Company were performing strongly, buoyed by positive news from their Western Australian projects. Most of their mines were expected to begin crushing within a month or two. On 14 January the companies announced a merger, with the London and Globe to be recapitalised at £1 million in £2 shares and promising generous dividend payments of 35% to existing ordinary shareholders. The terms were later revised to register a nominal capital of £2,000,000 in £1 shares.[25]

CHAPTER 10

As Rampant as Ever

HENRY GORE AND REGINALD MURRAY marked out a site for a test bore near the Maryborough to Castlemaine Road, about 1.6 km east of the Moolort railway station. Their goal was to locate the gutter and then select a site for the main shaft. By mid-February 1897 the bore was completed, having passed through 2.4 m of heavy wash at a depth of 92 m. A sample from the last core at the bottom yielded four specks of gold, which was an unusual result in diamond drilling, even in favourable conditions. By May, four bores had been drilled, and they had chosen the shaft site.[1]

Abraham Kozminsky was back in Australia but soon had to return to London on company business, important enough for him to miss his son Maurice's *bar mitzvah*. He was away until November, working with Whitaker Wright's team and identifying the best British suppliers for pumps and mining machinery.[2]

Henry Gore began calling tenders for other mine equipment, including timber for the 30 m long poppet legs and 60,000 super feet of timber for poppet heads, frames, braces, and other construction needs. This shaft would be enormous compared to other Victorian mines, internally measuring 22.5 by 7.5 feet (6.9 by 2.3 m) and divided into four compartments to accommodate pump plungers and rising mains.[3]

The capital raised in London was now flowing through to businesses in Victoria. Gore placed orders with Thompsons of Castlemaine for the temporary shaft-sinking equipment: an air compressor, an air receiver, a steam winding winch, a boiler feed pump, a return-tube steam boiler, pit-head pulleys, a feed tank, a pair of coupled high-pressure steam winding engines with winding gear, and a high-pressure steam capstan engine. The foundry agreed to delivery in 14 weeks.[4]

Gore chose contractor Jorgenson and Sons to erect the temporary poppet heads, steam winding and air compressor plant, and to set up a blacksmith's shop, store, and office. Additionally, he called for tenders from suppliers of ironmongery, oil, chandlery (candles), and other goods.[5]

On Kozminsky's initiative, Victorian Gold Estates took an option on 1,619 ha adjoining the northern boundary of their existing lease. Once their pumps had drained the lead, this option area might become significantly more valuable. The Minister of Mines required them to provide an additional £30,000 in working capital to hold the new area.[6]

Henry Gore initiated another series of bores to select the best site for a second shaft. The first bore, 75 mm in diameter and drilled by hand, encountered artesian water at 40 m, gushing at a rate of 12.6 l/s with warm, sulphurous water – an early indication of the conditions to come. The second bore passed through 1.2 m of timber, an old tree trunk from the era when the deep lead was a fast-flowing river. It bottomed in 2.3 m of wash at 118 m, revealing specks of gold. A third bore encountered wash at 104 m. Gore decided that the No 2 shaft would be in Bucknall's paddock, near the swamp, about 5 km south of the No 1 shaft.[7]

By the end of August construction at No1 shaft was advanced and the sinking machinery from Thompson's Foundry had begun to arrive. Gore called for tenders to sink the shaft to a depth of 100 m and ordered 400,000 bricks for the machinery foundations.

In England, Kozminsky placed orders for the permanent machinery – engines and pumps for No 1 shaft. The machinery would cost £30,000 and would weigh approximately 2,000 tons. The cost for the plant and shaft-sinking alone was estimated at £65,000. The pumps at each shaft would be designed to raise 5 million gallons per day (263 l/s), making it the most powerful pumping operation in Australia.[8]

SHAFT SINKING WAS a specialised skill within the mining fraternity. Because it was needed only for a limited time in the life of a mine, it was usually performed by miners working for a contractor. The well-dressed shaft miner wore loose-fitting trousers, often made of denim, and a short-sleeved, coarse grey flannel shirt. He wore leather lace-up boots with hobnails and tied bowyangs (straps or laces) around his knees. Of course, many miners wore old and cast-off clothing, including warm formal jackets and trousers that soon became ingrained with mud.

In the shaft, the miner might wear a felt hat hardened with candle wax, or often a sailor's sou'wester to keep the water from running down his neck. He usually wore a waterproof oilskin coat or jacket, but there was no point in wearing waterproof boots, as the water could rise to his knees or thighs while working at the shaft bottom. Discomfort was part of the job. The bowyangs took the weight of his wet trouser legs, reducing the discomfort from the weight of the trousers on his belt.

Upon arriving at the shaft, he would wait with his mates from the shaft crew while the kibble (a large bucket) was raised. The flap doors on the shaft-sinking compartment would close, and the kibble would be lowered to rest on the doors. Depending on the size of the kibble, two or three miners would climb into it, or place one leg in while holding onto the rope. The kibble was then raised, the doors opened, and they were lowered, upon a signal, to the bottom of the shaft. A line, hanging close to the kibble and suspended from the knocker in the headframe, could be used to signal to the winder driver to stop or start the winder if necessary. In the early phases of sinking, each miner might wear a policeman's whistle around his neck to signal if the knocker failed.

Upon arriving at the bottom of the shaft, the miners would climb out of the kibble and send it back up for any needed materials such as shovels, picks, crowbars, drills, hammers, or explosives, depending on the phase of work at the shaft bottom.

If they arrived after a blast, their shift would be spent shovelling broken rock into the kibble and sending it to the surface. Blasting was usually done on one side of the shaft only, so they worked from a solid surface down into a pit that might be four feet deep on the opposite side. As the kibble travelled up and down, the miners had to be careful to stand aside from its arrival position. A gentle bump on the head sometimes reminded the miner to step aside. They were entirely dependent on the winder driver, who controlled the speed of the kibble. The winder driver had marked on his dial where the bottom of the shaft was and slowed the descent to avoid a violent arrival.

By blasting only half of the shaft bottom at a time, the effectiveness of the explosives was enhanced, and it freed up a working surface for the drillers to make an early start on the next round of blast holes. Keeping one corner of the shaft lower also created a sump for the pump, but this was only possible every second blast, as the pump position was fixed. All this work was conducted in a cascade of water coming from any wet seams in the shaft above. Candles were kept in jars or bottles under ledges to prevent them from being extinguished.

The snorting pump worked continuously, and its imperfect seal often sprayed more water into the working area. Shaft timbering did not extend down to the shaft bottom, as blasting could damage it, so for some distance below the last framed timber set, the miners worked against exposed rock walls. They carefully barred down any loose or dangerous rocks before moving below them as they arrived in the kibble.

BY THE END OF 1897, the No 1 shaft had reached a depth of 15 m and was progressing at a rate of 6 m per week, using pneumatic rock drills and explosives. Henry Gore arranged for bores to be drilled along the main road from Moolort to Joyce's Creek to assess the width of the gutter between the two shafts.

In an interview with the *Colonial Goldfields Gazette*, Whitaker Wright discussed his new ventures, including the British America Corporation and Western Australian properties. While Victorian Gold Estates was mentioned, he dismissed it as a speculative investment.[9]

The contract for constructing the permanent plant for No 2 shaft was awarded to the Phoenix Foundry in Ballarat. The plant included a 400-horsepower triple expansion pumping engine, equipped with a condenser. The pumping gear alone would weigh over 14 tons. Instead of timber, the travellers and bobs were made from rolled steel plates 1¼ inches (32 mm) thick. The 26-inch pumps in the shaft were also constructed from steel.

The winding plant featured two 18-inch bore by 42-inch stroke engines with heavy 9-foot (3 m) diameter winding drums, each with its own brake. The capstan engine, with a 14-inch bore and 36-inch stroke, would be primarily used for raising and lowering the pump components. The air compressing plant included a 16-inch bore steam engine with a 14-inch bore air cylinder and a steel air receiver 8 m long.

Three 150 pounds per square inch (psi) Lancashire boilers, each 7 feet 6 inches (2.3 m) in diameter, were also part of the setup. The spur gear for the pump, weighing 18 tons, was the largest casting ever produced in Ballarat. To complete the contract, the Phoenix Foundry had to hire additional staff.[10]

Figure 23 16-foot diameter spur gear
Maldon Vintage Machinery Museum

By early February 1898 the first load of English machinery for No 1 shaft was enroute by ship. The Colonial Directors Joseph English, Abraham Kozminsky, and Alexander Peacock visited the mine, where they were shown around by Henry Gore and Reginald Murray. The No 1 shaft had reached a depth of 31 m, and during the visit, they marked out the location for the No 2 shaft and discussed the possibility of sinking a No 3 shaft. A spur line was being surveyed from the Moolort railway to the No 1 shaft site for the delivery of machinery and supplies.[11]

In March, Henry Gore invited tenders for erection of the permanent poppet heads, braces, steam winding and air compressor plants at the No 1 shaft. He then called for tenders to sink the No 2 shaft to a depth of 122 m and for the supply of lime and mortar for building the engine foundations. When asked about the timber requirements for the mine's operation, Gore estimated that it would need approximately 150,000 super feet of sawn timber annually, 200,000 feet of props, and between 25,000 to 40,000 feet of panelling, in addition to firewood and other timber. He said that the timber supply from the Trentham Forest would likely be depleted within two or three years, after which they would need to source timber from the Otway Ranges. Timber from Gippsland had already proven unsuitable due to its poor growing conditions.[12]

The Victorian Conservator of Forests Mr Perrin was also worried about timber – not about its supply but about the destruction of native forests. In his report he said:

> The miner is just as rampant as ever for the timber, only now it is the young forest he is just as eager to devour, as in the old Ballarat days the matured forest was swallowed up by the great gold fields.[13]

As anticipation grew, worker camps and cottages began to appear around a new village known as North Moolort. A baker set up an oven near the No 1 shaft, and another was established at the No 2 shaft by June, likely offering a menu rich in Cornish pasties.[14]

The Charlotte Plains Group

WHITAKER WRIGHT'S SUCCESS in raising capital for Moolort boosted Victoria's profile on London markets. The dormant Charlotte Plains project stirred back to life in May 1897. After the sales agreement was renegotiated the Pioneer company received a deposit of £2,500 from the London buyers. The Pioneer company, as vendor, would now receive 40,000 shares (down from 50,000) while the English promoters received 40,000 shares and provided £20,000 for working capital in exchange for additional shares, so that the total value of shares issued was £100,000. There was no public subscription; if more working capital was needed up to £50,000 could be raised by issuing more shares.[1]

In August 1897 George Maitland King, a former Queensland planter and now chairman of the Charlotte Plains Proprietary, travelled from London to Victoria to finalise arrangements for starting work. George Bryant was appointed mining manager. Bryant was born in Maryborough and after leaving school aged 13 he had worked progressively as a blanket washer, trucker, braceman, miner and shift foreman before being appointed mining manager at the United Leads claim at Majorca, then at Chalks No1 mine.[2]

Bryant began sinking the new shaft in early 1898, only 25 m from the old Pioneer shaft. Measuring 14.5 by 7.5 m, it was designed to accommodate two 20-inch pumps and a winding compartment for double cages. The company was considering using electric pumps, which had already proven successful in the anthracite mines of Pennsylvania. The shaft was completed to a depth of 105 m in July. Timber for the 27 m long poppet legs was cut in the bush south of Darnum, near Warragul in Gippsland.[3]

As at Moolort where a town was already taking shape, a 120 ha site for the new Pioneer township was marked out, with allotments being offered for sale. The price of land in nearby Baringhup was also rising.[4]

The neighbouring New Havilah Company was located between the

Figure 24 Charlotte Plains mine, Pioneer shaft on the left
Dunolly Museum

northern boundary of Chalk's No 3 mine and the southern boundary of
the Pioneer Company's ground. Havilah was the land of gold mentioned
by Moses in the second chapter of Genesis; the company's name was often
misspelled as Havillah.

The New Havilah had drilled bores in 1891 and started sinking a shaft on
its lease but, like many others, it had been affected by the financial crash. In
mid-1896, after Reginald Murray predicted that the Carisbrook lead would
extend from Chalk's No 3 into the New Havilah ground, the company was
sold to a London group of investors with strong ties to BHP, largely the same
group who now held the Charlotte Plains Proprietary. By February 1898 their
shaft had reached a depth of 30 m, but a month later work was halted due to
water inflow. Initially, there was no formal relationship with the Charlotte
Plains Company, although much of the ownership overlapped.

As the market thrived, the Charlotte Plains directors decided to sell part of
their lease. The northern area, where boring results suggested the Carisbrook

and (presumed) Berry leads converged, was sold to Junction Deep Leads of Victoria Limited. This new company, owned by two Western Australian companies – Whittaker Wright's West Australian Gold Fields Limited and Hampton Plains Estate Limited – had an authorised capital of £160,000, including £30,000 in working capital. No public shares were issued.

The Charlotte Plains, New Havilah and Junction companies, all represented by Drysdale Brown, decided that they would share the costs of establishing a centralised coal fired electric power plant. This initiative marked the first time in Australia that electric power would be distributed to multiple mines, where it would be used for hauling, pumping, puddling, and lighting. They established the Deep Leads Electric Transmission Company in London and signed a contract with TG White and Company, electrical engineers from New York, to supply and test a complete power plant. The General Electric Company of New York would provide the electrical systems, while the engines and boilers would be supplied by the Buckeye Company from Salem, Ohio.[5]

The introduction of the new electrical technology generated significant excitement in Victoria, largely due to its expected lower cost compared to the rising expense of firewood. Local authorities approved the construction of 6,600-volt above-ground transmission lines across public land and roads. The *Tarrengower Times* enthusiastically reported that:

> The 'Deep Leads Electric Transmission Co.' will not only supply the motive power for the Charlotte Plains Proprietary, New Havilah, and Junction Deep Leads mines, but will supply the power for electric trams, which will traverse the plains, and also illuminate the new town at the mines. The day is probably not far distant when Maldon, Maryborough, Dunolly, and the surrounding towns will also be illuminated from the Deep Lead Electric Transmission Works. [6]

The power station, with its massive chimney, was to be constructed next to the Charlotte Plains mine. A railway spur line would be used to deliver coal and supplies. Initially, the plan was to install a waterproof 250-horsepower electric motor at each of the three participating mines, in a chamber off the shaft, to power the pumps.[7]

IN MAY 1899 a new company, the Victorian Deep Leads Limited, was floated. This company had secured a 4,047 ha lease that included the anticipated junction of the Berry-Loddon-Moolort deep lead system, immediately north of the Victorian Gold Estates ground. The northernmost project in the Loddon Valley, it would join the electrification scheme. The lease had been acquired by West Australian Goldfields Limited and the Hampton Plains Estate Company, based on the data sent to London in 1897. The Capital was £350,000 in £1 shares and the vendors received £260,000 in fully paid shares.[8]

The directors of the Victorian Deep Leads company were Hugh Godfray, a London solicitor and director of Peak Hill Gold Field Limited, which operated a mine in Western Australia; Major (retired) the Honourable Denis Lawless, third son of Baron Cloncurry, who held shares in hotels at Lawlers and Menzies, Western Australia; Major-General Sir James Heriot Maitland, a highly decorated soldier with the Royal Engineers and Chairman of the New Havilah Company; and RC Ogilvie, a prominent English civil engineer and director of Sons of Gwalia Limited, who was involved in several Western Australian mining companies and the Perth Electric Tramways.

Edward Wyman was appointed Managing Director; he also managed the Junction Deep Leads of Victoria, the Deep Lead Electric Transmission Company, and the Kalgoorlie Electric Light and Power Company.

Besides Drysdale Brown, the local Victorian advisory board included Frederick Moule; Ernest Lidgey, a geologist and officer in charge of the Victorian Mining Department in London, who was expected to join the Local Board upon his return to Victoria after resigning from his official position; and William Blair Gray, a mining engineer and local councillor based in Maldon. Moule was a Melbourne solicitor, a member of the Melbourne Club, a founding member of the Royal Melbourne Golf Club, and President of the Victorian Law Institute. Gray, a Scotsman and marine engineer, had arrived in Victoria in 1856 and initially worked as a construction contractor. His experience had led him to become an expert in gold extraction.[9]

CHAPTER 12

Victorian Gold Estates

BY MID-1898, surface works at Whitaker Wright's Victorian Gold Estates properties were progressing well. The No 2 shaft was the same size as No 1 shaft, divided into four compartments – two for winding and two for pumping – with a planned depth of 122 m. The bottom of the shaft would extend 15 m below the gutter, and then a 300 m drive would be needed to access the wash. Meanwhile, No 1 shaft had already reached a depth of 70 m, cutting through solid slate rock.[1]

While work proceeded on site, signs of trouble were starting to show at the London and Globe office in London, and the share price was falling. When the financial accounts were finally presented, months behind schedule, commentators found them vague and unconvincing. The details of transactions and assets were unclear, and significant write-offs had been made without sufficient explanation. A large portion of the assets consisted of 'shares held in various companies,' which could only be realised if sold at their stated valuations.[2]

The *Westminster Gazette* remarked:

Of all the meagre and disappointing reports, this is surely one of the worst.[3]

In September Alfred Hess, writing for the *London Critic*, questioned when the Victorian Gold Estates would deliver the promised one million pounds to London and Globe shareholders. He predicted that London and Globe company itself was headed for a significant fall, as it needed substantial funds to support its various ventures. And Hess did not know that Whitaker Wright was siphoning off huge amounts of cash to develop his personal estate in Surrey.[4]

The general meeting held on September 20, 1898 was packed, with many shareholders unable to enter the room. Lord Dufferin, the new chairman who had replaced Sir William Robinson following his death, gave a lengthy speech. He defended the directors' high standards and emphasised that they had no control over the fluctuations in the share price. He also cautioned against trusting everything reported in the press and gave a brief overview of the company's projects, including the Victorian deep leads.

Dufferin had reason to be defensive. Besides the financial concerns about the London and Globe, allegations had surfaced that the company, or Whitaker Wright himself, had paid a bribe to the editor of the *Pall Mall Gazette* to secure favourable coverage. These claims had emerged after the editor's death, and Wright had not been able to provide a satisfactory explanation for the payment.[5]

Dufferin explained that the company's primary focus was the Baker Street and Waterloo Railway (later known as the Bakerloo line), a 5 km electric railway being built as part of London's rail network. This project, while potentially profitable once sold or floated, was currently consuming a significant portion of the company's funds. To demonstrate confidence and stability, the London and Globe had moved from its previous headquarters to a seven-year lease on the former Bank of Scotland building, located next to the London and Westminster Bank.[6]

IN OCTOBER KOZMINSKY applied for a lease of 1,330 ha near Majorca, with plans for another capital raising in London. Describing this lease area as a 'nice modest slice', the Weekly Times remarked that:

> John Bull has as many eyes as Argus, and a land hunger that would have done honour to Gargantua.[7]

On the northern end of the Majorca lead, three English companies were already established: Drysdale Brown's Charlotte Plains Proprietary, the New Havilah, and the Junction Deep Leads of Victoria. A growing sense of competition was developing between Kozminsky's and Drysdale Brown's groups.

The plant and machinery for both Gold Estates shafts were designed by Hugh Reid, a consulting mining engineer from Ballarat. Reid, who had previously served as foreman at the Phoenix Foundry for 18 years, oversaw the manufacturing of all the locally made machinery and the installation of both plants.[8]

The new machinery for the No 2 shaft was completed at the Phoenix foundry in late October 1898. Although the boilers at No 1 shaft had been designed to burn coal, which was expected to be a more cost-effective fuel than the increasingly scarce firewood, those at No 2 shaft would burn firewood. Horse-drawn wagons were hauling the machinery to No 1 shaft, on a tramway which was built to the same gauge as the government railway line.[9]

Dodwell Henry Browne, previously the mining manager at the nearby Chalk's No 3 mine, was appointed as mining manager and took charge of both shafts at the beginning of 1899. Browne, originally from New Zealand, had left school at 15 and had worked in mining, including shaft sinking for 5 years, before becoming a mine manager at Creswick. He then managed several mines at Smeaton and Rutherglen and had overseen the shaft sinking for the Madame Berry mine.[10]

By December, No 1 shaft had been sunk to a depth of 137 m but work on No 2 shaft was paused due to excessive water inflow. Once the No 1 shaft plant was completed and the two 20-inch pumps were installed at the shaft bottom, work began on driving from the shaft toward the lead. Meanwhile, at No 2 shaft, approximately 300 tons of machinery had been delivered from the Phoenix Foundry, with another 300 tons pending delivery. Contractor James Knox of Ballarat was hired to erect the plant, which required about 150,000 bricks.[11]

It was customary to hold a ceremony and to name the main engines when starting new mining machinery. This event was usually performed by the wife or daughter of a visiting dignitary or company official. On a hot Friday in February Henry Foster, the Minister of Mines and Water Supply, attended the machinery start-up ceremony at No 1 shaft. The event was well-attended by the directors, several dignitaries, and 'a large assemblage of gentlemen from Melbourne, Castlemaine, Maldon, and Newstead,' many accompanied by their ladies. Melbourne visitors arrived by special train, and around 300 people were present. Among the features noticed by the guests was a prominent plaque on the chimney bearing the names of the officials responsible for the project.[12]

The guests were gathered in the engine room which was decorated with flags, and bunting was draped over the lofty poppet legs. Tables were laden with a substantial lunch, snacks, and refreshments. The ladies were seated at the head table alongside prominent mining figures including Drysdale Brown and politicians including Alexander Peacock. Although several lengthy speeches were delivered, their impact was diminished by the constant noise of shuffling feet and the echoing clamour of the wooden shed and cast-iron machinery.

Miss Nellie Foster, daughter of the Minister of Mines, and Esther Kozminsky, wife of Abraham Kozminsky, performed the christening ceremonies. They broke three bottles of champagne over three different flywheels, each time amidst enthusiastic cheering and the distribution of pieces of the ribbons that had been used to suspend the bottles. The engines were named Victoria (in honour of the Queen), Ruth (after the Kozminsky's two-year-old daughter, who was present), and Nellie (after Miss Foster). The benefits of English capital were clear to everyone present, from the Minister for Mines to Mrs. Campbell of the McIvor Hotel in Maryborough, who provided the catering.[13]

Figure 25 Celebrating the start of machinery
at Victorian Gold Estates No1 shaft
after an image held by Maldon Vintage Machinery Museum

IT SEEMED A TURNING point had been reached: Victorian Gold Estates was in capable hands and on solid footing. Two weeks later, Kozminsky departed Melbourne for London on the SS *Barbarossa*, leaving his family behind. He anticipated being away for six months, marking his third trip to London on behalf of the company. Costs were escalating and were expected to exceed initial forecasts. It was likely that the Victorian Gold Estates funds, including the £80,000 lodged with the government and the remaining £20,000 in working capital, would soon be depleted. Kozminsky intended to meet with the London directors and discuss the situation with Whitaker Wright, who was facing challenges on multiple fronts.[14]

Interest in Victorian projects remained strong in London in early 1899. Capital raisings for Victorian mining projects had grown steadily, with nine companies registered in 1896 with capital of £985,000, ten in 1897 with £841,500 in capital, and twelve in 1898 with £1,370,000 in capital. This brought the total to 31 companies with an aggregate nominal capital of £3,196,500 over three years. However, most of these were hard rock quartz mines and not deep lead mines. The main British-owned deep lead mines included the Ascot Deep Main Lead at Ascot, the Mount Greenock Estates at Talbot, and the Victorian Gold Estates, Charlotte Plains Proprietary, Junction Deep Leads, and New Havilah Limited in the Moolort area.[15]

Work at the Victorian Gold Estates mine continued, with progress on several fronts. No 2 shaft was being sunk, No 1 shaft was receiving its final touches, and work was ongoing to drive two levels from it. By April, the upper (intermediate) level had been driven 128 m into very soft sandstone when it broke into the washdirt, causing an inundation with water flowing at 480,000 gallons per day (25.2 l/s). This scenario had been anticipated, and flood doors were closed to restrict the flow to less than the pump capacity while the water was being removed. The lower level, where work was still in progress, had reached 52 m from the shaft.

Still, finances were strained and somewhat unfairly, a gossip column in the Melbourne newspaper *Table Talk* wrote with double entendre about the situation:

> Victorian Gold Estates at Moolort, over which the champagne corks were popped at a recent date, is now struggling to keep its head above water.[16]

Anticipating that the mine would soon be in production, employees submitted petitions to the local council and the Railways Department, requesting workmen's trains to run from Maryborough to Moolort. But was production truly imminent? In May Kozminsky gave a detailed interview to the *British Australasian* newspaper, confirming that he was in London to 'consult with the directors on future developments.' While it remained unsaid, he was increasingly concerned about Whittaker Wright's behaviour and the stability of the London and Globe group.[17]

While Abraham Kozminsky was still in London, shareholders in Melbourne convened a meeting to wind up his Tasmanian New Kozminsky Company. Although tributers had found some ore on the lease, it was not sufficient to sustain a public company. This situation was just a distraction for Kozminsky, who was focused on getting ongoing financial support for the Victorian Gold Estates work in Victoria.[18]

The launch of the No 2 shaft machinery in early September was a more subdued affair than the previous launch, though it still featured food and several toasts. The dignitaries present included Joseph English, chairman of the local advisory board; Henry Gore, mining superintendent; ER Meekison, chief inspector of the Mines Department; and PG Middleton, managing director of the Phoenix Foundry Company in Ballarat.[19]

The machinery for No 2 shaft was almost identical to that of No 1, but the No 2 shaft machinery had cost several thousand pounds less than the imported equipment for No 1. In No 1 plant, the massive pinion wheel had been cast in several pieces for easier transport, whereas in No 2 it was cast in one piece, making it stronger and more rigid. The pump bob sent from England for No 1 was primarily made of timber enclosed in steel plates and bolted together. In contrast, the Phoenix Foundry's bob for No 2, weighing about 27 tons, was made from steel and expected to last much longer.

A Roots blower, powered by a steam engine on the surface, provided fresh air to the underground working areas at No 1 shaft through ducting. The drive from No 1 shaft reached the wash in September 1899. It needed about 30 m to reach the location where specks of gold had been seen in the surface bores. However, although driving continued in the wash, no discovery of gold was announced, despite the two levels advancing at a rate of 25 to 30 m per month. By year's end, the face of the bottom level was about 520 m from the shaft, with an additional 700 m needed to reach the gutter. It was increasingly clear that the No 1 shaft was in the wrong position.

Sixteen men were working in No 2 shaft, with four on each shift, and this number was increased to twenty-one men in the New Year. The temporary sinking plant from No 1 shaft, having fulfilled its purpose, was put up for sale.

The new settlements around each shaft were growing, with expectations that operations would soon employ five hundred men at each site. By this time, £90,000 had been spent on the lease.

AT THE VICTORIAN GOLD ESTATES annual meeting in London on 22 December 1899, the chairman reported that the company's funds had been exhausted. However, he reassured attendees that the London and Globe Finance Corporation had been lending additional funds to keep the company operational and promised that, as a major shareholder, it would continue to do so. Reported in Melbourne, this statement provided some reassurance to those Australians supplying and working for the operations. Yet, doubts were growing about the future.[20]

Kozminsky had drawn his own conclusions. After returning to Melbourne in late November he promptly put his house and its entire contents up for sale. The advertisement described the items as 'beautiful modern household furniture,' detailing the elegant and tasteful furnishings and art of a wealthy family. This sudden sale likely raised questions among those not closely acquainted with the family. Was Kozminsky facing financial difficulties? A week later, Lord Loch resigned as a director of the London and Globe Finance Company. Ominously his replacement was Mr. Leman, the private solicitor of the Marquis of Dufferin.[21]

At the end of March 1900, Abraham Kozminsky, along with his wife Esther and daughter Elsie, set sail for Marseilles aboard the RMS *India*. They were joined by Esther's 26-year-old sister, Sadie. While Sadie returned after nine months to be married, the Kozminsky family continued, on what became a nearly two-year trip around the world. The eldest son Maurice stayed in Melbourne, as he was a student at Geelong Grammar.[22]

In the same week that the Abraham Kozminsky family sailed for Europe, his brother Simon's wife Emma announced the sale of the Kozminsky goldsmith, silversmith and jewellers' business, which had been owned in her name. Abraham may well have been a part owner, either since its establishment or since Simon's insolvency in 1895. Was this further evidence of Kozminsky 'clearing the decks', anticipating the collapse of Victorian Gold Estates following what he had observed at the London and Globe office? Perhaps he wanted to remain hard to find until the situation settled down.

After sailing for Europe, Abraham Kozminsky would no longer play any role in the mining company he had founded. However, he was not in hiding, as he would attend Lord Loch's Suffolk funeral in June 1900.[23]

CHAPTER 13

Shareholders Want Their Money Back

WORK AT THE SHAFTS went on uninterrupted while the loans from the London and Globe continued to flow. The busy pace continued, even when miner Thomas Hefford fell 30 m to his death after accidentally stepping into the No 2 shaft. He left a widow and four children.[1]

Additional drainage bores were drilled up from the drives at No 1 shaft as the drives were extended. In August 1900, the company announced to the Stock Exchange that they had struck payable gold in a 1.2 m thick layer of wash in the No 1 shaft workings. The gold was described as an excellent sample – rough, heavy, and well water-worn.[2]

Encouraged by this discovery, the directors promptly ordered two puddling machines and planned to add four more, with a new engine to drive them. At No 2 shaft, skids to guide the cages were installed, and a cage and water tank were commissioned. Meanwhile, workers were cutting chambers at both 113 m and 125 m levels to begin driving out from the No 2 shaft.[3]

An article widely circulated in Australian newspapers in early October highlighted a promising spring season for both agriculture and mining. It particularly emphasised the prospects for the Victorian Gold Estates mine, stating that the results would 'richly reward English investors for their heroic enterprise.' By this time, the lower level at No 1 shaft was nearly one kilometre long, the wash drive was being prepared for production, and the puddling machines were being erected.[4]

The mine's future seemed assured. However, behind the scenes, Whitaker Wright was planning a reorganisation and refinancing of the venture. The company had borrowed around £45,000 from its parent company, which was now struggling financially. To address this, the lease would be split, and a new company would be formed around each shaft. New investors would repay the loans and provide fresh capital.[5]

A new company, Loddon Valley Goldfields Limited, was formed to take

Figure 26 Loddon Valley Miners
after an image held by Dunolly Museum

over the No 1 shaft and a lease covering the promising area accessible from that shaft. The London directors included the Earl of Warwick (chairman), AC Bicknell, and G Leveson-Gower. The Australian advisory board consisted of Joseph English and Alexander Peacock, with Reginald Murray appointed as consulting geologist and Henry Gore as consulting engineer. The authorised capital was £750,000, with shares valued at £5 each. Of this, £50,000 was allocated as working capital, while the Victorian Gold Estates company, as the vendor, was granted 140,000 fully paid shares.[6]

A separate company, Moolort Goldfields Limited, was formed to take over No 2 shaft. The *London Morning Leader* described the plan as:

> A striking illustration of the methods of multiplication which find favour in Whittaker (sic) Wright finance. …the Loddon Valley Goldfields, is paying £170,000 in cash and £530,000 in fully-paid shares for one-half of the original £350,000 property. For the other half £700,000, wholly in shares, is being received from the Moolort Goldfields, Limited, so that the multiplication of paper has been at the rate of four to one. No prospectus of the Moolort company has been issued to the public at present, but the foregoing details may be made a note of for reference purposes. They will probably be required before the new century is far advanced.[7]

Then, on the last day of the year, the Melbourne Argus ran the headline:

London Share Panic. Crisis on the Stock Exchange. Dealings in Lake View Consols. Many Failures.[8]

The London and Globe Finance Corporation had failed to secure a loan to meet its obligations which fell due at the year's end. Cheques it had sent out were dishonoured and returned. The collapse triggered a cascading effect, with 29 members of the London Stock Exchange being 'hammered' – the most significant event that could occur on the Exchange. When this happened, a member of the managing committee would rise, hammer his desk with a mallet, and announce the names of members in default, signalling their insolvency. This would bring the trading floor to a standstill.

Whitaker Wright had been locked in a months-long battle with Charles Kaufmann, his former consulting engineer in Western Australia, over control of Lake View company, with both parties engaging in short selling of shares. Wright was caught, and the price of Lake View shares collapsed. Wright had been pursuing a high-risk strategy that relied heavily on securing finance. A key setback occurred when he failed to sell all the shares in the Baker Street and Waterloo Railway. As underwriters, the London and Globe Finance Corporation were left holding 50% of the stock, having already invested £700,000 in the project.

A comprehensive list of the London and Globe's interests was published, which included the Victorian Gold Estates. Faced with mounting financial difficulties, the directors of London and Globe decided to voluntarily wind up the company. Lord Dufferin, who had resigned as chairman the previous week, was already enroute to South Africa, where his son had been seriously wounded in the Boer War and would die a week later.

The collapse of the London and Globe Finance Corporation sent shockwaves around the world. The *British Columbia Mining Record* referred to the event as a reflection of 'the corruption of English finance.' However, the publication offered a nuanced view of Whitaker Wright, stating:

> The *MINING RECORD* has always drawn a sharp distinction between his mining and financial methods. The first show daring, grasp, invention, prudence, and despatch; the second, a complete disregard of ordinary prudential calculation.[9]

In Melbourne, uncertainty loomed over what would happen next. The newly formed companies, Loddon Valley Goldfields and Moolort Goldfields, were each capitalised at £750,000. Additionally, Berry Glengower Goldfields Limited had a capital of £350,000 in £1 shares, having acquired a lease from the Loddon Valley Pioneer Syndicate. Another company, promoted by Horatio Bottomley's Associated Financial Corporation, announced a 1,012 ha lease near the Talbot railway station. This venture was capitalised at £650,000 in £1 shares, with £50,000 allocated for working capital. *The Economist* criticised these ventures, attacking them as clearly overcapitalised, which they indeed were.[10]

Meanwhile, the wash drives at No 1 shaft were yielding only small amounts of gold, meaning that the newly completed puddlers would have no work even after the engine was installed. The bottom level had now been extended well over a kilometre from the shaft without reaching the gutter, confirming that the shaft had been sunk in the wrong position. Then, on February 8, a major setback occurred when one of the massive pumps at No 2 shaft broke through its iron casting. Since the pump wasn't under heavy strain at the time, it was likely a manufacturing defect at the Phoenix foundry. Fortunately, the remaining pump was able to maintain the water level on its own until the damaged part could be replaced.[11]

In February 1901, as a formality, shareholders in the Victorian Gold Estates company, which held shares in the two new ventures, resolved to liquidate the company and distribute its remaining assets. Shareholders were expected to receive between 3 and 4 shillings per share. The transfer of leases and operating licenses to the new companies was then approved.[12]

Adelaide investors were hit hard by the collapse of the London and Globe Finance Corporation. The *Adelaide Critic* remarked:

> Vic. Gold Estates, from its two 'pups,' Loddon Valley and Moolort Goldfields Co., hauled in £170,000 in cash and 1,230,000 £1 shares, with the selling price of Moolort being £700,000 in shares. What use is this scrip unless to paper the Vic. Estates' board-room? Anyway, if the British public subscribed any money for these two shows, they must be asses.[13]

A few days later, the publication added:

The glowing reports furnished by Mr. Reginald Murray regarding the prospects have not been fulfilled. Altogether, the Gold Estates appears to be the biggest fiasco Victoria has yet encountered, and it will be interesting to watch its final shuffle. Even if it did get a good wash, the returns would never cover the capital sunk.[14]

The frustration among investors intensified. In June, *The Argus* featured a bold headline: 'A Gold Mining Company Shareholders Want Their Money Back.'[15]

By August, the situation worsened at No 2 shaft (now Moolort Gold Mines) when water breached the upper level and washed a substantial amount of sand into the pumps, causing them to become clogged. With the sand settling and the water level rising in the shaft, nothing could be done immediately. Henry Gore convened a meeting of experienced mine managers to devise a plan of action. He decided to wait a month before lowering a new pump – a draw lift – into the water to address the issue.[16]

In September, *The Argus* published a detailed analysis of the situation by their mining reporter. The analysis noted:

The task undertaken by the ... Loddon Valley Goldfields and Moolort Goldfields and...the Havilah Gold-mining Company, the Charlotte Plains Proprietary, the Junction Deep Leads of Victoria, and the Victorian Deep Leads, is, however, one of exceptional magnitude and importance. If successful, the operations of these ventures will, in addition to proving their own ground, be the means of providing for the exploitation of 15 miles of lead, extending from the Moolort claim to the Spring Hill and Central Leads mine, at Kingston, together with the continuation of the lead north beyond the boundary of the Victorian Deep Leads leases. Years of work will thus be available for a large mining population, and an enterprise which, to some extent, fell under the baneful influence of the London and Globe collapse in Great Britain will make headway with rehabilitated reputation.[17]

At this time the pumping capacity of the mines in millions of gallons per day was planned to be:

Moolort Goldfield	5.0
Loddon Valley Goldfields	5.0
New Havilah	2.6
Charlotte Plains	2.6
Junction Deep Leads	2.6
Victorian Deep Leads	2.6
Chalk's No 3	2.8

The article highlighted that if all pumps were operational, they could deliver more than 23 million gallons per day (1,208 l/s), but that 18 million might be a more realistic estimate. At this time the Moolort shaft was flooded, the Loddon Valley was still working to reach the gutter, and the remaining mines were all focused on driving a single bottom level to the gutter.

Given that the two lead systems were only 5 km apart, it was anticipated that once the Charlotte Plains and New Havilah mines began draining the gutter, it would alleviate some of the pressure on the Moolort and Loddon Valley pumps.

MEANWHILE IN LONDON, the compulsory liquidation of the London and Globe Finance Corporation continued, with claims from Loddon Valley Estates shareholders and the Lake View Syndicate threatening to prolong the process in the courts. After Mr. Hughes, the Australian secretary of Loddon Valley Estates, travelled to London to investigate, he reported optimistically that the company should not incur any losses.[18]

By then the Kozminsky family was enroute home from San Francisco after twenty months away, travelling on the RMS *Ventura* via Honolulu and Samoa to Sydney. In December 1901, they settled into 'Marina,' a rented house in St Kilda. Kozminsky had severed ties with Moolort and avoided the associated drama. Abraham Kozminsky began placing regular advertisements to buy mines or mining properties, for which he would invest development capital. However, this does not seem to have led to any acquisitions. His investments would soon take him, with his friend Sir Alexander Peacock, in a different direction entirely.[19]

The first meeting of creditors of the London and Globe Finance

Corporation was held in London in December 1901. They learned that the company faced unsecured liabilities of £1,142,000, while its assets amounted to only £424,000, leaving a significant shortfall.[20]

The official receiver explained the events leading to the company's downfall. The directors had been taking 5% of all dividends paid, and he spelled out the totals; Lord Dufferin (£4,097), the late Lord Loch (£4,250), Whitaker Wright (£4,250), Lord Edward Pelham Clinton (£4,250), and Lieutenant-General Gough Calthorpe (£4,250). In addition, Wright had received an annual salary of £2,000 as managing director – this was all real cash, not paper profits.

By contrast, the company's first-year profit of £989,679 was largely an unrealised paper profit, mainly stemming from the promotion of the Ivanhoe Gold Corporation, with only £182,000 representing actual cash. A subsequent £782,000 in cash was lost in speculations involving the Lake View company in Kalgoorlie. By September 30, 1900, the company had been 'absolutely and hopelessly insolvent' according to the receiver and to hide this Wright had inflated the value of its assets on the balance sheet.

The Victorian properties were central to this financial deception. In promoting the Loddon Valley Goldfields for the Victorian Gold Estates, the London and Globe Finance Corporation included a property called the Options Block, purchased through Kozminsky by the Victorian Gold Estates for £10,000 but listed in London and Globe's books at £100,000 – a tenfold inflation. Additionally, 200,000 shares in the Victorian Gold Estates, valued at £200,000 in London and Globe's records, were shown as worth £704,000. These valuations stemmed from the promotion of the Loddon Valley and Moolort Goldfields after they took over Victorian Gold Estates properties. The total capital of the Victorian Gold Estates was £350,000, but because of those two sham transactions the company was entitled to receive £1,400,000 in cash and shares.

Little of these massive financial manipulations was documented in the minutes of the London and Globe. The official receiver concluded that, apart from Whitaker Wright, none of the directors was aware of the full extent of what was happening. The company also made speculations in Baker Street and Waterloo Railway shares, and Loddon Valley Goldfields shares to the tune of £218,000, with no trace of these transactions in the books. There was clearly more to the deception, and further revelations were expected.

The Australian bank accounts were now empty, and operations at the mines ground to a halt. Dodwell Browne resigned as mining manager in June 1902 and went off to manage the Spring Hill and Central Leads mine at Smeaton. He was replaced by Charles Hope Nicolson, now termed General Manager. Nicolson was the eldest son of a well-known policeman who had been involved in the pursuit of several bushrangers including Harry Power and the Kelly gang. But soon, with no funding in sight, Nicolson took a six-month leave and went to Western Australia. Although the pumps at both shafts were kept running with a trickle of funds advanced from England, no other activity occurred.[21]

Charlotte Plains Consolidated

ON THE NORTHERNMOST lease, held by the Victorian Deep Leads company, the boring results had been promising and by the end of 1900 they had completed a new shaft to a depth of 107 m. William Capron, who had previously managed the Chalk's Junction, Chalk's No 3, and Main Leads mines near Carisbrook, was appointed as manager. Although the shafts at Victorian Deep Leads, Charlotte Plains, and New Havilah had now been completed, progress at those mines was halted until the power station was commissioned.[1]

The boilers for the Deep Leads Electric Transmission Company had arrived on site by mid-1899 but delays in the arrival of power station components meant that it was not completed until early 1901. The power station was first tested in March 1901, with the Minister for Mines and other dignitaries in attendance. Drysdale Brown was now the chairman of the local boards for all four mining companies and the Electric Transmission Company.[2]

The New Havilah and Charlotte Plains pumping systems were identical,

Figure 27 Charlotte Plains Mine
Museums Victoria

Figure 28 The Electric Power Station
after Weston & Edwards, Maryborough, printers, 1902

and it was planned that the Junction Deep Leads would be the same. The New Havilah was the first to be operational. The pumps, weighing 77 tons, were housed in a concrete-lined arched chamber 14 m long and 7.6 m wide, located 104 m below ground level. The concrete was placed using the Monier system, which incorporated iron bars for reinforcement. Monier's Victorian agents, engineers Monash and Anderson, had previously used this system for bridge construction, including Wheeler's Bridge on the Creswick-Lawrence Road. John Monash later gained prominence for his military and engineering achievements.[3]

The three-throw, double-acting pumps were powered by electric motors. Each plunger was 11 inches in diameter with a 36-inch stroke, and with the cranks set at 120 degrees to each other, the water flow was nearly continuous. Initial trials showed that the system might raise nearly 3 million gallons per day (158 l/s) with the pump operating at 30 revolutions per minute, though this was never achieved in steady operation.[4]

The pump compartment in the shaft was designed to be compact, only

Figure 29 Pump at New Havilah mine
after Weston & Edwards, Maryborough, printers, 1902

needing to fit an 11-inch diameter rising main and an electrical supply cable. An iron water-lock door, made by the Phoenix Foundry, could be closed to protect the pumps in the event of flooding.

The pumping system at the Victorian Deep Leads company was notably different, powered by two electric motors situated on the surface. Each motor drove a set of reduction gears through nine Manilla driving ropes and a friction clutch, which helped to absorb mechanical shocks at the motors and ease the loads at start-up. These gear sets drove cranks that operated bell-bobs at the shaft collar, which in turn operated pump rods in the shaft.

The two pump rods each operated Cornish plunger pumps located at depths of 95 m and 41 m below the surface. The lower set of pumps fed the upper set, which then sent the water to the surface. Both sets of pumps, with diameters of 20 inches and 8-foot strokes, delivered water into a single 22-inch diameter rising main. This pumping plant was designed to raise 2.6 million gallons per day (137 l/s).

English capital was good for the Victorian economy. The plunger pumps

Figure 30 New Havilah flood door
after Weston & Edwards, Maryborough, printers, 1902

were manufactured by Humble and Nicholson of Geelong; the bell-bobs and rocking posts were made by W Anderson and Sons of Melbourne; holding down bolts and tension rods were supplied by Mephan Ferguson of Footscray; and the sweep and connection rods came from the Australian Forge and Engineering Company in Williamstown.

However, the rising main pipes were supplied by the Piggott Company of Birmingham, England, and the rope transmission system was sourced from Robert Poole and Company of Baltimore, USA. The machinery was designed and installed by Kelly and Lewis, Melbourne.

The power station, by the time it was completed, featured three steam engines, each delivering 600 horsepower from 150 psi steam, with each engine, excluding the generator, weighing 36 tons. It was equipped with six 300-horsepower Babcock and Wilcox boilers to generate steam. The powerhouse was a showcase of new and innovative technology for managing steam and water and for controlling engines.

Figure 31 Engines in the power station
after Weston & Edwards, Maryborough, printers, 1902

Three General Electric revolving-field generators, each producing 3-phase alternating current at 6,600 volts, fed four transmission lines – one for each of the mines. Each mine had a sub-station to reduce the voltage for driving the motors. The power station switchboard, mounted on nine marble panels, controlled the generators, exciters, and feeders and was equipped with fuses and lightning protection.

Construction at the Charlotte Plains shaft continued. In January 1902, four 30 m long poppet legs, 76 cm across at their wider end, were delivered from the Otway Forest. The pumps began operating in May once the poppet legs were in place. Due to the ongoing Federation drought, local farmers immediately began using the water for irrigation, with the excess water flowing into the Loddon River.[5]

Additional funding was required, so the Charlotte Plains Proprietary and New Havilah companies were merged to form a new company, the Charlotte Plains Consolidated Gold Mines Limited. The New Havilah shaft became known as No 1 Shaft, and the Charlotte Plains shaft as No 2 Shaft, though

Figure 32 Generators in the power station
Museums Victoria

people continued to refer to them by their original names. The new company was capitalised at £200,000 in £1 shares, issued as paid up to 15 shillings each, with the ability to call £65,000 in working capital if needed. One-third of the shares were held in Victoria by the original Pioneer Company, while the remainder were held in England.[6]

Drysdale Brown was appointed chairman of directors of the Consolidated company, and William Capron became General Manager of the combined operations, which covered nearly ten kilometres of leads with widths ranging from 213 to 366 m, according to the boring results. A Melbourne stock market joke emerged that the mines were intending to pump the Murray River dry.[7]

Electric winders, powered by 75-horsepower motors, were installed at both shafts. The underground development was sized to allow the use of electric locomotives, and appropriate rails were installed. Two Ganz locomotives were taken underground at the Charlotte Plains mine. These ran on direct current, which required conversion from alternating current supply using a motor-generator set. The use of electric locomotives underground was not a risky strategy, as they were already in use at the Great Southern No 1 and the Chiltern Valley Gold Mining Company mine at Rutherglen. At each of those mines a small generating plant on the surface was used to supply the locomotives.[8]

The pumps at both shafts functioned as expected, causing the water level in the lead to fall steadily, so in late August 1902 there was hope that

Figure 33 Ganz electric locomotive
after Light Railways, April 1986, p 22

tunnelling could soon resume. However, the neighbouring Chalks No 3 mine had ceased pumping, possibly waiting for Charlotte Plains to lower the water level in their mine. The English directors of Charlotte Plains instructed their manager to halt pumping unless Chalks No 3 resumed operations. The issue was escalated to Ewen Cameron, the newly appointed Minister of Mines, who advised the parties to resolve the matter themselves. Reluctantly, Chalks No 3 resumed pumping.[9]

By the end of 1902, one steam engine and generator set in the power station was supplying power to the Charlotte Plains and New Havilah shafts. A second generating set was ready to power the Junction Deep Leads and Victorian Deep Leads when needed, while a third remained in reserve.

The Loddon River

THE DEEP LEAD PROJECTS were about to pump large volumes of water into drains and creeks which discharged into the Loddon River. There was no regulation governing this situation and it seems little thought was given to the possible environmental effects, either by the mining companies or the government authorities. The Loddon River had already been polluted by mining waste for a long time.

As it flows north from the Dividing Range, the Loddon River receives no water from tributaries beyond Eddington and unlike most rivers, it diminishes due to evaporation and seepage. By the time it reaches Kerang, it is usually no bigger than the other creeks in the area. In earlier times, the section of the river below Kerang was known as the Murrabit, and during dry periods it turned into a series of waterholes. In most years when the Murray River flooded, its waters backed up into the Loddon floodplain for about 16 kilometres.

By 1890, numerous irrigation trusts had been established from northeast of Kerang to Koondrook. Channels were dug, and creeks deepened to irrigate wheat crops using the annual floods of the Murray River. This irrigation boosted wheat yields fourfold, to about 20 bushels per acre. Once the reliability of irrigation was proven, farmers began diversifying into lucerne, fruit, and vineyards.[1]

Laanecoorie Reservoir was built by contractor Andrew O'Keefe for the Victorian government from 1889 to 1891. This was the second irrigation scheme for Victoria after the Goulburn Weir. Gunbower Creek was diverted into Kow Swamp to irrigate over 52,000 ha in the lower Loddon Valley around Kerang. This happened around the same time the Chaffey Brothers were developing large-scale irrigation at Mildura, and water from the Goulburn River was being diverted into Waranga Swamp near Rushworth, which became a reservoir for the Campaspe region. At Bridgewater, a weir created a large lake, where a steamboat operated summer excursions for two years before unexpectedly sinking while being tied up at the riverbank.[2]

While these irrigation schemes were being established, mining in the hilly upper reaches of the Loddon and its tributaries in the Castlemaine district caused a lot of sludge to enter the river. Miners slurried and reworked the old alluvial ground around Castlemaine and Chewton, particularly after the Coliban River scheme diverted water northward through channels to supply Castlemaine and Bendigo. This water was used for sluicing in the hills south of Chewton, around Fryerstown and beyond. Sludge flowed through Barker's Creek, Forest Creek, Campbell's Creek, Fryer's Creek and others into the Loddon River. Formerly deep waterholes that had once been home to large cod were filled with sludge. Some residents on the river flats had to build levy banks up to 1.5 m high to protect their gardens and fields from the sludge, which gradually made its way down the river toward the Murray.[3]

The Federation Drought, lasting from 1891 to 1903, was one of the

Figure 34 Laanecoorie weir circa 1900
State Library of Victoria

most severe droughts ever recorded in Australia. Large parts of the country received less than 40% of their typical annual rainfall in 1902, which was the driest year on record. Many farmers who relied on the Loddon River for stock and irrigation expressed frustration with the irrigation trusts and pushed for the government to do more. There were public discussions about building a large dam on the Murray River above Albury to ensure a steady year-round water supply for irrigation. Expanding the Waranga storage was also considered.

In May 1899, Loddon Valley landowners gathered in Newstead to protest the granting of new dredging leases, fearing that dredging would further devastate the river flats and cause silt buildup in the waterworks and weirs. There were reports of cattle refusing to drink the muddy downstream water. Additionally, drainage and runoff from towns, which had previously been diluted by the river's flow, now became a health concern.[4]

By late 1900, the Loddon River at Eddington had silted up due to reduced water flow caused by the Laanecoorie Reservoir, forcing the construction of a new tank for the town's water supply. The drought worsened, and by 1901, cattle were getting trapped and dying in the river's muddy bed. Meanwhile, 40% of any water that made it as far as Bridgewater was being diverted into irrigation channels.[5]

In this situation the water that might be delivered into the system by the Moolort mines was a potential benefit, not a problem. It would be received with gratitude by residents and irrigators downstream. Only later did some concerns arise about the quality of that water.

Before the drought the irrigation trusts had expected to receive large volumes of water from the Loddon River. For example, the Tragowel Irrigation Trust had initially irrigated 78,000 ha using water drawn from the Laanecoorie reservoir, distributed through 600 km of channels. However, by 1902, the reservoir had completely dried up. In October 1902, the town water supply in Kerang began to fail as all available river water was being diverted to upstream irrigators. Meanwhile, dredges began working the bed of the upstream Loddon River itself near Castlemaine.[6]

The irrigation trusts were now unable to provide the promised water to irrigators, leading to widespread financial difficulties. As a result, both the irrigators and the trusts began to default on debt repayment, prompting the government to pass the Water Supply Advances Relief Act. In October 1902, Melbourne's Lord Mayor launched a public appeal for funds to aid Victoria's drought-stricken regions. By the time the appeal closed a year later, it had raised nearly £19,000. Any water from the Moolort mines would be welcome.[7]

The Federation Drought began to break late in October 1902 when flooding rains drowned sheep and destroyed any remaining crops. The Loddon River overflowed its banks, submerging the Loddon Blocks dredge at Guildford. While the rain was initially a relief, it was followed by weeks of hot weather that dried out crops and grass, leaving sheep again struggling to find food. Even the rabbits seemed to disappear. Despite the late rains, total rainfall for 1902 was only half the long-term average, with most of it falling in the final quarter of the year.[8]

And yet, during the summer of 1902–03, the situation became so dire that the Maryborough Council considered sourcing its town water from the deep lead mines. Dr. Howell, the Government Chemist, noted that while the water didn't fully meet hygienic standards, it could be used for domestic purposes in extreme circumstances. However, he advised *against using it* in steam boilers for locomotives.[9]

In early 1903, frequent thunderstorms caused flooding on the Loddon River. In July, Baringhup experienced significant flooding, threatening the Bridge Inn and Loddon hotels. The river flats were submerged once more in September, and Newstead was flooded in November.[10]

In July 1904 Henry Gore, in his address as President of the Chamber of Mines of Victoria, referred to the benefits flowing (literally) to landholders from the water pumped from the deep lead mines. Something like 8,000 million gallons of good drinking water (he said) was being pumped each year and this, after passing over the land in channels, flowed into the Loddon River and its tributary creeks. During the drought thousands of stock had benefited.[11]

Gore must have been aggregating all the pumping from deep lead mines in the Loddon catchment to arrive at his estimate, which equates to about 22 million gallons per day (1,152 l/s). Even so, it seems an exaggeration.

Just how important was this contribution during the drought? If we take one irrigation trust as an example, the Dry Lake Irrigation Trust was licensed to draw up to 100 cubic feet per minute (47 l/s) from the Loddon River between July and October, and 20 cubic feet per minute (9.4 l/s) from November to April, as long as the river maintained a flow of at least 200 cfm (94 l/s). So, the flow from the deep lead mines was significant in comparison.[12]

In September 1904, a Water Bill was introduced that defined the Victorian government's authority to control waterways and prevent pollution. This legislation established the State Rivers and Water Supply Commission and transferred existing waterworks into state ownership. Among these were the Laanecoorie, Bridgewater, and Kinyapaniel weirs on the Loddon River.[13]

In February 1905, horses grazing along Joyces Creek and the Loddon River became ill, showing symptoms such as staggering, refusal to eat, and blindness. Initial suspicions pointed to water from the Moolort mines, although horses further down the creek remained unaffected. The sick horses quickly recovered when moved away from the water. Further investigation indicated that the issue might be due to sludge from dredging operations upstream rather than Moolort water. Barkers, Forest, Tarrengower, and Sandy creeks were described as 'channels of liquid mud flowing into the Loddon'. It was suggested that Moolort mine water could be used to clarify the water in the Loddon River.[14]

Pumping from the deep lead mines had depressed the water table, drying up many natural springs and bores that had been used for watering stock. A conference of municipalities in April 1905 considered the motion:

> That this conference is of opinion that while the extensive pumping operations in deep lead mining companies are draining the local sources of water supply, making the river more than ever necessary for stock, the dredging operations are rendering the water not only unfit for use, but they are causing wholesale destruction of stock having access to it. The silt is rapidly filling the waterhole and river channels, and also the Laanecoorie weir basin, and the whole water supply of the district is being jeopardised.[15]

The motion was passed, only after the reference to the deep lead mines was removed, leaving the blame entirely with the dredgers.

In July 1905 Alexander Clarke, a grazier from Joyce's Creek, successfully sued the Loddon Gold Dredging Company for polluting the river that flowed through his Park Hill property, making the water unfit for cattle to drink. He also obtained an injunction to prevent further pollution. The defendants argued that 'custom' granted them the right to discharge their debris into the stream. However, Judge Chomley ruled that such a custom had not been proven to exist, noting that while pollution had been occurring for over 40 years, the practice itself had not been established before 1851. Henry Gore commented that the decision posed a serious threat to the mining industry, as 'many so-called rivers had been practically sludge channels since the early fifties.'[16]

The Victorian Government formed a Sludge Abatement Board in February 1905. The stated aim was to regulate the disposal of sludge, sand, and debris from alluvial and lode mining in Victoria to prevent pollution or damage to watercourses, such as rivers, streams, lakes and reservoirs, and agricultural and grazing lands.[17]

The Sludge Abatement Board first reported in April 1906, when there were 30 pump dredging plants in operation and the Loddon River was silted up above Eddington. Sludge had accumulated in the Laanecoorie Reservoir, and once the stored water was depleted, the ordinary flow, along with water pumped from the deep lead mines, cut a channel about 4 m wide and 800 m long through the sludge in the basin. This sludge was then deposited in the riverbed for roughly 1,200 m below the weir.

The Board also reported on the mineralisation of the river water:

> For the past seven years a considerable volume of nearly clear but slightly mineralised water has been pumped from the Deep Lead claims lying to the south into the Loddon. There is evidence that this has had the effect of considerably improving the quality of the water in the Laanecoorie Basin in summer for washing and cooking purposes, but there is no certainty that it has been improved for irrigation. Indeed, one witness said that flowers seemed to die if regularly watered with it in the usual way. We consider, however, that on the whole the Loddon water is not now more mineralised in summer than it was in 1887.[18]

The Board concluded that effective management of dredge sludge was necessary but did not provide further comments on the deep lead operations.

Farmers had come to rely on water from the deep lead mines and were using it to irrigate pasture for dairy herds. This ensured there was enough cream available over the summer to keep the Newstead butter factory operational. But lucerne crops irrigated with water from the Loddon River were failing, and it was claimed that drinking the river water had caused illness in half of the children at the Kerang school. Alexander Peacock blamed these issues on the historical pollution, saying that the new sludge abatement regulations should be allowed time to take effect.[19]

CHAPTER 16

Bewick, Moreing and Co.

AFTER WHITAKER WRIGHT'S financial collapse, the Loddon Valley and Moolort companies remained idle. However, behind the scenes in London, Charles Moreing was engaged in negotiations with the official receiver and had found investors to advance funding to keep the pumps going. Bewick, Moreing and Co. had been consulting engineers to Whitaker Wright's West

Australian Exploring and Finance Company since it was floated in 1894, giving Moreing familiarity with Wright's assets.

By 1903 Bewick Moreing had a large staff and several representative offices, with Australasia a particular focus. Bewick Moreing were the leading mining engineers in Australasia, in the same way that Wernher Beit and Company were in South Africa and John Taylor and Sons were in India.

Charles Algernon Moreing, the very active managing partner, lived with his family in Watford, Hertfordshire. His junior partner Herbert Clark

Figure 35 Herbert Hoover as a young mining engineer, Perth, 1897
State Library of Western Australia

Hoover, who lived in London, was responsible for all the company's mine management contracts, which were primarily in Australia. Hoover acted as the front man for the company in Australia, but it was primarily Moreing who dealt with the London company owners and directors who were their clients. To Australians it was Hoover who appeared to be the decision maker, but really Moreing pulled the strings.[1]

Moreing was born in the New South Wales town of Braidwood in 1855.

Orphaned at nine, he was sent to live with his uncle Charles Moreing, an architect and surveyor in St Leonards on Sea, Sussex. To avoid confusion, he became known as C. Algernon Moreing. He went to a local preparatory school, then to King's College. In 1874 Moreing became a trainee and student of Thomas Bewick in Northumberland. Bewick was an experienced railway and mining engineer who owned the consulting firm Bewick and Partners, Ltd., which also owned and operated a profitable lead mine.[2]

Moreing furthered his experience at the Wohlfahrt lead mine near Rescheid, Germany, and at the Saint-Étienne-du-Valdonnez coal mines in southern France. He became fluent in French, a skill that would later influence his career. He also developed a passion for mountain climbing and, upon returning to England in 1881, joined the Alpine Club, a London-based gentlemen's club where membership required having climbed a 'reasonable number of respectable peaks.' That same year, he was promoted to Associate Member of the Institution of Civil Engineers.[3]

In 1881 Moreing married and was named consulting engineer in the prospectus of the British Australian Gold Mining Company, which had a property at Hill End, NSW. The questionable venture was led by Lord Robert Montagu, with vendors set to receive £130,000. Moreing, still young, was likely given this opportunity through his connection with Bewick. Shortly afterward, the Hawkins Hill Consolidated Gold Mining Company floated the same property, but this time with only £21,000 in vendor consideration. The new company was headed by the Duke of Manchester, featured an entirely new board, and notably did not include a consulting engineer.[4]

This experience is notable as an example of the dubious world of mining promotion that Moreing was learning to navigate and to exploit. *Vanity Fair* remarked that:

> The whole thing has a very suspicious appearance, and we strongly advise the Duke of Manchester to withdraw from it as quickly as possible.[5]

Moreing then travelled to the Cape Colony, as South Africa was then known, to serve as Managing Engineer for the French Diamond Mining Company, which owned a group of claims in Kimberley. Discovered in 1871, the Kimberley diamond field had grown into South Africa's second-largest town, with a population of around 40,000. The mine was open cast, and Moreing had to contend with unstable ground which caused slips into neighbouring claims and later prompted the need for a shaft and underground working.[6]

By 1885, the partnership of Bewick and Moreing had been established. Moreing travelled to Nevada to assess the Garfield properties, a group of eight shallow, high-grade gold and silver mines that had been founded two years earlier. Reports in the press mentioned that 'well-known English engineers and experts' had estimated the ore reserves to have a net value between £60,000 and £250,000. When the Garfield company was floated in May 1886, the prospectus promised annual profits of £30,000. Moreing returned to the mine to serve as Managing Director and Engineer on behalf of Bewick Moreing.

Despite plans to expand its operations, the company never added to its original five-head battery, and its first annual profit was just £3,708. By June 1889, the company only managed to break even, and it was wound up in October of that year.[7]

Moreing then focused his efforts on creating the *Telegraphic Mining Code, Alphabetically Arranged for the Use of Mining Companies, Mining Engineers*, with the first edition published in 1888. The book was a success and went through several editions, later co-authored with Thomas Neal. The code served two primary purposes. First, it provided confidentiality; for instance, the word 'Achatina' meant 'you should not accept his statements without confirmation,' a meaning understood only by those who owned the code book. Second, it offered cost savings on international telegrams, which were typically charged by the word. By condensing complex messages into a few coded words, users could reduce costs and alleviate congestion in the telegraphic system.[8]

By 1889 Moreing had advanced significantly in his career, becoming a Member of the Institute of Civil Engineers and a Fellow of the Geological Society. In 1891, he became a director of the Mozambique Company of Lisbon, which held a 50-year concession for land in Central Mozambique, granted by the King of Portugal. The company, floated in Paris, aimed to exploit the region's mineral and other resources primarily using local manpower, partly through a system of forced labour. Alongside the Duke of Marlborough, Moreing served as a director on the Paris Board and acted as the company's agent in London. In an interview, Moreing stated that the success of the new company would rely heavily on English management and capital. Plans were also underway to establish a company to build a 290 km railway connecting the concession area to a new port at Beira on the Pungwe River.[9]

When asked about its prospects he commented:

> Melbourne between forty and forty-five years ago did not exist, Port Philip Bay was then just as Beira is to-day. Gold was discovered in Ballarat, and Melbourne has become the largest and wealthiest city in Australia.[10]

Later an un-named journalist wrote:

> Charles Algernon Moreing is a Bagstock when slyness is concerned. He has the facial contour lines of a strong man, the auburn hair of a fighter, and a discretion born of a life-long contact with the science and practice of markets.[11]

Major Joseph Bagstock was a character in Dickens' *Dombey and Son*. By 1896, Bewick Moreing had secured several management contracts in Western Australia. Seeking experienced staff, Moreing hired Herbert Hoover to join the Coolgardie office.

HERBERT CLARK HOOVER, born in 1874 in West Branch, Iowa, shared a striking similarity with Moreing – both had been orphaned at nine and were subsequently raised by an uncle. Hoover graduated from Stanford University as a geologist in 1893 and spent two summers working with the Geological Survey of Arkansas. After a brief stint in the Grass Valley mining district, he secured a position with the renowned mining engineer Louis Janin. This job involved extensive travel, evaluating prospects and mines, and came with a substantial salary.

By the time Hoover was interviewed by Moreing in London in April 1897, Thomas Bewick had fallen ill and was no longer active in the business. Bewick passed away in August of that year, but the firm continued to operate under his name. At just 23 years old, Hoover made the journey to Australia, arriving first in Albany, before traveling to Perth to catch the train to Coolgardie. Aware of the risks, he had taken the precaution of organising life insurance. Typhoid fever was rampant among Bewick Moreing's staff in Australia – every one of the firm's thirty-six engineers had contracted the disease, and six of the fifty-three employees had died.[12]

In Western Australia, Hoover's role involved extensive travel and reporting on mining prospects. He recommended the purchase of the Sons of Gwalia mine near Leonora and subsequently served as its first mining superintendent for seven months. In 1898, Moreing transferred Hoover to China to serve as a technical adviser to the Chinese provincial director general of mines. During the Boxer Rebellion, Hoover facilitated the acquisition of the valuable Kaiping coal mines by an Anglo-Belgian company formed by Moreing.[13]

While enroute to China, Hoover had married fellow Stanford geology student Lou Henry. By 1901, the Hoovers had returned to London, where Herbert was made a partner in Bewick Moreing and Co. He took on responsibility for managing all the mines operated by the company, most of them being in Western Australia.

In early January 1902, Hoover travelled to Perth with his wife Lou and he spent the next two months inspecting all fifteen Western Australian mines managed or worked under option by Bewick Moreing. The journey was demanding, covering 3,000 km by train, 400 km by coastal steamer, and 1,200 km by horse and trap. Impressed by the success of new automobiles in London, Hoover resolved to bring one on his next Australian visit to alleviate the burden of travel. The Hoovers departed Fremantle for London in early April.

MOREING SAW WHITAKER WRIGHT'S financial collapse as an opportunity which he discussed with Hoover. The former Victorian Gold Estates properties, although still in early development stages, had positive geological reports and the pumping machinery was already in place, although it was in poor shape. A big fund raising would be needed.

In March 1903, the Official Receiver of the London and Globe put the Options Blocks lease and two large parcels of shares from the two mining companies up for tender. Moreing orchestrated the acquisition process, with Francis Govett's brokerage house initially securing the purchase. Ownership then transferred through a series of legal steps to a group of former shareholders in the London and Globe company.[14]

In May 1903, the London and Globe Deep Lead Assets Company (soon to be renamed Consolidated Deep Leads) was formed, with a capitalisation of £200,000 in four-shilling shares, of which £150,000 was allocated for working capital. The new company acquired a controlling interest in both the Loddon Valley and Moolort companies, as well as the Options Block leases, for the bargain price of £50,000. The leases collectively covered 4,600 ha.[15]

The new directors of the Consolidated Deep Leads had no prior connection with the London and Globe. They were Philip Lyttelton Gell, director of the British South Africa Company, Robert Logan, chairman of the National Bank of New Zealand, Sir Gerard Smith, a former Governor of Western Australia, and William Elder, a director of the English, Scottish and Australian Bank.

Bewick Moreing were appointed as the general managers and engineers. Samuel Body, formerly the manager of the Duke United mine at Timor, was

Figure 36 Philip Lyttleton Gell
Wikipedia

appointed as the mining manager for both mines, while Charles Nicolson came back from Western Australia as General Manager.[16]

In June, the scheme for reconstruction was approved. The capital of the two companies, Loddon Valley and Moolort Goldfields, was written down from £750,000 to £160,000, with shares priced at £1 each and paid up to 15 shillings. Underwriters would receive 20 percent of the profits for the first two years.[17]

Hoover and Moreing devised the plan, recommending a joint expenditure of £30,000 to demonstrate the value of the properties. The capital raising had provided about £37,500 in working capital for each company. Hoover also proposed that the Victorian Government establish a water board to mandate contributions from the nearby companies for pumping. While work at the Charlotte Plains and New Havilah mines was proceeding, operations at the Junction Deep Leads and Victorian Deep Leads had stalled. Both were waiting for the others to draw down the water level.[18]

Hoover arranged for Dr Waldemar Lindgren, his former supervisor in the Sierras and a leading figure in the United States Geological Survey, to visit Victoria and assess the deep lead projects. Moreing wrote to the Victorian Attorney General, praising Lindgren as 'the greatest living authority on deep-lead mining.' Moreing promised that Bewick Moreing's associates would invest £500,000 if Lindgren's report was favourable and if the Victorian government supported the initiative. The key support sought was for the government to require all leaseholders to contribute to the costs of pumping.[19]

Moreing pressured the directors of the Victorian Deep Leads company to recapitalise and resume pumping, hinting that failure to do so could result in losing their lease. His efforts

Figure 37 Waldemar Lindgren
US Library of Congress

succeeded, and a reconstruction scheme raised £32,000 for that company, deemed sufficient to complete the drives, drain the wash, and install a puddling plant. Bewick Moreing was entrusted with managing this project as well. Moreing then turned his attention to the Junction Deep Leads company, securing an informal cooperation agreement with Drysdale Brown.[20]

In September 1903, the Consolidated Deep Leads company held a meeting in London chaired by Lyttelton Gell. He confirmed that Bewick Moreing were behind the entire scheme. The London and Globe Deep Lead Assets Company, which held approximately 60% of the shares in both the Moolort and Loddon Valley goldfields, had played a significant role in inducing the

Victorian Deep Leads Company to undergo reconstruction. It was believed that the Junction Deep Leads company would follow a similar path.

Gell outlined the company's strategy to consolidate all leases on the field into a single entity. Besides the Loddon Valley, Moolort, and Victorian Deep Leads, they had also secured the Rodborough Estate to the south and were negotiating with neighbouring properties. Gell suggested that the company's influence with the local electorate, landholders, and the state government would enable them to enforce cost-sharing for dewatering efforts. He referenced the *Kimberley principle* as a precedent, which mandated that all parties benefiting from collective action either contribute their fair share or forfeit their rights.

He said:

> We cannot work as we hope to do, and put British capital and British brains into this undertaking if it means that a certain number of fellows who are doing nothing but sitting on addled eggs are going to stop the road. We must persuade or oblige them to contribute their share, or see if we can get the state to confiscate their estates in favour of those who will.[21]

Gell emphasised Hoover's extensive knowledge on the subject and noted that Hoover would soon visit the property. He also highlighted that Dr Waldemar Lindgren, recognized as the leading authority on deep-lead mining and geology, was conducting a general survey of the company's deep lead interests. Furthermore, Gell assured shareholders that they would benefit from the expertise of Bewick Moreing's team of mining engineers. At the same meeting, Moreing pronounced:

> I have not the slightest doubt that before we meet again, very great progress will have been made, and it is even possible we may be working the deposit by next time you meet.[22]

After Lindgren arrived in Melbourne in August 1903 he visited mines at Kyneton, Lauriston, and Malmsbury on his journey north. While Moreing had already conveyed confidence in the presence of gold and outlined a practical plan for water removal, Lindgren's role was to provide a comprehensive assessment of the entire district. His report was intended to guide decisions on which acquisitions and projects should take priority, offering a strategic direction for the potential operations in the area. However, there was a strong expectation in London that he would somehow confirm, without physical access, the presence and quantity of gold.[23]

In mid-October 1903, Hoover arrived in Perth with his wife Lou, baby Herbert Junior, and a French Panhard motor car. They travelled by train to Kalgoorlie, where Lou stayed with friends. Hoover accompanied by his friend, the journalist and mining engineer James Curle, and the local Bewick Moreing manager, William Loring, then embarked on a motoring tour of nine properties. The group travelled as far as Mount Sir Samuel, covering about 800 km in total. The Panhard car averaged about 25 km per hour, though readers of the Laverton and Beria Mercury might have believed otherwise after reading:

> Morgans saw its first motor car on Monday last. Mr. H.C. Hoover passed through Murrin Street with his car like a flash of greased lightning. He outran the Perth train with a couple of days to spare.[24]

Hoover later noted that the car operated 'most of the time' and could cover 200 km per day, compared to just 65 km per day with horses. However, poor road conditions posed significant challenges. To clear the roads, they negotiated a 'fee' of three bottles of beer with an Afghan camel team. Despite this, breakdowns caused by dust in the carburettors and punctures from sticks and horseshoe nails were common, leading them to wrap the tires in steam hose for protection. Initially, Bewick Moreing had used camels and then horse-drawn carts to travel between the mines. Eventually they would replace the horse relays with four cars saving, said Hoover, US$5,000 to $10,000 per month.[25]

The Hoovers sailed for Melbourne on 20 November, arriving four days later. Hoover was well received in Melbourne, as befitted the representative of so much English capital. Bewick Moreing had done good things in Western Australia, and the same was expected in Victoria. Hoover lost no time in visiting the Moolort mines, being briefed by his local engineers on the condition of the machinery.[26]

The pump at the Loddon Valley (No 1) shaft, designed for 5 million gallons per day (263 l/s), had initially achieved only 2 million gallons per day (106 l/s). However, after modifications in October 1902, its capacity had increased to 3.5 million gallons per day (184 l/s). This improvement had allowed underground work to resume, with nine drainage bores operating above the north drive and four in the east main drive. Meanwhile the Moolort (No 2) shaft was poorly designed with weak foundations and was capable of less than 20% of its design capacity. It was apparent to Hoover that both plants needed further upgrading.

Whitaker Wright

THE PROSECUTION OF WHITAKER WRIGHT for the alleged falsification of balance sheets began in late August 1903. Wright had deceived his fellow directors and caused the downfall of several firms in the City of London, along with devastating countless investors. One stockbroking firm alone lost £356,000 and subsequently defaulted. For more than two years, liquidation proceedings had delayed any potential criminal prosecution. Despite his actions, some individuals who had profited from Wright's manipulations remained sympathetic toward him. However, the case was relentlessly pursued by investigative journalist Alfred Arnold. In early 1903 Wright fled to Paris and then to the United States but was later extradited and returned to England by detectives.

It was revealed that Wright had been manipulating share transactions between the companies he controlled, often just a day or two before the balance sheet was finalised – sometimes on the very day. He did this to create the illusion that the companies were thriving, showing substantial profits and a healthy profit-and-loss account as each balance sheet was prepared. These transactions were typically not documented in the company minutes.[1]

One example involved a reported profit of £504,000, supposedly made by the London and Globe Finance Corporation through the conversion of £1 shares in the Victorian Gold Estates into shares of the two new companies. This conversion occurred just before the balance sheet was drawn up. However, the shares of one of the new companies, Moolort, were never actually issued.

The Victorian companies played a significant role in Whitaker Wright's fraudulent activities. Shareholders in his companies suffered substantial losses, with the reported figures being London and Globe (£2.0M), British America Corporation (£1.5M), Standard Exploration (£1.5M), Victorian Gold Estates (£0.35M), Loddon Valley Goldfields (£0.75M), Moolort

Goldfields (£0.75M), Columbian Proprietary (£0.5M). In total, the losses amounted to £7.35 million.[2]

The judge delivered a summary against Whitaker Wright, and within just an hour, the jury returned a guilty verdict on all counts. Whitaker Wright stood in the dock to receive his sentence – his face pale, twitching slightly yet still maintaining the dignified composure that had characterised him throughout the trial. Sentenced to seven years imprisonment, Wright appeared to accept the punishment without flinching. Bowing slightly to the judge, he said calmly, 'All I can say, my lord, is that I am innocent of any intent to deceive anyone.'[3]

Wright exited the courtroom through a private door, accompanied by his solicitor, Sir George Lewis, the assistant superintendent of the Law Courts, and a tipstaff. The four men proceeded to a consultation room near the court. After spending half an hour and having a glass of whisky, Wright went to the toilet unescorted. Upon his return, he appeared unwell, collapsed, and died. It was later determined that he had taken potassium cyanide. A search of Wright's body revealed another capsule of cyanide and a loaded pistol. He was buried in the graveyard of Witley Church near Godalming in Surrey, close to the lavish estate he had developed.

Into the Wash

IN 1903 THE CHARLOTTE PLAINS CONSOLIDATED was facing its own financial challenges. In the previous twelve months, pumping by the company and Chalks No 3 had only managed to lower the water level at the old Pioneer shaft by 12 m. A reorganisation offered 260,000 new shares to existing shareholders in the original companies. This plan aimed to raise £43,333 through bi-monthly calls of 3d per share.

At a Sydney presentation in June, Drysdale Brown detailed the company's expenditures and progress. He reported that £183,000 had been spent since 1889 on boring, shaft sinking, and infrastructure, including the electric power station. Twenty-one bores, each around 12 m long, had been drilled up into the wash from the drives. The company was pumping over six million gallons per day (315 l/s) and anticipated reaching the old riverbed within nine months. Drysdale Brown also mentioned that each new bore showed the presence of both coarse and fine gold in the wash.[1]

Concerns were mounting over the future supply of timber for mining and firewood. Forestry authorities in the USA had predicted the complete depletion of global timber supplies, as consumption was outpacing regeneration by one-third. In response, the US government had established nearly five million Ha of forestry reserves to slow this trend. In Victoria, a Forests Protection League was formed, highlighting the risks to the mining industry due to the rapid depletion and alienation of forests.

The cost of mining laths (split boards) had nearly doubled over the previous 30 years, and prices were continuing to rise. Each increase of 1 shilling per hundred laths, 1 shilling per hundred feet for props, and 1 shilling per ton for firewood would add £600,000 annually to the costs at the Loddon Valley goldfields. Within an eight-mile radius of Maryborough, there were no props left to cut. Mines in the Charlotte Plains group were sourcing timber from 40 km away. Although a million acres of virgin red gum

Figure 38 Main drive at New Havilah
Note use of timber and elevated rails for drainage
Weston & Edwards, Maryborough, printers, 1902

forest lay 400 km west of Maryborough, the prohibitive cost of rail transport made it more economical, according to the *Adelaide Critic*, to import timber from Puget Sound in North America.[2]

In early 1904, the Charlotte Plains and New Havilah shafts continued to drain the lead while awaiting the start of gold mining. Drysdale Brown gave an address on the advantages of electric pumping, referring to a report by the manager of the Spring Hill and Central Leads mine, who had compared the costs of various pumping systems, adjusting for their differing capacities. He noted that an amount of pumping, which cost £2,100 using the Cornish beam engine at the old Lord Harry mine, could be done for £700 at the Chalks No 3 mine with a compound condensing engine. The Charlotte Plains electric pumps, however, could achieve the same for just £406.[3]

In April 1904, the company began constructing a three-mile spur railway line from the Maryborough line, at a cost of around £3,000. While unsuccessfully lobbying the government to fund the siding and railway,

Drysdale Brown forecast that the project would create jobs for at least 1,200 men, excluding the large workforce needed to split timber in the forest and transport firewood and mining timber.[4]

Drysdale Brown emphasised that the companies had already invested £150,000 in Victoria, most of which had gone to wages for working men, iron founders, mechanics, miners, woodcutters, carters, and others. Specifically, £62,000 had been spent on locally manufactured machinery, £53,000 on wages, and £12,000 on fuel, stores, and cartage. Additionally, £7,700 had been paid to the Railway Department for freight, £2,200 to the Mines Department for lease rents, and £6,700 to the Customs Department for duties.[5]

The miners' trains were now running from Maryborough. Despite the government's refusal to fund the spur line, the company proceeded with the construction, and by June 1904, wood and coal were arriving by rail.[6]

In May 1904, Drysdale Brown announced his candidacy for Nelson Province in the Legislative Council elections. Nelson Province encompassed a region including the larger towns of Ararat, Carisbrook, Clunes, Creswick, Dunolly, Maryborough, St. Arnaud, Stawell, Talbot, and Timor. He campaigned on issues of mining development, closer settlement, and water conservation, securing an easy victory alongside Hans Irvine, a mine and vineyard owner. Jim Brown would henceforth be known as Mr J. Drysdale Brown MLC.[7]

Prominent Maldon resident William Gray, a director of nine mining companies including Charlotte Plains Consolidated, was re-elected to the legislative council at the same time. At an election rally, Gray stated that the company would need to spend an additional £20,000 to manage water extraction. However, he projected that each fathom of washdirt would yield £3 in gold for an operating cost of £2. He estimated it would take ten years and £600,000 worth of gold recovery before shareholders would see a return on their investment. This statement was met with applause by his audience, who were electors set to benefit from the company's expenditures, rather than English investors waiting for a return.[8]

In June 1904 the company installed a 12-inch high-lift Sulzer centrifugal pump and electric motor, which together weighed 16 tons. This enhanced pumping also helped reduce the water level at Chalks No 3, sparking speculation about which company would be first to get to the washdirt in early 1905. Investors could monitor the water levels by viewing a chart displayed in the window of Baring Chambers on Market Street in Melbourne.[9]

The Charlotte Plains pumps had reportedly set a world pumping record. Combined, the Chalks No 3, Charlotte Plains, and New Havilah mines were raising 13.5 million gallons per day (710 l/s), all of which was now being channelled into the Loddon River.[10]

BY FEBRUARY 1905, the face of the main drive at Charlotte Plains was 961 m from the shaft, while at New Havilah it was 670 m from the shaft. Both drives were being prepared for haulage with electric locomotives. Boring upward from the drives was successfully draining the wash and yielding promising gold colours. The puddlers from the old Pioneer shaft were being relocated to Charlotte Plains, and new puddlers were to be installed at New Havilah.[11]

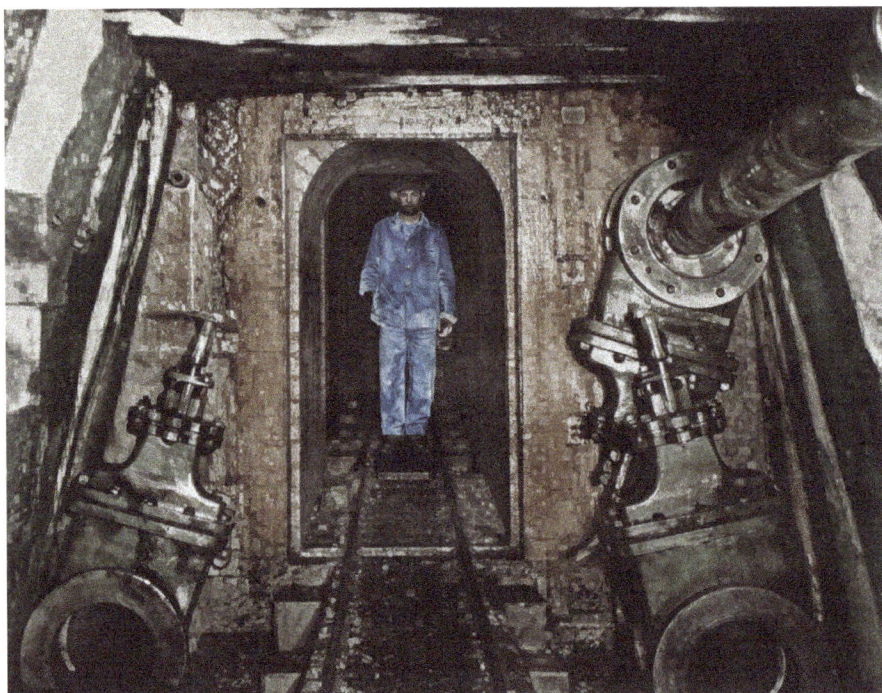

Figure 39 Charlotte Plains flood door protecting the pump chamber
Weston & Edwards, Maryborough, printers, 1902

Figure 40 Drilling drainage bores upward at Charlotte Plains mine
Weston & Edwards, Maryborough, printers, 1902

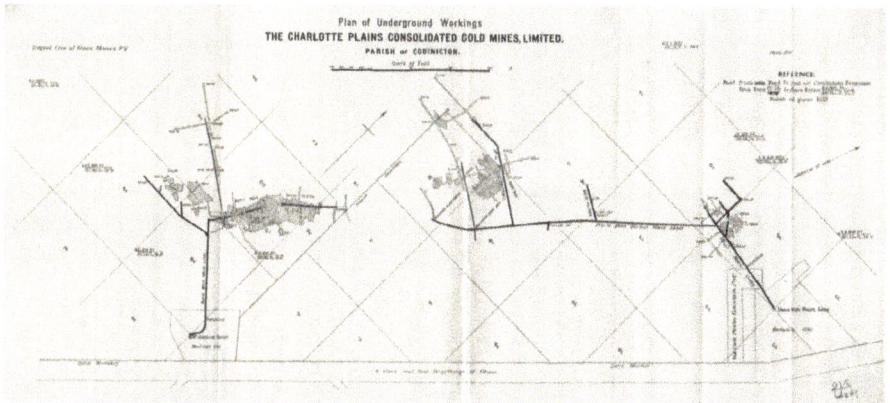

Figure 41 Plan of Charlotte Plains Underground workings
Geological Survey of Victoria, 1909

The supply of firewood had become problematic, with the delivered price rising to 8 shillings per ton, more than half of which was due to rail freight. Local firewood sources had been exhausted, including a 388 ha reserve known as O'Keeffe's. The company began replanting this reserve with young trees to secure future firewood supplies.[12]

In July 1905, the directors announced that after three years of pumping, both mines were preparing to enter the wash. The leases were nearly dewatered, with low water pressure reported at the New Havilah bores and some dry holes at Charlotte Plains. The installation of the puddling machines had been delayed by wet weather but was ongoing.[13]

By the end of November, three parties of miners were working on driving the wash at New Havilah and two groups at Charlotte Plains, with what seemed to be satisfactory gold yields. One small patch produced 12 dwt of gold. The puddlers required additional work, as the driving gears had proven inadequate.[14]

The manager at Charlotte Plains, William Capron, had been ill for several months and missed the excitement when the puddlers began operating in January 1906. They were processing material from eight parties of miners working in the wash. The first batch, brought from the northern end of New Havilah, produced 35 ounces of smelted gold from 36 fathoms, nearly an ounce per fathom. Drysdale Brown expressed his delight at the results, and soon after invited Premier Bent and other dignitaries to visit the mine. The visitors travelled more than one kilometre in an electric train through an electrically lit drive to visit the production area.[15]

Extracting the Wash

TWO SYSTEMS WERE used for extracting wash dirt in alluvial mining, depending on whether the wash layer was over 1.2 m thick or less. These systems were called blocking and panelling.[1]

When the wash was over 1.2 m thick, the blocking method was used. In this method, the wash dirt on either side of the main drives was divided into 120 foot (36.6 m) wide blocks, often referred to as cross-drives. From these cross-drives, truck roads were driven at 32-foot (9.8 m) intervals, leaving a strip of ground 16 feet (4.9 m) wide on either side of each truck road. The wash dirt was then removed in strips 8 feet (2.4 m) wide, with the height depending on the thickness of the wash. As the material was extracted, the roof was supported by laths resting on round timber cap pieces, which in

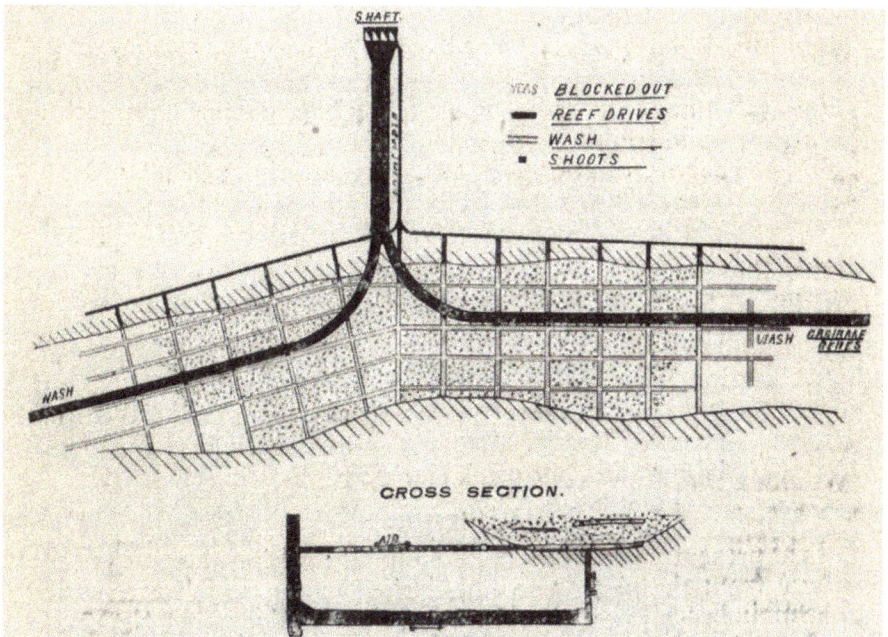

Figure 42 Plan and elevation view of extraction
Wilkinson, 1905, p 263

turn were held up by 15 cm diameter legs. The height of these legs varied according to the thickness of the wash.

Blocking was done on a contract basis, with miners paid per running foot, and the width of the cut being 8 feet (2.4 m). This method was used at the Charlotte Plains mine.

When the panelling method was necessary – typically when the wash was less than 1.2 m thick – the process of dividing the wash into blocks and laying truck roads was the same as in the blocking method. The washdirt, which could range from just 10 cm to 1.2 m thick, was removed in strips of 4 feet 6 inches (1.4 m) wide. When the wash was less than 76 cm thick, and the ground was loose, additional country rock was removed to create a working space of 76 cm in height, as this was the minimum required for miners to work. While this may seem extremely low, such working heights were common in coal mines then and until recent times.

As the washdirt was extracted, the roof was supported by laths held up by panelling props – round or split timbers 6 cm thick and ranging from 76 cm to 1.2 m long, spaced about 15 cm apart. Panelling was also done on contract, paid per fathom, with a fathom measuring 2 m long, 1.4 m wide, and varying in height with the thickness of the wash.

A crew consisted of six miners and five truckers who extracted the washdirt and transported it within the extraction level. The mining company supplied all their tools and equipment except candles, which were paid for by the miners because it was impossible to police the theft of candles, which were in demand in every home.

The box trucks were filled at the working faces, then pushed along the extraction level to the top of the balance shaft. From there, they were lowered one at a time into the main drive using a cage controlled by a friction brake. As the full truck descended, an empty one – or one loaded with supplies – was raised in the second compartment. Otherwise, a windlass was used to transport timber and other supplies up from the main drive to the top of the jump-up.

Once the full trucks reached the main drive, they were moved onto a siding. Three rail lines were laid at the bottom of each balance shaft: one for the main road, one for full trucks, and one for empty trucks. When enough trucks were filled with wash, they were moved to form a train, which was then hauled by an electric locomotive to the shaft. There, the trucks were hoisted to the main brace, which was about 21 m above ground level. The washdirt was then tipped into the puddlers located 2 m below the main brace.

CHAPTER 20

Australian Commonwealth Trust Ltd.

AS 1904 BEGAN, Bewick Moreing continued their move into the Victorian deep leads, purchasing 20,000 shares in the Berry United company for their syndicate. Berry United was the northernmost mine on the Madame Berry field, located about 20 km south of the Moolort shaft. The London and Western Australian Exploration Company, chaired by Moreing, also shifted focus to Victoria, proposing a £25,000 investment in deep lead projects.[1]

Hoover secured contracts totalling £11,000 with local firms for new pumping equipment. The Melbourne firm of Kelly and Lewis was tasked with rebuilding the Loddon Valley (No 1 shaft) pumps, while Austral Engineering took on the Moolort (No 2 shaft) project. Hoover announced that both steam plants would be upgraded to handle the 5 million gallons per day (263 l/s) they had originally been designed for. To utilise the increased pumping capacity the reef drives would be advanced swiftly, with numerous new holes bored upwards to drain the lead.

The Adelaide *Critic* greeted this news enthusiastically:

> Bewick, Moreing, & Co. deserve a vote of thanks from 1,200,000 Victorian people for importing American and South African ideas about machinery into Victoria. The funeral of the last cousin Jack miner and director will mark the beginning of a new epoch in Victorian mining. These uneducated, ignorant, rough Cornish miners, with their ingrained meanness and low-grade intellects are keeping back Victorian mining to a disastrous degree.[2]

After Herbert and Lou Hoover returned to London, the financial engineering continued. Moreing became chairman of a new company, the Australian Commonwealth Trust Ltd. Consolidated Deep Leads held 50,000 shares in the Australian Commonwealth Trust, 60,000 shares in Loddon Valley (out of a total of 100,000 shares), and 80,000 shares in Moolort (out of 100,000). The Australian Commonwealth Trust's role was to serve as a financial corporation overseeing the management and control of all the deep lead assets.[3]

The Trust was entitled to one-fifth of the annual profits for ten years from both Loddon Valley Goldfields and Moolort Goldfields, with the companies having the option to buy out this obligation after four years. The Trust also shared a one-fifth interest, under the same terms, with West Australian Goldfields. Additionally, it held 23,500 shares in Berry United, controlled leases at Avoca, and owned 30,000 shares in the Great Berry Proprietary Company.[4]

Bewick Moreing's activities in eastern Australia were managed out of Melbourne by an American graduate of the Columbia School of Mines, Charles Herzig. Hoover appointed his old college friend, engineer Deane Mitchell, as manager of the deep lead projects. Not yet 30 years old, Mitchell was 172 cm tall with a square chin, dark eyes and brown hair, an energetic American like Hoover. The mining companies joined the Victorian Chamber of Mines, with Bewick Moreing represented by Mitchell, while Charles Nicolson, the mine manager at the Moolort shaft, represented Loddon Valley Goldfields.[5]

Figure 43 Deane Mitchell 1921 from a passport application

Sir Alexander Peacock was appointed chairman of the local advisory board for both the Australian Commonwealth Trust and Consolidated Deep Leads. Noting that these advisory boards were intended to serve as a link between the London directorate and the Victorian operations, the *Argus* commented:

> It will therefore fulfill an important function, as the lack of knowledge in London mining circles regarding deep lead mining is something woeful.[6]

Peacock had become Premier of Victoria in 1901 and had been knighted in 1902. However, he had lost a vote of no confidence in the same year and was now in opposition to the conservative premier William Irvine. There was little public concern about any conflict of interest, with several prominent politicians also active in mining and other industries.

Waldemar Lindgren's report, made public in June, focused on the Moolort Goldfields, Loddon Valley Goldfields, Options Block, and Victorian Deep Leads. He mapped the course and depth of the leads based on boring results, confirming the earlier work of geologists like Murray and Lidgey. Lindgren estimated that once the pumps had been upgraded the leads could be reached within 2.5 to 3 years.[7]

Lindgren's calculations, based on his estimates of gold content, suggested that the Moolort mine could generate a profit of £400,000 over a fifteen-year period. He predicted a similar profit for the Loddon Valley mine, despite its faulty pumps and the need for a new shaft. The Loddon Valley and Moolort shafts together were still only raising a little over 4 million gallons per day (210 l/s). The Charlotte Plains and New Havilah shafts were pumping 50% more than this. While the other two properties showed promise, they required further evaluation before any conclusions could be drawn.[8]

Bewick Moreing published a preface to Lindgren's report, highlighting their plan to boost pumping capacity from 4 million to 13.5 million gallons per day (709 l/s). However, at least one journalist questioned how the gold content could be estimated without direct access to the lead and some trial mining. Borehole results were not considered a reliable basis for gold calculations, as gold specks were rarely recovered in such tests.[9]

BY NOW, TWENTY-FOUR English mining companies were operating in Victoria, engaged in alluvial and quartz mining. After a lot of engineering work, the Loddon Valley and Moolort mines gradually increased their combined pumping capacity to about 8 million gallons per day (420 l/s). However, in October, the flywheel of the Loddon Valley pump broke, taking it out of action for a month while repairs were made and temporarily halting mining activities.[10]

Consolidated Deep Leads held its general meeting in London in

December 1904. The Chairman reported that Hoover had been sent to manage the pumping operations, and his efforts had boosted the pumping rate to 9.5 million gallons per day (500 l/s), although the old pumps might not be able to sustain this rate. The Victoria Deep Leads mine was preparing to start pumping and share prices for the invested companies had risen, resulting in Consolidated Deep Leads having assets worth £39,000 more than their initial cost.[11]

The Chairman explained that the Moolort mines faced persistent issues with their Cornish pumping plant, a problem Bewick Moreing had been addressing since 1903. Despite efforts to rebuild the engines, which increased the combined horsepower from 234 to 700, new issues arose with the drive gear, necessitating the reconstruction of engine foundations, boilers, and bob pits. The mines had been plagued by problems with the pumps from the start, stemming from rushed construction under pressure from Whitaker Wright's London promoters in 1896. Since then, there had only been two years of effective pumping.[12]

The frequent machinery breakdowns at both properties were a significant source of frustration. The names of the original Victorian Gold Estates management team had been displayed in a plaque on the chimney stack. Following another breakdown, Deane Mitchell climbed a ladder and chipped off the names with a hammer and chisel. *The Adelaide Critic* remarked:

> It was the best thing he could do, as the owners of those names were not easily reachable. What he should have done instead was leave the names in place and add the total cost of repairs below them.[13]

The annual meeting of Loddon Valley Goldfields was held in May 1905. The chairman, Mr. Simpson, announced that the new 7 m diameter gear wheel, cast by Austral Otis Engineering in Melbourne, was likely one of the largest in the world. This upgrade was expected to enable the No 1 shaft to consistently raise 5 million gallons per day (263 l/s), although he had previously claimed that this rate had already been reached at a meeting six months earlier.

The Consolidated Deep Leads company was concentrating its efforts on the Loddon Valley shaft, where the pumping engines were consuming 1,600 tons of firewood per month. In July 1905, a beam engine with a 26-inch lift was being installed at that shaft to add a further capacity of 2.6 million gallons per day (137 l/s). Supplied by machinery merchants Cameron and Sutherland of Ballarat, this engine was now the largest pump in Victoria. It was operational by November.[14]

A steam-powered Keystone core sampling drill, recently developed in the USA, was brought in by Bewick Moreing through the Australian Commonwealth Trust to rapidly evaluate deposits across central Victoria. The ten-ton machine could drill 10 m per day in ordinary ground or 3 m per day in hard rock. Many optioned areas were abandoned following an assessment with this drill.[15]

The drill provided a clearer understanding of the bedrock profile at Moolort, confirming what everyone already knew, that the Loddon Valley shaft was badly located. Consequently, a new shaft, to be known as the Keystone shaft, was begun closer to the lead, 1400 m northeast of the No 1 shaft. This new shaft was designed to pump ten million gallons per day (525 l/s) and include two hoisting and two pumping compartments. It was expected to reach a depth of 137 m and be completed by the end of 1905. The new shaft would save about 1,200 m of underground tramming.[16]

James Curle, the special mining correspondent of London's *Economist*, a friend of Hoover's and a supporter of Bewick Moreing, wrote that the presence of gold in payable quantities in the leads had been established. He said that while promising gold prospects had been identified through bores, predicting the gold content of the wash remained difficult. Curle emphasised that the primary challenge was overcoming the water issues. He concluded:

> If the water is overcome, I believe these mines will produce a substantial amount of gold and generate good profits; on paper, they are very promising mining ventures.[17]

However, he also wrote:

> ... it is conceivable that the water in those mines never will be mastered, and that when the companies have come to the end of their finances they will give up in despair. I, however, believe that before such a financial position is reached, the water will have been overcome and the 'wash' will be in the course of development.[18]

When the Herbert and Lou Hoover returned to Melbourne in early August 1905, Charles Herzig organised a grand reception with over sixty guests, featuring a band and a fortune teller. Among the attendees were Deane Mitchell, Sir Alexander Peacock, and their wives.[19]

Hoover's primary purpose for the Melbourne visit was to represent Bewick Moreing in negotiating the purchase of a vast stockpile of zinc-rich tailings from the South Broken Hill Company, anticipating that a new process would be developed to recover the metal. While Hoover was the front man, Moreing was involved behind the scenes. Hoover travelled to Broken Hill and the contract was signed on September 15. Additional contracts were negotiated with other mines, totalling two million tons of tailings which were estimated to contain 700,000 tons of zinc, 300,000 tons of lead, and 20 million ounces of silver.[20]

This deal led to the creation of Zinc Corporation Limited, which eventually evolved into today's Rio Tinto. The syndicate proponents were William Lawrence Baillieu, Francis Algernon Govett, Arthur Terrill, London stockbroker Lionel Robinson and William Clarke. The directors of the new venture included WL Baillieu, Charles Herzig, Herbert J Daly, and, in London, Herbert Hoover and William Clark. The Zinc Corporation had its office in Melbourne and was managed by Bewick Moreing.[21]

Hoover met with the Victorian Minister for Mines, proposing the establishment of a 'pumping trust' to ensure fair contributions from all participants towards the cost of pumping. The Minister responded that the department already had significant discretion to handle such matters and had done so previously. Hoover was surprised to hear this and remained unconvinced that the existing arrangements would be sufficient to satisfy London investors given the large sums required.[22]

After consulting with his Bewick Moreing colleagues, Hoover decided to suspend operations at the Moolort (No 2) shaft and relocate its pump to the Loddon Valley (No 1) shaft. This move would allow for necessary repairs and upgrades at both locations. The minister granted a six-month suspension of labour conditions at No 2 shaft. Hoover said that the combined pumping capacity at the Loddon Valley (No 1) and Keystone shafts would be 12 million gallons per day (630 l/s), a significant downgrade on earlier announcements. Charles Nicolson, the mine manager at the Moolort shaft, was made redundant and returned to Western Australia. Herbert and Lou, along with their infant and nurse, departed Melbourne on October 10.[23]

Big Dog Engineers

THE LARGE-SCALE OPERATIONS organised by Bewick Moreing, particularly the move to the new Keystone shaft, put considerable financial pressure on Loddon Valley Goldfields, forcing it to increase its capital by creating 80,000 new £1 shares in February 1906. The mine was buzzing with activity as nearly 100 men dismantled the machinery and buildings from the Moolort shaft and transported them to the Keystone shaft using a combination of traction engines, large wagons, bullock teams and horse teams. Thirty tons of Oregon pine logs up to 30 m long were delivered to the new shaft for pump rods. Four massive poppet legs, each 30 m long and 1.2 m diameter, were transported from Warburton in the Yarra Ranges.[1]

The sheer volume of mining-related transport disrupted the normal activities of the Moolort community. The railway sidings became overwhelmed, with wagons piled up and blocking access, so that the local farmers were unable to load chaff and their other produce onto the trains. In July, a large public meeting was held to address these concerns, with attendees resolving to bring the issue to the attention of the Tullaroop Shire and potentially escalate it to the state parliament if necessary. The tension between mining operations and local agricultural interests highlighted the broader economic and social impacts of the deep lead mining boom on the region.[2]

Pumping at the Loddon Valley shaft continued, with the wash nearly drained by October 1906, before a heavy flow of water suddenly led to a suspension of work at the shaft. Despite this setback, the development crew quickly shifted their focus to other tasks, including the crosscut linking the 152 m level of the new Keystone shaft to the existing workings. This crosscut, 2.4 m high and 3.7 m wide at rail level, showcased the scale of the engineering efforts. Two large chambers were cut at the 138 m level, with winzes sunk from these chambers to facilitate further development.[3]

Bewick Moreing's General Manager William Loring was now responsible for an expanding range of copper, gold, and coal mining ventures in eastern Australia. In January 1907, Deane Mitchell returned from Western Australia, where he had been sent to manage the Oroya-Brownhill mine. He was given responsibility for all the Bewick Moreing deep lead projects in Victoria. One of these, the Berry United mine, was a large pumping project but was well south of the Moolort operations and unaffected by them. Another, the Cathcart, was five miles southwest of Ararat.[4]

At the end of January, Mitchell supervised a renewed attempt to access the wash at the No 1 shaft. Miners started work along the bank of the old river, about 6 m above its bed. Early returns from 20 tons of wash were modest – 48 shillings per fathom, with direct working costs of 32 shillings. Nevertheless, much richer yields were anticipated once they could access the riverbed itself.[5]

The public mood in Victoria around the deep lead mines remained optimistic despite some negative press coverage. The mines were decked out in bunting to welcome a visit by the Governor, an event extensively covered by the Melbourne papers. Afterward, the McIvor Hotel was granted permission to advertise that it was 'Under the patronage of His Excellency the Governor, Major-General the Honourable Sir Reginald Talbot, K.C.B.'.[6]

Despite the positive public relations efforts, some journalists were sceptical. One noted:

> The water isn't beaten, and Bewick-Moreing's new pumps couldn't have got
> it down to the point talked about unless the old plant had been at work for
> years. Even now only a bit of the lead is drained, and it will take 12 months,
> if not more, to get to work in the wash.[7]

Herbert Hoover returned to Australia, this time alone, in February 1907 for an extended visit. His travels took him to Kalgoorlie, Broken Hill (twice), Melbourne (twice), and Emmaville in north Queensland. His primary missions included investigating gold theft in Kalgoorlie, advancing zinc recovery research at Broken Hill, and addressing the deep lead situation. Hoover later recorded that he advised that the deep lead project be abandoned. The exact timing of his advice and the specific recipients were not documented, but it marked a critical turning point in the project's history.[8]

Hoover worked closely with WS Robinson and RPC Baillieu on the Zinc Corporation project. Robinson, two years younger than Hoover, had just resigned as commercial editor of *The Age* newspaper and begun an interest in mining and business that would make him one of Australia's leading industrialists. Robinson's older brother Lionel was a London stockbroker and a member of the Zinc Corporation syndicate. His firm friend Richard Percy Clive ('Joe') Baillieu, almost the same age as Hoover, was a partner in the family stockbroking company of EL Baillieu & Co.[9]

Hoover, still only 33 years old, was weary from constant travel and the pressure of work, much of which he attributed to the unreasonable demands of his boss Moreing. One Sunday, Robinson and Baillieu were looking forward to joining Hoover for Sunday lunch. They had set off from Melbourne that morning by steam train, enjoying the scenery of the Mornington Peninsular, before changing to a horse-drawn buggy at Mount Martha. They might have gone by car, but recent experience favoured a train ride. Just a few weeks earlier they had tried to drive the sixty miles from Melbourne to Sorrento in a Clement Talbot car. They got as far as the stretch between Aspendale and Frankston, where they got stuck in the sand and had to be pulled out by a couple of horses.[10]

Mount Martha was a coastal summer retreat on the Peninsular railway line, a place of mansions like Glynt, Yellow Robins, The Chalet, and Green Gables, and guest houses like Mount Martha House and Grandview. The lunch invitation had come from Hoover, who was still a car enthusiast, and they arrived to find him lying on his back, covered with grease, under a Porthos car. Hoover had a lot on his mind and perhaps work on the car provided an escape from these worries. It certainly had his attention, because he stayed under the car all lunch time and most of the afternoon, leaving his guests to dine alone.[11]

LODDON VALLEY GOLDFIELDS LTD, now under severe financial pressure, applied to the Victorian state government for a £20,000 grant. To throw some of that pressure back on the government the company argued that it had been misled by the optimistic results from the government's boring operations and the reports sent to London, which had influenced its investment decisions. They admitted that their original pumps were inadequate, and that the volume of water encountered had far exceeded expectations. The results from driving across the wash had been disappointing and costs were running at £1,500 to £1,600 per month. The company stressed that halting the pumps would make it impossible to restart them and would have a detrimental effect on other deep lead mining operations.

In July 1907, Cabinet reviewed the application and approved a grant of £8,000, contingent on the company providing matching funds. The grant was intended to be used for driving and proving the lead. To secure the loan, the government took a mortgage over the lease and part of the mine's plant. Having already spent £237,000 and struggling financially, the company now needed to raise additional funds from its shareholders. A new entity, The Loddon Valley Goldfields (1907) Ltd., was established with a registered office in Sydney. The new company's capital was set at £240,000 in £1 shares. The old company, burdened by loans from Consolidated Deep Leads and facing financial difficulties, went into voluntary liquidation.[12]

Sydney's *Bulletin* remarked critically on the situation, stating:

> Bewick, Moreing & Co. are the big-dog engineers; but they haven't shifted the universe since they have been in Victoria, though they had no stint of Bull's cash to help them.[13]

In August, a London shareholders' meeting was convened to discuss the reconstruction. Sir Gerard Smith revealed that only an eighth of a mile of the old riverbed had been tested out of a total expected length of four or five miles. While some rich patches had been discovered, they were very localised, and the overall ground proved unpayable. The gold was spread over a wide area rather than concentrated in a deep gutter as anticipated. Herbert Hoover spoke cautiously. He did not recommend abandoning the mine but acknowledged that it was impossible to say what would happen with the geology.[14]

Each shareholder was required to contribute 5 shillings to retain their position, raising £58,000 if fully subscribed, and the financial engineering continued. In October, it was announced that Consolidated Deep Leads

Ltd. (which held the Loddon Valley and Moolort mines) and the Australian Commonwealth Trust were planning to amalgamate into a new entity: the Australian Deep Leads Trust.

This new company would have a capital of £350,000 and would acquire the assets of the Loddon Valley, Moolort Goldfields, Victorian Deep Leads, and the Berry United, all of which needed more funding. The existing companies would be liquidated, and shareholders would receive shares in the Australian Deep Leads Trust. Each shareholder would be issued four-shilling shares, with three shillings deemed paid up.[15]

When the company reports were published Sydney's *Bulletin* observed:

> Those two London PROMOTING AND GAMBLING CONCERNS, the AUSTRALIAN COMMONWEALTH TRUST and the CONSOLIDATED DEEP LEADS present figures which show how completely and utterly 'busted' they are.[16]

By December 1907, there was renewed activity at the Loddon Valley mine. The puddlers were relocated to the Keystone shaft, and additional workers were employed. However, the Victorian Deep Leads company decided to suspend all work at their mine until the results from the Loddon Valley trials were available. The previous year's pumping had not significantly reduced the water level at the Victorian Deep Leads as anticipated.

The first result from the relocated puddlers at the Keystone shaft, reported in April 1908, was 414 ounces from 740 fathoms.[17]

Leaving Lou and their new baby in London, Hoover travelled to Burma after the Loddon Valley shareholders meeting, where he endured an arduous programme of travel and mine assessment in tropical conditions. On his return he had a final falling out with Moreing. At the end of January 1908, the company announced that:

> Owing to ill-health caused by continuous overwork, Mr. HC Hoover is retiring from the active management of Messrs Bewick, Moreing, & Co.[18]

Hoover had been unhappy with his role in Bewick Moreing and wrote privately that Moreing 'had proved a wholly impossible partner'. Taking a few weeks on the beach at Brighton, England he wrote '... I could not stand

Moreing any longer than necessary – having given practically 5 years to that mess'.[19]

Surprisingly, not all London investors had given up on the deep leads. Bewick Moreing managed to raise £40,000 in January 1908 to develop the Berry United mine. This mine was the closest on the Berry lead to the Moolort shaft, though it was still seventeen miles to the south.[20]

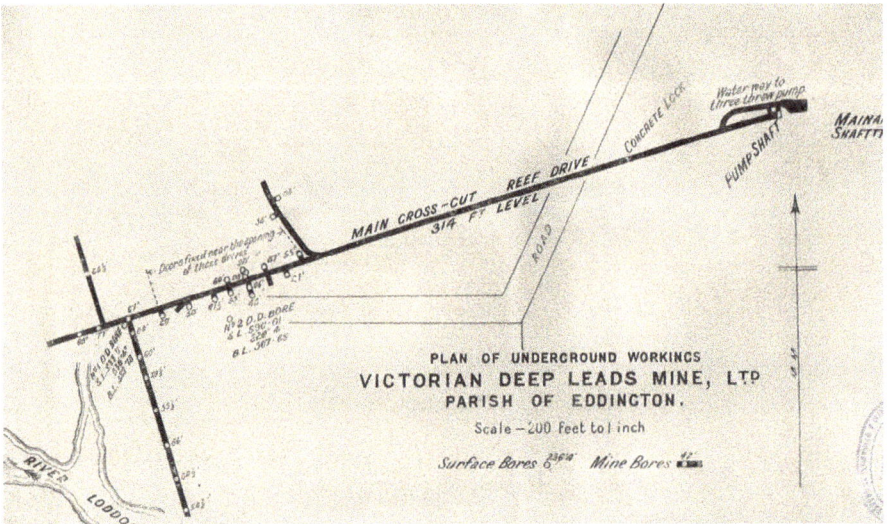

Figure 44 Plan of Victorian Deep Leads underground workings
Geological Survey of Victoria, 1909

CHAPTER 22

The Junction Dispute

WILLIAM CAPRON DIED in February 1906, aged 49, and was succeeded as General Manager of Charlotte Plains Consolidated by the mining manager George Bryant. In a stroke of misfortune, the manager's residence burned down a few weeks later. Fortunately, plans and records had been duplicated in Melbourne, so no significant information was lost.[1]

In April Charles Moreing, along with William Loring, the General Manager for Bewick, Moreing in Australia, and Mr. Reid from the London board of Charlotte Plains Consolidated, embarked on a familiarisation tour of the deep lead projects. At both Charlotte Plains and New Havilah two puddlers were operating, reportedly yielding the excellent results of 12 dwt to 1 oz of gold per fathom (4 to 6 dwt per square metre). Still, as an experiment that smacks of desperation, the Charlotte Plains manager planned to sluice all low-grade material from above the level of the washdirt to find out if it might be profitable.[2]

At the time of that visit, the main reef drives extended 1,800 m at Charlotte Plains and 800 m at New Havilah. Ventilation was managed by a Roots Blower, which pushed air through a 63 cm diameter pipe, which reduced to 41 cm at the mining faces. However, only a quarter of the surface-drawn air reached the faces due to leakage and the effects of atmospheric pressure changes with depth and temperature. It was still humid, hot and unpleasant at the face. There were plans to drive an additional 430 m to connect the two mines, which would significantly improve ventilation. Connecting the old Pioneer shaft would also help ventilation and it could be used for lowering timber, freeing up the main hoist.[3]

The initially promising results did not continue. Over the first six months of the year, the mine produced only 355 oz of gold, a figure far too low to offset the significant pumping costs. With an average grade of just over 12 dwt per fathom (4 dwt per square metre), the operation ran at a substantial loss, leaving shareholders frustrated. Their dissatisfaction found focus on the Junction Deep Leads company, a partner in the electric power project.[4]

The Junction Deep Leads had done no pumping since 1902 and despite raising capital in March, it had not resumed operations. Instead, the company had leased its share of electric power to the Victorian Deep Leads company, effectively forcing Charlotte Plains to dewater the Junction's portion of the lead at no cost. This arrangement meant that while the Charlotte Plains mine bore the burden of the pumping expenses, Junction Deep Leads was poised to start mining the following year without having contributed to the pumping efforts. This angered the Charlotte Plains shareholders.[5]

John Paull, still a significant shareholder through the Pioneer company, was particularly outraged by the Junction Deep Leads company's inactivity and perceived unfairness. He sought government intervention, applying to have the Junction's lease forfeited. His case was supported by witnesses such as Drysdale Brown, Reginald Murray and Henry Gore. However, the Junction lawyers proposed calling back Drysdale Brown and cross-examining him.

Paull was advised by his lawyer that the cross examination of Drysdale Brown:

> …was likely to be lengthy and to have reference to matters which he considered would involve the consideration of issues which were not pertinent to his application.[6]

Clearly, Drysdale Brown had reasons for not wishing to be cross-examined. He had been one of the promoters of the Victorian Deep Leads company and had been on the local board of the Junction Deep Leads. His conflict of interest would be painful to unravel. He persuaded John Paull to withdraw the application for forfeiture of the Junction lease. It cannot have helped that Sir Alexander Peacock, his friend and a fellow member of parliament, was acting as attorney under power for the Junction company.[7]

Instead, on 1 August, a group of about 20 shareholders led by Drysdale Brown approached the Victorian Minister for Mines, Donald McLeod, with a petition. They objected to an agreement that had been made between the Department of Mines and Moolort Goldfields Limited which exempted the Junction Deep Leads from contributing to the cost of pumping, as long as two pumps were working at Moolort. The shareholders asked McLeod to either revoke the Junction's exemption or compensate the Charlotte Plains company for the extra pumping expense. McLeod promised to consider the issue.[8]

The petition included a breakdown of Charlotte Plains' historical expenditures, highlighting the high operating costs, particularly in wages and electric power:

- Pioneer Company: £29,000
- Wages to miners: £44,332
- Rail freight (firewood, etc.):   £10,102
- Lease rents: £827
- Electric power: £57,993
- Plant: £38,328
- Stores: £2,889
- Telegrams and postage: £800
- Mining timber: £2,300
- Sundry: £4,576
  Total: £191,147

In response to growing shareholder dissatisfaction, Drysdale Brown organised an inspection visit to the Charlotte Plains mine to demonstrate progress and bolster confidence. He arranged for a special train from Melbourne, followed by a lunch hosted by George Bryant. Around sixty gentlemen and a few ladies attended the visit, where they posed for photographs in front of the mine buildings. [9]

In September the mine's puddlers processed 230 ounces of gold, maintaining an average yield of about 12 pennyweights per fathom. Drysdale Brown was optimistic, estimating that mining costs were around 8 pennyweights per fathom, leaving a margin for profit once the water levels were sufficiently lowered. He compared the current washdirt favourably to the rich wash found by mines in the Majorca lead, which had historically been profitable.[10]

Wood had proven to be a more economical fuel for the power station than coal. Despite the electrical plant now consuming 645 tons of firewood per week, Drysdale Brown noted that maintenance costs were minimal, indicating the infrastructure was operating efficiently. His efforts to engage shareholders and demonstrate the mine's potential profit helped alleviate some of the growing concerns over the company's performance.

Despite steady production at Charlotte Plains, the company struggled with labour shortages, particularly in hiring and retaining miners. Drysdale Brown successfully lobbied the Victorian Railways to introduce special workers' trains from Maryborough to Carisbrook, Charlotte Plains, and Moolort, beginning in late October. The mining companies subsidised 25% of the train fares, making it easier for miners to commute to the mines.[11]

Figure 45 Carpenters at Loddon Valley Mine
Dunolly Museum

By this time, there was broad consensus that the mine had reached a stage of steady production, with panelling operations confirming the expectations from boreholes. At the Charlotte Plains a horizontal drive had advanced to the edge of the gutter, and a western branch was being driven to connect with the New Havilah workings. Three rises had been established into the wash, and wash drives were being developed to facilitate gold extraction.[12]

George Bryant projected that once four puddling machines were operational, the mine would need to process and hoist 90 tons of washdirt and mullock per day, requiring a workforce of 230 men. However, by this point, only 1,200 ounces of gold had been recovered from 1,877 fathoms, an average yield of 12 pennyweights per fathom (3.6 dwt/ sq m). Bryant remained optimistic that large-scale operations would reduce costs to around 8 pennyweights per fathom, allowing for profitable operations.[13]

All the deep lead mines in Victoria were facing a precarious situation by late 1906, as investor confidence was beginning to erode and share prices fell. Mine owners attempted to bolster support by feeding optimistic promotional material to the London press. Maps purported to show the courses of deep leads as if they were well understood, and forecasts of low working expenses and high gold yields – like those made by George Bryant – were widely circulated.[14]

The Victorian Mines Department went public in urging caution, stating that the lowest recorded working cost for a deep lead mine in Victoria was 10 pennyweights of gold per fathom, and the average cost was more than 11 pennyweights per fathom. Furthermore, a promotional pamphlet titled 'The Victorian Deep Leads Manual' was criticised for being misleading in many aspects, prompting Melbourne's *Age* to call upon Bewick Moreing, recognised as experts in the field, to clarify the situation. Compounding the uncertainty, November brought the news of financial restructuring for both the Victorian Deep Leads and Moolort Deep Leads companies. To counter concerns about George Bryant's forecasts, Sir Alexander Peacock highlighted Bryant's six-year tenure at the Main Leads North mine, where £22,500 had been paid out in dividends.[15]

In December 1906, the longstanding dispute between the Charlotte Plains company and the Junction Deep Leads Company reached a turning point when the Victorian Minister of Mines demanded that the Junction company show cause why it should not contribute to costs. However, the case was further delayed due to an application in London to wind up the jointly owned Deep Leads Electric Transmission Company.

Frustrated by the delay Drysdale Brown, on behalf of the Charlotte Plains company, pressed for an immediate resolution and requested a backdated contribution of £75 per week from the Junction. Finally in mid-February 1907 the Minister ordered the Junction Deep Leads Company to make a significant back-payment of £1,560 and to continue paying £60 per week going forward, with the threat of losing their lease if they failed to comply. This ruling would set a precedent in Victoria for the equitable sharing of pumping costs among neighbouring mining companies.[16]

Despite this victory, the Charlotte Plains company was far from profitable. By the end of 1906, the mine had only produced 1,845 oz of gold – a stark contrast to the 10,847 oz produced by the nearby Chalks No 3 mine in the same period.[17]

CHAPTER 23

A Ghastly Failure

WORKERS WERE NOW present in their hundreds in the underground mines and surface works, processing the wash and hauling supplies. Every house in the nearby town of Baringhup was fully occupied, and residents were actively seeking land there to build new homes.[1]

In February 1907 Governor Sir Reginald Talbot, along with yet another group of dignitaries, toured the bustling deep lead mines. Drysdale Brown showed them around Charlotte Plains mine and powerhouse, where smoke poured from the tall chimney. The visitors then travelled on to Moolort by horse-drawn cabs where Sir Alexander Peacock, representing Bewick Moreing, took the governor, dressed in oilskins and wading through water in the drives, on a similar tour.[2]

Charlotte Plains mine was suffering from a shortage of miners. The discovery of the *Poseidon* nugget, weighing 860 oz (26.6 kg) at Tarnagulla had caused a sensation and many of the miners quit their jobs and went off to Tarnagulla to dig for gold. George Bryant was forced to advertise for experienced alluvial miners, promising consistent work, the highest district wages, a dry mine, and a train service from Maryborough and Carisbrook to Charlotte Plains for every shift.[3]

The miners' trains ran to the Charlotte Plains mine throughout 1907. Although tickets cost four shillings each – more expensive than Melbourne metropolitan trains – they were popular with the miners and the Maryborough community. But Drysdale Brown was annoyed at the high freight rates being charged by the Railways Department and he decided to reduce the subsidy being paid for the miners' tickets. When the Railways Department increased prices by sixpence in response, there was a vigorous protest. On 11 November about 50 men refused to board the afternoon shift train, disrupting work at the mines.[4]

The trains did not yet run to the two Moolort mines and when the

Maryborough Traders' Association called for this, 32 residents of Moolort raised a petition against it. They would prefer that miners lived and spent their earnings closer to where they worked. The larger towns of Maldon and Maryborough were in competition for the business and employment opportunities created by the mines, and the railway service gave Maryborough a clear advantage.[5]

John Paull led a deputation from the Maldon Traders Association to the council, advocating for a telephone connection to Baringhup. The country telephone system was gradually improving, though it was another year before the Charlotte Plains mine was connected to a network that included Carisbrook, Maryborough, Talbot, Dunolly, Avoca, Clunes, Creswick, and Ballarat.[6]

Money was again running short, so Drysdale Brown announced another financial reconstruction in mid-March 1907. He said that although they had yet to find good washdirt, Reginald Murray had inspected the mine and indicated that they were 'likely to get into good washdirt any day'.[7]

The formation of a new company named Charlotte Plains Consolidated Gold Mines Limited was completed in May. This new entity was capitalised at £390,000, comprising 780,000 10-shilling shares, each paid up to 9 shillings per share. The board of directors for the new company included EV Reid, GHM King, SM Ferguson, HFL King, HA Plumb, and M Horner. The new company had £39,000 available for its operations. The previous company had spent £300,000 including £100,000 from Australian investors and £200,000 from English investors.[8]

Gold production at the Charlotte Plains mine began to increase gradually, initially reaching around 200 ounces per month, ramping up to over 300 ounces in June and 400 ounces in July. In August, an interesting find was made at the Charlotte Plains mine – a quartz specimen containing nearly an ounce of gold. This discovery confirmed the presence of quartz reefs beneath the lead, which could potentially develop into viable quartz mines, like those at Ballarat West. The gold returns for August also showed improvement, with 480 ounces smelted. Both shafts seemed to be accessing a richer part of the lead, and production increased to around 600 ounces per month over the following six months.[9]

In June 1907, the English company that owned the Junction Deep Leads mine went into liquidation. The Minister of Mines, Donald McLeod, granted a temporary suspension of the labour covenants, provided the liquidators continued to pay the £60 per week contribution to the pumping costs. They failed to do this and never paid any of the £5,000 they ultimately owed for pumping costs. Despite this, McLeod did not void their lease, leading some to speculate that Sir Alexander Peacock, still representing the Bewick Moreing group, might be influencing the situation. Eventually the company was wound up, and the plant was sold off in June 1908.[10]

At the New Havilah shaft, the pumps were now only needing to raise one million gallons per day (53 l/s) to keep the water down. The three-throw plunger pump at the Charlotte Plains shaft was raising three million gallons per day (158 l/s), with the centrifugal pump kept in reserve. The quality of the washdirt in the leading drives was believed to be improving, and Drysdale Brown was hopeful that no further capital would be needed from shareholders.[11]

But the improved gold production was still insufficient to cover costs. George Bryant believed that they were mining on the flanks of the lead and that the rich deep ground had not yet been reached, so a lot more driving would be needed to access it. The company was now paying over £1,000 each fortnight in wages, directly employing five hundred men and indirectly supporting around 1,400 people in the district[12]

In mid-1908 rumours began circulating that part of the workforce would be laid off. While Drysdale Brown denied rumours that English shareholders were not paying calls, George Bryant confirmed that more time and money would be needed to for the mine to become profitable. But the London shareholders really had reached their limit – no additional funds would be provided. The company had spent £307,655 but had earned only £36,600 from gold sales and was in debt for an additional £16,000.[13]

In a last-ditch effort to salvage the situation, Drysdale Brown organised yet another reorganisation and the London directors agreed to transfer the property and assets to a new Australian company. This company, registered in Melbourne, would have a greatly diminished capital of just £23,400 in one-pound shares. Shareholders from the old company would be given the opportunity to purchase one share for every forty they held in the previous company. The purchase terms included three shillings and fourpence on application, the same amount on allotment, and the remainder to be paid through future calls.[14]

However, the reorganisation was still underway when cash ran out, despite a clean-up of 584 oz of gold in mid-June. George Bryant had to suspend all operations on 30 June 1908, resulting in 250 men losing their jobs. To prevent the rising water from carrying sand and debris into the mine workings, the lock doors were secured throughout the mine.[15]

Now doing all the pumping itself, Chalks No 3 faced rising water levels and asked the Mines Department to compel Charlotte Plains to continue pumping. Meanwhile, the Prentice and Southern mine at Rutherglen, which had already invested £193,000 in development and received £30,000 in government assistance, sought an additional £10,000 from the government. This mine had been pumping 3 million gallons per day (158 l/s) for the previous ten years.[16]

THE CLOSURE OF THE CHARLOTTE Plains mine in June 1908 was followed by the announcement of the Keystone mine's permanent closure just four days later. Many of the Keystone miners quickly found new positions at the Cathcart mine in Ararat and the Berry United mine at Creswick, both managed by Bewick Moreing. Tragically, eight days before the closure, eighteen-year-old John Bennet suffered severe injuries when he was caught between the cage and the timbers at the Keystone shaft.[17]

In 1900 Whitaker Wright had divided the Victorian Gold Estates' assets between two companies: Loddon Valley Goldfields Limited, which took over the No 1 shaft, and Moolort Goldfields Limited, which took over the No 2 shaft. Under Bewick Moreing's management, the plant and equipment from the Moolort property had been moved to the Keystone shaft. Recently a contractor had been engaged to sink a new shaft at a better location for the Moolort company, but this work was halted with the closure of the Keystone mine, and the Moolort company went into hibernation.

A meeting of the Loddon Valley Goldfields Limited was held in London on 17 August. Chairman Sir Gerard Smith expressed his belief that the

Loddon Valley had 'proved to be a ghastly failure' and admitted that it was difficult to determine how much money had been spent on the property. He explained that the great underground river, while potentially valuable in its upper reaches (in the Berry system), appeared in the lower areas to be a vast, shallow basin. If the gold had been concentrated into a narrow channel, the property could have been highly profitable. However, without reaching the further bank of the river, and with gold values only sufficient to cover extraction and treatment costs while leaving nothing for pumping and development, the situation was dire.[18]

Smith advised the investors that they had lost their money and that the only course of action left was to accept the loss with as much philosophical fortitude as possible. A lengthy report from Bewick Moreing was read out to the meeting. Moreing spoke against any further investment, and the vote to give up on the Loddon Valley project was unanimous. The Victorian government confirmed that it would enforce its mortgage.[19]

CHAPTER 24

If Collins Street Were a River Bed

EMPLOYEES AND THEIR FAMILIES were in shock, and the nearby communities were devastated. George Bryant and his son William, who was an engine driver at the mine, were now both unemployed. A month later, while cleaning a shotgun at his Charlotte Plains home, William accidentally discharged the weapon, fatally injuring his infant son Percy. "I didn't know it was loaded," said William. George Bryant bought a hotel and store at Amherst, but he couldn't keep away from mining and would take a position as manager at the Cathcart Plains mine the following year. [1]

Since 1906, the Victorian government had invested £80,000 and advanced loans of £90,000 to support the mining industry. These funds were used for exploration bores, cutting tracks, building roads, establishing laboratories, and printing promotional materials. Of the loans, £49,000 had been repaid. Politicians debated the situation, noting that English companies had collectively spent over £1.5 million which had helped support the Victorian economy. Cabinet had to consider whether the industry's potential justified further assistance. In August, the Minister introduced the Mining Development Bill for a second reading, which was approved. The Bill allocated £100,000 to support the industry, including gold and coal mining. [2]

In the third week of August, the state cabinet agreed to advance loans of £6,000 to the Charlotte Plains company, £3,000 to the South Star quartz mine in Ballarat, and £10,000 to the Prentice and Southern deep lead mine at Chiltern. In response, Drysdale Brown immediately registered a new company named the Charlotte Plains Gold Mining Company Limited. He anticipated it would take four months to set up the mine, and once fully operational, it would employ 400 men and inject £2,000 each week into the Maryborough district.

Beside Drysdale Brown, the directors of the new company included Herman Schlapp and Macpherson Robertson. Schlapp was an American metallurgical engineer who had joined BHP in 1886 and built the first Port Pirie smelters. He had retired from BHP in 1893 to become a consultant and company director. Macpherson Robertson was born in Ballarat in 1859 and was the founder of the chocolate and confectionery company MacRobertsons, which had grown to become Australia's largest confectionery company. Robert Roberts, who had previously been the underground manager at the New Havilah shaft, was promoted to Mine Manager to replace George Bryant.[3]

The Director of the Victorian Geological Survey, Edward Dunn, issued a report on the Charlotte Plains mine. The main development work done during 1908 included extending the main bottom level westward and some panelling in the lead. The western blocks, closer to the presumed main gutter, yielded 17 dwt per fathom (5 dwt/sq m). Dunn estimated that £10,000 and 3 to 4 months would be required for the new company to ascertain the mine's value.[4]

Robert Roberts began issuing regular reports on the mine's development, although there was no significant gold production. In October he reported 2 oz per fathom; in November, 93 oz from 89 fathoms; and in December, 140 oz from 104 fathoms. According to previous cost estimates, this should have been quite profitable. The miners' train service, which had been stopped at the beginning of July, was resumed in mid-November. Drysdale Brown also successfully applied to have the Junction Company's seven leases forfeited to the Charlotte Plains company. No work had been done on these leases for nine months, and the plant had already been removed for sale or scrapped.[5]

At the November budget hearings, the £6,000 advance to the Charlotte Plains company again raised concerns about Drysdale Brown's potential conflict of interest. In response, it was noted that 95 men were employed at the mine, with expectations that this number would increase to 500 by the end of 1909. In January 1909, Drysdale Brown was appointed Attorney General in the new ministry, while WL Baillieu was named Minister of Public Health and Commissioner of Works.

Despite a Christmas break, the mine reported solid production figures, cleaning up 238 oz from 236 fathoms in January and 206 oz from 239 fathoms in February. By this time the mine had pumped nearly 14,000 million gallons (53,000 megalitres) in three years. Drysdale Brown calculated:

If Collins-street were a river bed, that water would fill it ten feet deep, and would stretch out for 420 miles long. The Yarra as wide and deep as it is at Queen's Bridge – 300 feet wide and ten feet deep – would have to be 140 miles long to hold all the water. If it were put into four hundred gallon iron tanks and they were placed side by side, they would form a line stretching round the earth at its widest part and lapping over more than a thousand miles.[6]

Gold production at the Charlotte Plains continued at an average rate of 207 oz per fortnight, translating to roughly 1 oz per fathom. The west main level was being extended rapidly, though production from the New Havilah shaft had been suspended. The operation was sustained by calls on shareholders.[7]

In May 1909, Drysdale Brown firmly refuted rumours that the company was poised for closure, asserting that 'the prospects and outlook are better and more encouraging at present than at any time since the company commenced operations.' Demonstrating confidence, the company had also bought out its partners in the electric company for £3,250.[8]

However, shortly thereafter, a pump failure caused the mine to lose 38 shifts while repairs were made, severely impacting cash flow. Many miners laid off during this period found employment elsewhere. Over the previous six months, the company had spent £14,458 and earned approximately £9,300 from gold sales. On 9 August, Drysdale Brown was forced to announce the closure of the mine and the cessation of pumping operations.

Drysdale Brown convened a general meeting of shareholders to address the situation. He reported that yields had been disappointing, with only narrow runs of payable wash. The company was the sole remaining operator pumping but faced challenges with poor-quality and scarce fuel. They had relied on the Mines Department reports, but the situation was now deemed hopeless, with an operating loss of £5,134 incurred over the previous six months. The company owed £34,016 to creditors and Drysdale Brown had personally lost £12,000. The meeting resolved to sell the property, if possible, but it wasn't.[9]

CHAPTER 25

Liquidation

IN JANUARY 1909, a liquidator was appointed to The Loddon Valley Goldfields (1907), Ltd. He acted swiftly, auctioning off buildings, stores, and equipment, including a double-seat buggy and a bicycle. Larger equipment was put up for public tender, while the mortgaged remainder was auctioned on behalf of the government. The primary buyers were machinery merchants Miller and Company and Cameron and Sutherland of Ballarat. Meanwhile, thieves moved into the abandoned sites and took what they could, with an emphasis on brass and copper items.[1]

The Moolort Public Hall which had become an important social centre for the farming community, was hauled three miles from Moolort North to a new site on the public road. A resident's working bee quickly put up fences, gates and a water tank.[2]

The big items at the Keystone shaft were offered by tender in October 1909. These included:

> the whole of the Magnificent Triple Expansion PUMPING PLANT, complete with Three Lancashire Boilers, 2 iron bobs, gear and rods, poppet heads, air compressor and receiver, Rootes blower, electric lighting plant, powerful capstan engine and gear ... and all buildings covering the same. Separate tenders will be received for the 26-inch single cylinder Pumping Engine and Gear, also Capstan Engine, gear, etc., which are not erected.[3]

The Keystone pumping plant was purchased by the South Langi Logan mine at Ararat, while the boilers were acquired by the State Coal Mine at Wonthaggi. The government put the mortgaged large steam engines up for tender in July 1910 and declared the leases void in October 1911. After purchasing the equipment, the machinery merchants only moved it when it was resold. Meanwhile, thieves continued to target the site, with reports of brass fittings being stolen as late as 1918.[4]

The remaining private buildings were either removed, demolished, or destroyed by unexplained fires. The Moolort North post office, telephone exchange, coffee palace, and residence burned down in October 1910, prompting the transfer of postal services to the railway station. The cause of the fire was not determined. The railway residence at Moolort station was relocated in 1912. The Moolort State School closed in 1913, although the building remained and was reopened later.[5]

The Charlotte Plains mining leases were declared void in May 1910. Despite rumours of interest from several parties, no sale of the leases had materialised. The electric power plant, including engines, boilers, generators, switchgear, and pumps, was sold in 1913. The electrical engineer's and mine manager's houses, along with other buildings and water tanks, were sold in 1914, a process overseen by Drysdale Brown. By 1918, the corrugated iron from the power plant and mine buildings had been repurposed as the roof for the new Maryborough butter factory.[6]

HAVING RAISED CAPITAL before abandoning the mines, Loddon Valley Goldfields Limited and Moolort Goldfields Limited held assets exceeding £60,000 in cash and shares, which caught Algernon Moreing's attention. Herbert Hoover, no longer a partner at Bewick Moreing, had been in southern Russia assessing the Maikop oil fields and had secured several options, forming the Maikop and General Petroleum Trust. The Maikop oil boom of 1910 saw the flotation of over fifty companies in London, inspired by Hoover's ventures.

In 1911, Moreing floated the Maikop Oil Company Limited and the London and Maikop Oil Corporation Limited, winding up the two deep lead companies and transferring their assets. These companies weathered the Maikop oil crash of 1912 but were eventually liquidated following the Russian Revolution.[7]

After the closure of the deep lead mines, dredging and other mining activities upstream were also significantly reduced and subjected to stricter regulations. As a result, the water quality in the Loddon River improved considerably, leading to a rise in market gardening and dairying. By 1927, the Bridgewater area downstream of Moolort was producing over 1,000 tons of tomatoes annually. Today known as Bridgewater-on-Loddon, the town offers skiing, fishing, swimming, walking, canoeing, kayaking and wineries to attract visitors. The surrounding district pursues mixed farming and grazing.[8]

CHAPTER 26

Afterward

WITH THE BUILDINGS, machinery, houses, and rail spurs gone, Moolort has returned to its quiet rural past. The brick and concrete foundations of the mining machinery remain to varying degrees at each shaft site. The most notable remnants include the foundations of the power station at the Charlotte Plains mine and the concrete arch for the Cornish beam engine at the Loddon Valley shaft. The large mullock heaps stand as markers at each site.

Aside from an overgrown concrete cricket pitch, no evidence remains of the town of Moolort North at the Loddon Valley mine or Pioneer Town at the Charlotte Plains mine. The relocated Moolort Hall was demolished in the later 20th century.

The 4 km spur line to the electric plant and Charlotte Plains shafts was used to remove stone from the mullock heap to make concrete, a practice that ceased in 1913. The line was dismantled in 1917. The spur line to the Keystone shaft was last used in 1910 to remove heavy machinery from the site, with the rails being removed by 1912. The railway line between Maryborough and Castlemaine, which opened in 1874, was closed between Moolort and Maldon Junction in 2004, making way for the Victorian Goldfields Railway to operate between Maldon and Castlemaine. Today any remaining railway infrastructure at Moolort is gone, replaced by modern grain silos now serviced by road trucks.[1]

The land around Moolort was mostly too rocky for ploughing, and the large basalt rocks at the surface were too difficult to remove by hand. As a result, there was limited cropping and little effort to clear the land or build stone fences. This changed in recent decades with the introduction of heavy machinery, which was used to excavate and stack the rocks, enabling broadacre cropping of wheat, oats, canola and other crops.

The few remaining Victorian deep lead mines closed in the years up to the first World War. The only serious subsequent attempt to revive deep lead mining was the Talbot Alluvials project of the mid-1930s. This was the first time that the price of gold and cost of labour and supplies had been favourable to mining since the war. The No 1 shaft pumping capacity was 550,000 gallons per day (29 l/s), the lead being much less wet than the Loddon or Berry leads. Talbot Alluvials encountered comparatively low grades but struggled on until closed by World War 2 in 1940.

Other deep lead mines operated at that time on a small scale including Chivers Alluvial (Havelock), Daylesford Deep Leads, Guildford Plateau, Trawalla Deep Lead, Yandoit, Yandoit South, Ross Creek and Gibraltar (Majorca). None was a success.

Since then, several projects have aimed to recover gold from deep leads elsewhere in Victoria using new technologies, including solution mining through boreholes, gravel pumping through boreholes and even submersible robotic excavators lowered down a shaft. However, none of these efforts have progressed to a practical stage. Environmental regulations would likely prevent the extraction of large volumes of water, which could affect farm bores or would discharge brackish water into local waterways. Modern safety standards would also prevent underground mining, even if miners could be found who were willing to take on the challenge. Most importantly, with all we know today, even a modern-day Abraham Kozminsky or Drysdale Brown would struggle to convince investors that the risks are worth the rewards.

The Lives of Key Figures After the Failure of the Moolort Mines

Presented here in the order of their appearance in the narrative.

Abraham Kozminsky (1853–1934)

Abraham Kozminsky did not pursue any other large mining projects after the failure of the Moolort mines. In 1906, he established the Austral Hat Mills in Abbotsford, a suburb of Melbourne. The company's directors included Kozminsky's eldest son, Maurice, and Sir Alexander Peacock. The business thrived, especially during World War I, when it secured military contracts to produce the Australian slouch hat. This may have created a potential conflict of interest for Peacock, who was again Premier of Victoria at the time. Maurice joined the army but died at the Somme in 1916 at the age of 32.

Citing ill health, Kozminsky sold the hat mills and wound up the company in 1922. His other interests included the Taxpayers' Association of Victoria, where he was a founding member and served on its council until his death. He also served as the foundation president of the Jewish Farmers' Agricultural Trust in Shepparton, a trustee of the East Melbourne Synagogue, a member of the Victorian Chamber of Commerce, and part of the committee of the Jewish Philanthropic Society. Kozminsky died in 1934 at the age of 80, leaving an estate valued at £44,281 to his children and grandchildren.[2]

James Drysdale Brown (1850–1922)

James Drysdale Brown represented the electorate of Nelson in the Victorian Parliament from 1904 until his death in 1922 in South Yarra. During his political career, he held several important positions, including:

- Attorney-General (1909–1913)
- Solicitor-General (1909–1913)
- Minister of Forests (1913–1915)
- Minister of Mines (1913–1915)
- Minister of Public Health (1913–1915)

Drysdale Brown believed that good government was rooted in efficient administration. A shrewd, though somewhat dour, administrator, he focused primarily on rural and environmental initiatives, such as promoting the use of Australian timbers and banning gold-dredging in rivers. Drysdale Brown never married and left his estate, valued at £10,337, to his nieces in Melbourne and New Zealand.[3]

John Paull (1847–1916)

John Paull continued his business as a draper in Maldon, where he also served as chairman of the South German Company, a director of several other mining companies, and a leading member of the Methodist Church. In 1910, he relocated to Moonee Ponds and passed away in 1916 at the age of 69, leaving behind an estate valued at £1,867.[4]

Henry Gore (1840–1909)

Henry Gore, a civil engineer, had served as the Member for Wellington in the Victorian Parliament from 1886 to 1892. His main passion was coursing (greyhound racing), and he acted as treasurer of the Victoria Coursing Club. He was also a director of several gold mining companies. Gore died in 1909 at the age of 68, leaving an estate valued at £2,084 to his widow and children.[5]

Sir Alexander James Peacock KCMG (1861–1933)

Sir Alexander Peacock was first elected to the Victorian Legislative Assembly for the seat of Clunes and Allendale, near Ballarat, in 1889. He served as an MLA for 43 years until his death, including three terms as Premier of Victoria (1901–02, 1914–17, and 1924). In 1901, Peacock opted not to run for the new Parliament of Australia and was instead elected Premier of Victoria. He was knighted in 1902 as a Knight Commander of the Order of St Michael and St George.

After 1906, Peacock held several key positions, including:
- Minister of Labour (1907–08, 1913–17, 1920–27)
- Minister of Public Instruction (1913–14, 1920–27)
- Treasurer (1914–17, 1924–27)
- Minister of Forests (1920–24)

In 1928, he was elected Speaker, a role he held until his death in 1933 at the age of 72. After his passing, his wife Millie successfully ran for his seat, becoming the first woman to serve in the Victorian Parliament.[6]

Reginald Augustus Frederick Murray FGS (1846–1925)

After the failure of the deep lead projects, Reginald Murray spent 14 months working as a geologist in Western Australia and visiting his son in Kalgoorlie. Upon returning to Victoria, he worked intermittently as a consultant. One of his ventures involved developing brown coal deposits near Altona to supply power to South Melbourne, but the project collapsed when one of the promoters absconded with the funds, leaving Murray financially embarrassed.

In his later years, Murray took occasional work for the Ballarat School of Mines and the Geological Survey of Victoria. His final report, *Bulletin 38*, was published in 1916 and covered the Tanjil or Russell's Creek goldfield, featuring a geological map and sections.

Murray became convinced he had discovered a deep lead gold deposit at Russell's Creek on the Tanjil River in Gippsland. In his final years he lived in seclusion, slowly digging a tunnel in pursuit of this potential gold strike. At the age of 79, Murray passed away in 1925, still uncertain whether he had found the deposit he sought. After his death, the tunnel was completed, but the wash proved worthless.[7]

Charles Algernon Moreing (1855–1942)

Charles Moreing remained the senior partner and chairman of Bewick, Moreing and Co., with branches in Coolgardie and Cue, Western Australia, as well as in Auckland, New Zealand, and Vancouver, British Columbia. In 1908, he participated in motor racing at Brooklands, competing alongside notable figures like Lord Montagu and Lord Churchill. Moreing became a celebrity in the mining world, and his arrival at Porcupine, Ontario, in 1911 caused a sensation, with crowds of prospectors flocking to his hotel, eager to present their business proposals.

Much of Moreing's reputation drew from the success of clients of Bewick, Moreing and Co., including several Cornish mines and major operations like the Sons of Gwalia and the Zinc Corporation in Australia. He retired in 1938 due to ill health and passed away in 1942 at the age of 87.[8]

Joseph English (1828–1910)

Joseph English continued his work as a diligent investor until his death, having made most of his wealth in the 19th century from properties on the Berry lead system, particularly the Madam Berry mine. As he grew older, he reduced his mining investments due to his inability to visit and inspect underground workings in person. English passed away in Moonee Ponds in 1910, at the age of 83, leaving an estate valued at £53,619.[9]

Herbert Clark Hoover (1874–1964)

After leaving Bewick Moreing, Herbert Hoover became an independent mining consultant and financier based in London. He focused much of his effort on raising capital, restructuring corporate organisations, and financing new ventures, earning the reputation of a 'doctor of sick mines.' Hoover made investments across every continent and had offices in San Francisco, London, New York City, Paris, Petrograd, and Mandalay. By 1914, he had amassed a personal fortune estimated at US$4 million.

When World War I broke out, Hoover voluntarily organised and led the Commission for Relief in Belgium, an international organisation that provided food to the country under German occupation. After the US entered the war in 1917, President Woodrow Wilson appointed him head of the Food Administration, where Hoover became known as the nation's 'food czar.' Following the war, he led the American Relief Administration, delivering aid to millions in Central and Eastern Europe, particularly Russia. Although he sought the Republican nomination in the 1920 US presidential election, he was unsuccessful.

Hoover served as Secretary of Commerce under Presidents Warren Harding and Calvin Coolidge. He was an unusually active and influential Cabinet member, earning the nickname 'Secretary of Commerce and Under-Secretary of all other departments.' Hoover played a key role in the development of air travel and radio, and he also led the federal response to the Great Mississippi Flood of 1927. He went on to win the 1928 presidential election, but his presidency was marred by the stock market crash of 1929, which signalled the beginning of the Great Depression.

In 1932, Hoover was decisively defeated by Franklin D Roosevelt in his bid for re-election. After leaving office, Hoover wrote numerous books and became a prominent critic of Roosevelt's foreign policy and the New Deal. In the 1940s and 1950s, his public reputation improved, particularly due to his work for Presidents Harry S Truman and Dwight D Eisenhower, including chairing the influential Hoover Commission. He passed away in 1964 and has since been the subject of many biographies and essays.

Philip Lyttelton Gell (1852–1926)

P Lyttelton Gell initially qualified as a historian, later became active in the administration of the Church of England. He held numerous directorships, including positions at Westralia Mount Morgans Gold Mines, Pilbarra (sic) Asbestos, and Huelva Copper and Sulphur Mines. In 1904, Gell leased Hopton Hall in Derbyshire, which he purchased in 1920, and he later acquired a house in Devon.

His primary business interest was the British South Africa Company, where he served as a director from 1899 to 1917 and again from 1923 to 1925. He held the position of Chairman from 1917 to 1920 and was President from 1920 to 1923. Gell passed away in 1926.[10]

Dr Waldemar Lindgren (1860–1939)

In 1905, Waldemar Lindgren co-founded the journal *Economic Geology*. By 1912, he was appointed head of the Department of Geology at the Massachusetts Institute of Technology (MIT). Over the years, Lindgren received numerous honours, being elected to the United States National Academy of Sciences in 1909, the American Academy of Arts and Sciences in 1912, and later the American Philosophical Society and the Royal Swedish Academy of Sciences. He was also a fellow of the Mineralogical Society of America and served as president of both the Geological Society of America and the Society of Economic Geologists.

Lindgren authored nearly 200 works, including *Mineral Deposits*, a widely used textbook. He passed away in 1939 in Boston.[11]

Deane Prescott Mitchell (1875–1965)

After the deep lead projects were shut down, DP Mitchell succeeded Loring as manager of Bewick, Moreing & Co.'s eastern Australian operations. Although many projects did not proceed, the Great Fitzroy Mines at Mount Chalmers in Queensland proved successful. Mitchell became Superintendent of the mines in June 1910 but left in March 1911 due to ill health.

He resigned from Bewick Moreing to join Herbert Hoover's group of engineers in London. Mitchell became a director, alongside Hoover, of the Irtysh Corporation Limited, which operated mines in Russia. He remained with the company throughout World War I and worked on other Russian ventures.

In his 1920 passport application, Mitchell noted that he had last left the USA in June 1919 to work for the Russo Asiatic Consolidated Company in London. His prior travels had taken him to Australia, New Zealand, Russia, England, Norway, Sweden, and Africa, and he had made 24 trips to the USA. Mitchell continued with the Russo Asiatic Corporation until at least 1928, when he visited Mount Isa in relation to the company's option over the Mount Isa Mines.

By 1939, Mitchell was living in Surrey, England, and after World War II, he returned to the USA. He passed away in 1965 at the age of 91.[12]

Figure 46 Electric company powerhouse, with Charlotte Plains mullock heap
Author's photo

Figure 47 Charlotte Plains site, powerhouse foundations on left
Author's photo

Figure 48 Keystone Shaft
Author's photo

Figure 49 Victorian Gold Estates No 1 shaft with Cornish pump wall
Author's photo

Figure 50 Cobbles from puddler at Charlotte Plains
Author's photo

Figure 51 Moolort shaft Victorian Gold Estates No 2 and mullock heap
Author's photo

A NOTE ON MEASUREMENTS

WHERE THE MATERIAL pre-dates the introduction of metric measurements under the *Metric Conversion Act 1970,* measurements are sometimes given in imperial form for clarity. In particular, the pump and pipe sizes make more sense in feet and inches.

The Australian currency of Pounds (£) Shilling (s) and Pence (d) was used prior to the introduction of decimal currency on 14 February 1966. There were 20 shillings in each pound and 12 pennies in a shilling. In 1966 one pound was equal to $2 of the new currency. No conversion is offered here, as to do so would be misleading and confusing. The value of £1 in the 19th Century bears no relationship to the value of $2 in 1966 or the value of a dollar today. Where it is meaningful, approximate equivalent values today have been calculated.

The weight of gold was (and is) measured in Troy Ounces. One ounce is approximately equal to 31.1 grams. Smaller measurements were pennyweights (dwt) equal to 1/20 oz. Some large nuggets were reported in pounds (one Troy pound is 0.37324 kg). Ore grades in hard rock mining were generally reported in pennyweights per ton (dwt/t).

Ore grades in deep lead alluvial mining were generally reported in pennyweights per fathom. In that context a fathom of alluvial ground was equal to 36 square ft, or 4 square yards. When reporting the yield of gold per fathom, the depth of the wash was not taken into account.

Throughout this book, gold production reports have been rounded to the nearest ounce. Reports of payments, accounts and debts have generally been rounded to the nearest £1.

Reports of pumping rates were originally published in several forms, such as gallons per hour, per day or per week. To standardise, these have been converted to gallons per day and litres per second.

ABBREVIATIONS

The following abbreviations are used throughout:

ft	feet
in	inches
m	metres
mm	millimetres
km	kilometres
oz	ounces
dwt	pennyweights
lb	pounds
g	grams
kg	kilograms
l/s	litres per second

METRIC CONVERSIONS

1 mile = 1.6 km

1 foot = 0.3048 m

1 Avoirdupois pound = 0.4536 kg

1 fathom = 6 ft (1.8288 m) as a measure
of length

1 fathom = 3.3445 square metres (as a measure
of floor area in a deep lead)

1 cubic yard = 0.7645 cubic metres

1 Troy ounce = 31.1035 gram (g)

1 Troy pound = 0.37324 kg

1 Troy ounce/long ton = 30.6116 gram/tonne (g/t)

1 Troy ounce/cubic yard = 40.682 gram/cubic metre

1 Troy ounce/fathom = 9.3 gram/square metre

1 acre = 0.4047 hectare (ha)

ACKNOWLEDGEMENTS

I am grateful to my wife Anthea Matley for her patience and encouragement during the research phase and for reading drafts along the way. I would also like to thank Joseph Poprzeczny who encouraged me to write this book and prodded me along whenever my enthusiasm began to wane. John Tully and Michelle Ross both pointed me to sources of information and read early drafts. Katherine Seppings reviewed an early draft and provided valuable guidance. Matthew Churchward at Melbourne Museum gave access to an important reference. Organisations that assisted and provided information included Carisbrook Historical Society, Maldon Vintage Machinery Museum, Dunolly Museum, Sovereign Hill, and Melbourne Museum. I would also like to acknowledge the late Tim Hobson, whose enthusiasm for mining history got my interest in the subject started nearly fifty years ago.

ENDNOTES

Introduction

1 Alluvial deposits are those formed by the action of flowing water, usually in a streambed. There are also eluvial deposits formed by in-situ weathering from quartz reefs. Both types are found in deep lead mining, but for simplicity I have followed the common usage of alluvial for both.

2 JG Douglas and JA Ferguson (Ed) *Geology of Victoria*. Geological Society of Australia Inc. 1988, p. 444; K Grimes, *The Ages Of Our Volcanoes*, Hamilton Field Naturalists Club, August 2013; The information on Mount Schank comes from its entry in *Wikipedia*.

3 The main deep lead areas are described in F Canavan, *Deep Lead Gold Deposits of Victoria*, Bulletin 62, Geological Survey of Victoria, 1988.

4 The geology is described in E Lidgey *Report of lecture on the deep leads of Victoria, and some indications of ore deposits*, Victoria Department of Mines Special Report 1898.

5 HC Hoover, *The Memoirs of Herbert Hoover. Years of Adventure 1874–1920*. Macmillan, New York, 1951, p. 88.

Chapter 1 Enough Gold to Turn the Brain

1 I told this story in more detail in PL McCarthy The Remarkable Life of John Phillips C.E. Mineral Surveyor in *Journal of Australasian Mining History* Vol 18, October 2021, pp. 62–84.

2 For the details we rely on letters and a pamphlet written by John Phillips as reported in *The Star* (Ballarat), 2 July 1859, p. 2.

3 *South Australian Advertiser*, 27 January 1881, p. 6.

4 *ibid*, p. 7.

5 The *Dauphin chart* drawn by the Portuguese between 1530 and 1536 is believed to be the earliest known map of Australia. It labelled the north-western coast of Australia Costa D'Ouro, the Gold Coast.

6 This quote and the story of these earliest gold discoveries is told in *The Mineral Resources of New South Wales* by E.F. Pittman, Government Geologist. Geological Survey of NSW. pp. 1–4.

7 *ibid*.

8 The story of the 1849 discoveries is told by Doug Wilkie in *1849 The Rush That Never Started*, Historia Incognita. Melbourne 2015.

9 *South Australian Register*, 30 July 1850, p. 4.

10 *South Australian*, 10 June 1851, p. 3.

11 *Ballarat Star*, 18 January 1870, p. 1.

Chapter 2 Ballarat

1   See the entry for William Cross Yuille in *Wikipedia*.
2   *Geelong Advertiser*, 23 November 1847, p. 2.
3   The separation from NSW is explained in the entry for History of Victoria in *Wikipedia*.
4   *Adelaide Times*, 4 October 1851, p. 2.
5   The first mention of Dunlop and Regan is in *The Argus*, 4 October 1851, p. 2; expanded in *The Argus*, 1 November 1930, p. 6. The story of the Ballarat discovery is covered in HJ Stacpoole, *Gold at Ballarat*, Lowden Publishing 1971. Dunlop's claim to the discovery is stated in his letter published in the Geelong Advertiser of 18 July 1853, p. 2.
6   This was described as 'half a hundredweight of gold' in *The Argus*, 30 September 1851, p. 2.
7   'The result has been, that the diggers are continually quarrelling, although before the levy and Doveton came down amongst them with his arrangements, they were at peace' see *The Argus*, 9 October 1851, p. 2.
8   *Geelong Advertiser and Intelligencer*, 26 September 1851, p. 2.
9   *Geelong Advertiser and Intelligencer*, 13 March 1852, p. 2.

Chapter 3 The Rush Now is Immense

1   I told the story of the discovery of the Canadian Nugget in more detail in PL McCarthy 'The 1853 Canadian Gully Nuggets, Ballarat, Victoria' in *Journal of Australasian Mining History* Vol 20, October 2022, pp. 73–85. The story was reported widely and in detail at the time. For example, see *Royal Cornwall Gazette*, 15 July 1853, p. 6, *Geelong Advertiser and Intelligencer*, 11 October 1853, p. 6; *Soulby's Ulverston Advertiser and General Intelligencer*, 23 June 1853, p. 2.
2   W Kelly, *Life in Victoria*, pub. Chapman and Hall London 1859, p. 216.
3   *Geelong Advertiser and Intelligencer*, 21 December 1853, p. 4.
4   *The Argus*, Melbourne, 10 February 1853, p. 5.
5   *The Argus*, Melbourne, 7 February 1853, p. 5.
6   *Geelong Advertiser and Intelligencer*, 11 February 1853, p. 2.
7   *The Albion*, Liverpool, 6 June 1853, p. 9.
8   The early history of deep sinking at Ballarat is given in R Brough Smyth, 1869. *The Gold Fields and Mineral Districts of Victoria*, Government Printer, Melbourne.
9   W Kelly, *Life in Victoria*, pub. Chapman and Hall London, 1859, p. 231.
10 Ibid.
11 *Geelong Advertiser and Intelligencer*, 2 September 1854, p. 4.
12 Notes on the Ballarat Goldfield by the District Mining Warden, Harry Wood, and published in R. Brough-Smyth, *The Goldfields and Mineral districts of Victoria* (1869).
13 *The Age*, Melbourne, 25 December 1856, p. 6.
14 *Geelong Advertiser and Intelligencer*, 3 October 1853, p. 5.

Chapter 4 Black Powder and Steam Engines

1   The arrival of the Serjeant family is recorded in the *South Australian Register*, 6 January 1849, p. 4.
2   The early technical innovations are explained by historian WB Withers in *Ballarat Star*, 8 February 1890, p. 1; CRC Pearce, First mine engine protected by gun, in *The Australasian*, 23 May 1931, p. 4.
3   *Ballarat Star*, 9 September 1869, p. 4; *Bendigo Advertiser*, 15 July 1856, p. 2.
4   *The Age*, 31 October 1859, p. 5; *The Sydney Morning Herald*, 4 July 1853, p. 2.
5   *Mount Alexander Mail*, 2 April 1879, p. 2.
6   *The Argus*, 7 February 1857, p. 4.
7   *The Argus*, 6 August 1855, p. 5; 16 August 1855, p. 5; *The Age*, 21 August 1855, p. 3.
8   *The Star*, 31 July 1856, p. 2; *Bendigo Advertiser*, 9 September 1856, p. 2; *The Star*, 22 July 1856, p. 2.
9   *The Argus*, 29 May 1849, p. 3; 4 July 1849, p. 2; *Geelong Advertiser*, 12 July 1849, p. 2.
10 *The Star,* 13 November 1856, p. 2.
11 *Bendigo Advertiser*, 10 July 1856, p. 2; *The Star*, 21 March 1857, p. 3, 3 April 1857, p. 2.
12 *Ovens and Murray Advertiser*, 2 May 1857, p. 2; *The Star*, 28 May 1857, p. 2, 3 June 1857, p. 3, 29 June 1857, p. 2, 20 July 1858, p. 2; *The Age*, 11 June 1857, p. 3; 8 August 1857, p.6; *Mount Alexander Mail*, 28 October 1857, p. 3.
13 *Brough Smyth*, pp. 471–472.
14 The size of a Cornish engine was described by the diameter of its steam cylinder.
15 *The Argus*, 27 April 1882, p. 9.

Chapter 5 265 Tonnes of Gold

1   *The Tarrengower Times*, 13 October 1906, p. 3–4.
2   The methods of shaft sinking were described in a series in the *Kalgoorlie Miner* by FD Johnson; 11 September 1902, p. 3, 12 September 1902, p. 3, 13 September 1903, p. 3.
3   *The Argus,* 23 May 1902, p. 7.
4   *The Argus,* 7 July 1904, p. 8.
5   KG Bowen, *An Analysis of gold production data for Victorian reef and deep lead mines*, Geological Survey Report No. 1974/ 12.

Chapter 6 We Had to Feel for the Water

1   My longer account of this tragedy appeared as PL McCarthy, *The Great Northern Junction Inrush*, The AusIMM Bulletin, August 2011. Also see *Ballarat Star* 18, 19, 20 October 1869, and *The Ballarat Courier*, 18, 19, 21 October 1869.
2   *Ballarat Star* 28 October 1869, p. 2.
3   LM Williams, *Diary of Disaster. The New Australasian Mine Tragedy* Creswick, 1882, pub. Hedges and Bell, Maryborough, 1982.
4   *The Argus*, 23 May 1902, p. 7.

Chapter 7 The Pioneer Mine

1   Lowe Kong Meng in *Australian Dictionary of Biography*, Volume 5, 1974.

2   John Paull's obituary appeared in the *Bendigonian*, 14 September 1916, p. 20.

3   The prospectus of the Pioneer company was published in *The Argus*, 19 March 1888, p. 10.

4   J Drysdale Brown in People We Know, *Punch* (Melbourne), 4 February 1909, p. 6.

5   The Pioneer company's problems were reported at the half-yearly meeting reported in the Tarrangower Times, 26 November 1892, p. 2.

6   See the *Wikipedia* entries for the Panic of 1893 and The Australian Banking Crisis of 1893.

7   The involvement of John Walker is explained in *The Age*, 4 May 1894, p.7, and the *Tarrangower Times*, 12 December 1894, p.3.

8   The sale of the mine was authorised at a meeting reported in *The Age*, 24 May 1895, p. 7. John Orlebar's departure from Warrnambool was reported in the *Hamilton Spectator*, 28 March 1874, p. 4. Frederick Dutton's obituary appeared in the *Advertiser* (Adelaide), 15 October 1930, p. 14.

9   *Financial News* (London), 20 September 1895, p. 2; *Tarrangower Times*, 30 May 1896, p. 2.

10   Registration of the company in London was reported in *The Age*, 15 October 1895, p. 7. The subsequent problems in London were explained at a meeting reported in the *Tarrangower Times*, 30 May 1896, p. 2.

11   One example of this obstruction by farmers appeared in a letter published in the *Bendigo Advertiser*, 12 January 1895, p. 3.

12   Parts of Howitt's report were published in *The Age*, 9 July 1895, p. 6.

13   *Ballarat Star*, 10 July 1895, p. 2.

14   *Geelong Advertiser,* 10 September 1895, p. 2.

15   *Weekly Times*, 14 September 1895, p. 35.

16   Reginald Augustus Frederick Murray in *Australian Dictionary of Biography*, Volume 5, 1974. The story about his speech impediment was told in *The Glengarry, Toongabbie and Cowwarr Journal*, 8 October 1925, p. 1.

17   The Creswick Gold Mines, in *The Argus*, 4 October 1895, p. 7.

18   The *Ballarat Star*, 30 October 1895, p. 4; 31 January 1896, p. 1.

Chapter 8 Abraham Kozminsky

1 Naturalisation certificate 158 (Victoria) Abraham Kozminsky, Certificate Date 5 May 1877, Native Place Krososhin, Prussia. See Wikipedia entry for Krotoszyn. His obituary was published in *Jewish Weekly News* (Melbourne), 21 December 1934, p. 8.

2 Formation of the partnership with Lyell, *The Argus*, 20 June 1889, p. 4; Lyell's insolvency *The Argus* 14 October 1890, p. 9.

3 Land Boomers 2 in *The Bulletin* Vol88 No 4523, 12 Nov 1966 p. 76. Also see Land Boom in the *Encyclopedia of Melbourne*, www.emelbourne.net.au.

4 For a description of Mount Dundas see *Daily Telegraph* (Launceston), 4 August 1890, p. 4.

5 Kozminsky's leases described in *The Colonist* (Launceston), 20 September 1890, p. 14.

6 The Mount Dundas company see *Australasian*, 31 January 1891, p. 28.

7 Claim jumpers see *The Argus*, 18 February 1891, p. 9.

8 *Zeehan and Dundas Herald*, 3 August 1894, p. 3.

9 The Kozminsky railway guide scandal, *Table Talk* (Melbourne), 23 April 1897, p. 10.

10 *West Australian*, 6 April 1894, p. 4; *Coolgardie Miner*, 21 April 1894, p. 2.

11 *ibid.*

12 *West Australian* 5 May 1894, p. 3; 18 September 1894, p. 3; *Australian Advertiser* (Albany), 8 June 1894, p. 3.

13 *Western Argus* (Kalgoorlie), 16 February 1895, p. 2; *British Australasian* (London), 11 May 1899, p. 12.

14 The comment on Western Australia was included in a review of the past year in *Weekly Times* (Melbourne), 5 January 1895, p. 23.

15 Mining statistics for 1894 in the *Bendigo Independent*, 29 December 1894, p. 2.

16 Ballarat mining review for 1894 in the *Ballarat Star*, 29 December 1894, p. 1.

17 The *Ballarat Star*, 22 December 1894, p. 4.

18 *The Argus*, 11 February 1895, p. 6.

19 *The Argus*, 13 February 1895, p. 6.

20 *The Kyneton Observer*, 16 February 1895, p. 4; *Weekly Times* (Melbourne), 23 February 1895, p. 21.

21 *Coolgardie Miner*, 24 November 1894, p. 7.

22 Death of Marks Kozminsky, *Jewish Herald* (Victoria) 17 May 1895, p. 9; Simon Kozminsky insolvency, *The Herald* (Melbourne), 15 June 1895, p. 2.

Chapter 9 Victorian Gold Estate Corporation

1   I am grateful to John Tully for the explanation of *Moolort*, Pers Com 22 Sept 2024.

2   *Tarrengower Times*, 28 December 1895, p. 3.

3   *British Australasian* (London),11 May 1899, p. 12.

4   Wright's life story is told in The Story of the London and Globe. The Case of Whitaker Wright. By Arnold White. *Pearsons Magazine* V 11 No 6 June 1904. pp 557–567.

5   Dan Plazak, A Hole in the Ground with a Liar at the Top, *The University of Utah Press.* 2006. pp. 234–252.

6   At the time of this float, Wright was described as 'a man of knowledge and integrity'. See *British Australasian*, 27 September 1894, p. 18.

7   *British Australasian*, 13 December 1894, p. 30; *The Colonies and India* (London), 15 December 1894, p. 29.

8   The prospectus of the West Australian Exploring and Finance Company appeared in the *London Evening Standard*, 26 September 1894, p. 4; the allegations are mentioned in Looking for Mr Wright. A tale of mining finance from the late Nineteenth century. By Jeremy Mouat. *Mining History Journal* 2003 pp 6–17.

9   Henry Macrory, *Ultimate Folly: The Rises and Falls of Whitaker Wright the World's Most Shameless Swindler*, Biteback Publishing, London, 2018, p. 98; The sale of the farm and estate was recorded in *Surrey Times*, 9 January 1897, p. 7.

10 The 1896 motor show is described in *Graces Guide to British Industrial History*; the Cinématographe in *The Sketch*, 18 March 1896, p. 7; the de Dion Tricycle in *Freeman's Journal*,16 June 1896, p. 3; the electric omnibus in *South Wales Daily News*, 20 May 1896, p. 8.

11 Wonderful Figures for Alluvial Mines in *The Bendigo Independent*, 18 April 1896, p. 4.

12 *The Mercury* (Hobart), 18 July 1896, p. 1.

13 *The Tarrangower Times*, 13 June 1896, p. 2.

14 William Luplau's obituary in *The Ballarat Star*, 16 May 1899, p. 2.

15 *The Tarrangower Times*, 4 July 1896, p. 3.

16 Details of the company in *The Age*, 2 July 1896, p. 5.

17 Kozminsky's return to Melbourne in *Passenger Lists*, May-August 1896, p. 250. Public Records Office.

18 *St James Gazette*, 3 November 1896, p. 16.

19 Zeals' involvement described in *The Age*, 29 October 1896, p. 5; mention of the Berry Lead in *Weekly Times*, 31 October 1896, p. 18; Moolort in *Newcastle Morning Herald,* 21 November 1896, p. 11.

20 Henry Gore's background in *The Muchison Times and Day Dawn Gazette*, 31 December 1896, p. 4.

21 Joseph English's obituary was published in *The Argus*, 23 September 1910, p. 7; Reginald Murray's story was summarised in *The Age*, 6 March 1939, p. 10.

22 *St James Gazette*, 3 November 1896, p. 16.

23 *Melbourne Punch*, 24 December 1896, p. 3; Davitt's comments in *The Age*, 31 December 1896, p. 6.

24 *The Murchison Times and Day Dawn Gazette*, 31 December 1896, p. 4.

25 *Truth* (London), 7 January 1897 p. 32; 14 January 1897, p. 34.

Chapter 10 As Rampant as Ever

1   *Wagga Wagga Advertiser*, Thursday 18 February 1897, p. 2.

2   His son's *barmitzvah, Jewish Herald*, 28 May 1897, p. 11; *The Homeward Mail from India, China and the East*, 9 November 1897, p. 1510.

3   A super foot in timber is a unit of cubic measure for lumber, equal to one foot square by one inch thick. It is also known as a board foot or a superficial foot.

4   The machinery orders are described in *Bendigo Independent*, 25 May 1897, p. 4; *Ballarat Star*, 2 March 1897, p. 4; *Mount Alexander Mail*, 31 May 1897, p. 2; *The Argus*, 4 June 1897, p. 2. Original handwritten orders 9097, 9197 and 9297 are held by the Maldon Machinery Museum, together with working drawings.

5   *Mount Alexander Mail*, 12 July 1897, p. 3.

6   *Table Talk* (Melbourne), 4 February 1898, p. 5; *Inquirer and Commercial News* (Perth), 4 June 1897, p. 11.

7   *The Argus*, 3 July 1897, p. 10; *Tarrangower Times*, 14 July 1897, p. 2; 25 August 1897, p. 3.

8   *Tarrangower Times*, 28 August 1897, p. 3; 24 November 1897, p. 2; *Barrier Miner*, 20 September 1897, p. 3; *Melbourne Punch*, 23 September 1897, p. 7; *Ballarat Star*, 19 November 1897, p. 4.

9   *Ballarat Star*, 15 December 1897, p. 4; *Kalgoorlie Miner*, 27 December 1897, p. 3.

10   *Geelong Advertiser*, 16 July 1898, p. 2; *The Age*, 29 January 1898, p. 10.

11   *Ballarat Star*, 7 February 1898, p. 1; *Australasian*, 12 February 1898, p. 41; *The Age*, 10 February 1898, p. 7.

12   Tenders called *Mount Alexander Mail*, 8 March 1898, p. 3; 6 April 1898, p. 3; Henry Gore on the timber required see *Mount Alexander Mail*, 21 June 1898, p. 2; *Ballarat Star,* 30 November 1898, p. 3. *Herald* (Melbourne), 29 November 1898, p. 2.

13   Mr Perrin's remarks quoted in the *Bairnsdale Advertiser*, 6 January 1898, p. 4.

14   The bakeries reported in *Mount Alexander Mail,* 7 June 1898, p. 2.

Chapter 11 The Charlotte Plains Group

1   After some haggling the shareholders seem to have been happy with the new deal. See *The Age*, 1 June 1897, p. 7; *Tarrangower Times*, 2 June 1897, p. 2.

2   Alex Stoneman, *Deep Leads Mines in the Central Goldfields Book 3 Moolort,* Carisbrook Historical Society, 2014, p. 16.

3   *Mount Alexander Mail*, 19 July 1898; The process of cutting down tall trees for the poppet legs is described in the *Warragul Guardian*, 2 August 1898, p. 2.

4   *Tarrangower Times*, 28 May 1898, p. 2; 8 June 1898, p. 2.

5   *The Argus*, 14 October 1898, p. 10; 15 November 1898, p. 6.

6   This quote comes from *Tarrangower Times*, 3 June 1899, p. 2; approval of above ground transmission lines, see *Mount Alexander Mail*, 1 July 1899, p. 2.

7   A description of the proposed plant was published in *The Age*, 13 August 1900, p. 7.

8   *The Daily Telegraph & Courier* (London), 3 May 1899, p. 4.

9   Moule's obituary appeared in the *Sun-News Pictorial* (Melbourne), 9 January 1945, p. 3; Gray's obituary appeared in the *Tarrangower Times*, 27 July 1904, p. 3.

Chapter 12 Victorian Gold Estates

1   *The Age,* 2 July 1898, p. 10.

2   *Pall Mall Gazette,* 20 September 1898, p. 4.

3   *Westminster Gazette,* 19 September 1898, p. 6.

4   The remarks by Alfred Hess were reported in the *Critic* (Adelaide), 10 September 1898, p. 18.

5   *Pall Mall Gazette,* 23 September 1898, p. 7.

6   The Chairman Lod Dufferin made a long defensive explanation of the company's situation, see *Morning Post* (London), 21 September 1898, p. 7.

7   *Weekly Times* (Melbourne), 8 October 1898, p. 12.

8   A detailed description of the plant was included in the annual report of the Secretary for Mines and Water Supply for 1898.

9   Progress at the site was described after a visit by a reporter in *The Age,* 2 July 1898, p. 10.

10   DH Browne's obituary appeared in *The Age,* 19 November 1940, p. 8.

11   The machinery and mining progress were described in *The Argus,* 21 October 1898, p. 7; 24 January 1899, p. 9; Dept of Mines *Annual Report* 1898.

12   *Mount Alexander Mail* 10 February 1899, p. 2; 11 February 1899, p. 2; *The Argus,* 11 February 1899, p. 11.

13   *Ballarat Star,* 11 February 1899, p. 4; *The Argus,* 11 February 1899, p. 11.

14   *Mount Alexander Mail,* 1 March 1899, p. 2; *British Australasian,* 11 May 1899, p. 12.

15   *Ballarat Star,* 2 May 1899, p. 4.

16   *Table Talk* (Melbourne), 31 March 1899. p. 5.

17   Workers trains see *The Age,* 24 April 1899, p. 9; Kozminsky's interview see *British Australasian,* 11 May 1899, p. 12.

18   *The Argus,* 11 August 1899, p. 8.

19   The No 2 shaft ceremony was reported in *The Argus,* 8 September 1899, p. 7.

20   *The Argus,* 8 February 1900, p. 7.

21   The sale of Kozminsky's household goods was advertised in *The Argus,* 16 December 1899, p. 2.

22   The Kozminsky family's departure was reported in *The Hebrew Standard of Australasia,* 30 March 1900, p. 8, their return in *Table Talk,* 12 December 1901, p. 39.

23   *British Australasian,* 28 June 1900, p. 11.

Chapter 13 Shareholders Want Their Money Back

1   *Bendigo Advertiser*, 26 February 1900, p. 3.
2   *The Age*, 6 August 1900, p. 8.
3   *The Argus,* 26 February 1900, p. 9; 17 September 1900, p. 8.
4   *Tatura Guardian*, 5 October 1900, p. 5.
5   *The Tarrangower Times*, 27 March 1901, p. 4.
6   *The Argus*, 4 January 1901, p. 7.
7   *The Morning Leader* (London), 28 December 1900, p. 2.
8   The basis of the share panic is explained in *The Argus*, 31 December 1900, p. 5, and 2 January 1901, p. 6.
9   *The British Columbia Mining Record*, August 1901, p. 38.
10 *The Age*, 3 January 1901, p. 5; *The Argus*, 23 January 1901, p. 8.
11 *Tarrangower Times*, 23 January 1901, p. 3; *The Argus*, 8 February 1901, p. 7.
12 *Tarrangower Times*, 13 March 1901, p. 4.
13 *Critic* (Adelaide), 9 February 1901, p. 20.
14 *Critic* (Adelaide), 16 February 1901, p. 21.
15 *The Argus*, 1 July 1901, p. 5.
16 *The Age*, 19 August 1901, p. 7; 20 August 1901, p. 7.
17 *The Argus,* 18 September 1901, p. 8.
18 *Kalgoorlie Miner*, 2 November 1901, p. 2; *The Age*, 26 November 1901, p. 8.
19 The Kozminsky family's activities are tracked in *Evening News* (Sydney), 3 December 1901, p. 4; *Australian Town and Country Journal* (Sydney), 11 January 1902, p. 43; *Western Mail* (Perth), 19 April 1902, p. 17.
20 *The Argus*, 23 January 1902, p. 7.
21 *The Argus*, 4 July 1902, p. 3; *Bendigo Advertiser*, 22 October 1902, p. 4.

Chapter 14 Charlotte Plains Consolidated

1   *Weekly Times* (Melbourne), 13 May 1899, p. 16; *The Argus,* 10 December 1900, p. 8.
2   *Evening News* (Sydney), 28 July 1899, p. 6; *The Argus*, 18 March 1901, p. 8.
3   A description of the plant is given in the *Ballarat Star*, 11 February 1901, p. 6.
4   *The Age*, 12 February 1901, p. 6.
5   *Ballarat Star*, 22 January 1902, p. 2; 7 June 1902, p. 2; *The Argus*, 17 February 1902, p. 8.
6   *The Argus*, 10 February 1902, p. 8; *Ballarat Star*, 1 January 1903, p. 3.
7   *Weekly Times* (Melbourne), 22 November 1902, p. 35; *Tarrangower Times*, 4 July 1903, p. 2.
8   *Australian Mining Standard and Electrical Record*, 5 May 1909.
9   *Tarrangower Times*, 20 August 1902, p. 3; *The Age*, 28 November 1902, p. 7.

Chapter 15 The Loddon River

1   *The Australasian*, 15 March 1890, p. 7; *Leader* (Melbourne), 29 March 1890, p. 13.
2   *Weekly Times*, 4 October 1890, p. 27; *Bendigo Advertiser*, 1 January 1901, p. 1; 4 December 1901, p. 3.
3   *Tarrangower Times*, 28 August 1886, p. 2; *Bendigo Independent*, 2 April 1906, p. 3.
4   *Mount Alexander Mail*, 2 May 1899, p. 2; 24 July 1903, p. 2; *The Age*, 5 September 1903, p. 12; *Bendigo Advertiser* 22 June 1901, p. 5.
5   *Bendigo Advertiser*, 28 October 1901, p. 5; 5 October 1900, p. 3; 4 March 1901, p. 4; 22 August 1902, p. 4; *The Age*, 6 September 1900, p. 7.
6   *The Argus*, 20 May 1902, p. 8.
7   *The Argus*, 10 March 1900, p. 13.
8   *The Age*, 22 October 1902, p. 5; 25 October 1902, p. 11; *Geelong Advertiser*, 27 October 1902, p. 4; *The Bendigo Independent*, 27 November 1902, p. 4; *The Argus*, 13 January 1903, p. 6.
9   Nikolai Beilharz, Drought of 1891 to 1903 reconstructed, *ABC Rural*, 16 July 2019; water famine in Maryborough, *Ballarat Star*, 15 November 1902, p. 2.
10 *Kerang New Times*, 28 April 1903, p. 2; *The Age*, 16 July 1903, p. 6; 19 September 1903, p. 12; *Mount Alexander Mail*, 30 November 1903, p. 2.
11 *The Argus*, 28 July 1904, p. 11.
12 *Kerang Times*, 11 April 1890, p. 2.
13 *The Australasian*, 10 September 1904, p. 9.
14 *The Age*, 10 February 1905, p. 6; 21 February 1905, p. 6; *Tarrangower Times*, 11 March 1905, p. 3.
15 *The Argus*, 3 April 1905, p. 8.
16 The Loddon dredging case was reported in *The Bendigo Independent*, 20 July 1905, p. 4; *Mount Alexander Mail*, 25 July 1905, p. 2; *The Australasian*, 5 August 1905, p. 41.
17 Sludge Abatement Board in *Public Record Office of Victoria, prov.vic.gov.au/archive/VA1403*.
18 *The Bendigo Independent*, 2 April 1906, p. 3; *Mount Alexander Mail*, 2 April 1906, p. 2.
19 *Ballarat Star*, 6 June 1908, p. 10; *The Age*, 27 March 1908, p. 4.

Chapter 16 Bewick, Moreing and Co.

1   The financial machinations and conflicts of interest of Hoover and Moreing are discussed in The Engineering of Herbert Hoover by Jeremy Mouat and Ian Phimister *Pacific Historical Review* Vol 77 No 4 pp. 553–584.
2   Thomas John Bewick in *Grace's Guide to British Industrial History*, at *www.gracesguide.co.uk*.
3   The record of Moreing's attempts and climbs exist in the *Annuaire of the Société des touristes du Dauphiné, Grenoble*; North of England Institute of Mining and Mechanical Engineers, *Transactions*, Vol.24 1875 p. XL111; *Charter, supplemental charters, by-laws, and list of members of the Institution of Civil Engineers* 1879, p. 112; *Coal and coal trade journal* v.19 1880, p. 570; *The Alpine Journal* Vol 10 (1880–82), p. 182; *The Engineer* v.52, 16 December 1881, p. 438.
4   *Vanity Fair* v.27, January 28, 1882, p. 49.

5   *Ibid*, p. 50.

6   *Reports of cases decided in the High court of Griqualand* v.1 1882–1883, pp. 171–184; pp. 467–500.

7   *St Stephen's Review* (London), 16 October 1886, p. 20; *The Globe* (London), 4 May 1886, p. 7; *Lloyd's List,* 5 December 1887, p. 4; *Glasgow Herald*, 13 July 1889, p. 5; *Commercial Gazette* (London), 23 October 1889, p. 20.

8   *The Iron Age*, 5 December 1889, p. 57.

9   *The Colonies and India*, 27 February 1889, p. 32; Mozambique Company see *Wikipedia*; *Surrey Advertiser,* 12 September 1942, p. 5.

10   *Pall Mall Gazette*, 23 October 1891, p. 1.

11   *The Argus*, 17 April 1911, p. 9.

12   Nash, p 53.

13   See entry for Herbert Hoover in *heritage.engineersaustralia.org.au.*

14   *The Australasian*, 21 March 1903, p. 49; Nash p. 308.

15   *The Brisbane Courier*, 30 May 1903, p. 5.

16   *Kalgoorlie Miner*, 8 July 1903, p. 3; *The Argus*, 3 August 1903, p. 8.

17   *The Argus*, 17 August 1903, p. 8.

18   *Examiner* (Launceston), 7 August 1903, p. 2; *The Tarrengower Times*, 23 May 1903, p. 3.

19   *The Argus*, 18 August 1903, p. 8.

20   *The Age*, 15 September 1903, p. 7;

21   *Examiner* (Launceston), 17 August 1903, p. 2.

22   Transcript of September 8, 1903 *Consolidated Deep Leads shareholders meeting* pp. 321–322.

23   *The Argus*, 17 August 1903, p. 8.

24   *Western Mail* (Perth), 14 Nov 1903, p. 41; *The Daily News* (Perth), Oct 1903, p. 1; *Sydney Mail and New South Wales Advertiser,* 4 November 1903, p. 1214; *Kalgoorlie Miner*, 6 November 1903, p. 3.

25   HC Hoover *The Memoirs of Herbert Hoover. Years of Adventure*. Macmillan 1951, p. 86.

26   *Mount Magnet Miner and Lennonville Leader*, 27 February 1904, p. 4.

Chapter 17 Whitaker Wright

1   *The Mercury* (Hobart) 19 October 1903, p. 7.

2   *Daily Telegraph* (Launceston) 22 February 1904, p. 8.

3   *Sunday Times* (Perth), 1 August 1926, p. 6.

Chapter 18 Into the Wash

1   *Sydney Morning Herald*, 26 June 1903, p. 9.

2   *The Advertiser (Adelaide)*, 31 December 1903, p. 4; *Critic* (Adelaide), 20 January 1904, p. 20.

3   *The Age*, 3 February 1904, p. 9; *Ballarat Star*, 8 March 1904, p. 3.

4   *Bendigo Advertiser,* 16 April 1904, p. 3; *Ballarat Star,* 25 October 1904, p. 2; *The Queenslander,* 21 January 1905, p. 39.

5   *Ballarat Star*, 12 February 1904, p. 4.

6   *Tarrangower Times*, 29 June 1904, p. 2; 20 April 1907, p. 4.

7   *Ballarat Star*, 17 May 1904, p. 1.

8   *Mount Alexander Mail*, 25 May 1904, p. 2.

9   *The Argus*, 8 June 1904, p. 8.

10   *The Age*, 5 September 1904, p. 7.

11   *The Tarrengower Times*, 29 April 1905, p. 2; *The Argus*, 3 February 1905, p. 8.

12   *Ballarat Star*, 1 February 1905, p. 6; *The Tarrengower Times*, 4 April 1906, p. 2.

13   *The Age*, 4 September 1905, p. 7; *The Argus*, 17 July 1905, p. 8; 4 September 1905, p. 8.

14   *The Age*, 11 December 1905, p. 7; *Ballarat Star*, 29 November 1905, p. 3.

15   *The Age*, 2 January 1906, p. 7; 1 February 1906, p. 6; *The Tarrengower Times*, 17 January 1906, p. 3.

Chapter 19 Extracting the Wash

1   This section is based on a longer article that appeared as Charlotte Plains Co. A Great Alluvial Mine, published by the *Tarrangower Times*, 13 October 1906, pp. 3–4, originally published in the *Australian Mining Standard*.

Chapter 20 Australian Commonwealth Trust Ltd.

1   *Ballarat Star*, 15 January 1904, p. 4.

2   *Critic* (Adelaide), 20 January 1904, p. 20.

3   *The Western Argus* (Kalgoorlie), 22 March 1904, p. 6; *Kalgoorlie Miner*, 18 June 1904, p. 3.

4   *Examiner* (Launceston), 21 June 1904, p. 2.

5   *Kalgoorlie Miner*, 31 March 1904, p. 3.

6   *The Sydney Morning Herald*, 17 May 1904, p. 6; *The Argus*, 17 May 1904, p. 8.

7   *The Argus*, 1 June 1904, p. 10.

8   *Daily Telegraph* (Launceston), 23 May 1904, p. 8.

9   Nash, p 311.

10   *Bendigo Advertiser*, 28 July 1904, p. 5; *The Age*, 3 August 1904, p. 9; *Ballarat Star*, 14 October 1904, p. 6.

11   *The Argus*, 17 January 1905, p. 8.

12   *The Argus*, 15 July 1905, p. 18.

13   *Critic* (Adelaide), 28 June 1905, p. 26.

14   *The Tarrengower Times*, 27 May 1905, p. 4; *Mount Alexander Mail*, 17 January 1906. p. 2; *Kalgoorlie Miner*, 12 October 1906, p. 3; *The Age*, 19 October 1905, p. 7; 8 November 1905, p. 11.

15   *Daily Telegraph* (Launceston), 27 March 1905, p. 6; *Morning Post* (Cairns), 22 September 1906, p. 2; *Kalgoorlie Miner*, 9 February 1906, p. 3.

16   *Gympie Times and Mary River Mining Gazette*, 23 May 1905, p. 2; *Ballarat Star*, 18 January 1907, p. 6.

17   *The Argus*, 28 August 1905, p. 8.

18   JH Curle *The Gold Mines of the World*, 1905; *The Argus*, 28 August 1905, p. 8.

19   *Table Talk*, 24 August 1905, p. 28.

20   *Financial News*, Wednesday 27 September 1905 'The negotiations in the matter have been conducted by Mr. Hoover, under the guidance of his firm, Messrs. Bewick, Moreing and Co., in London, and the whole of the arrangements on this side have been made under the advice and with the co-operation of that firm.

21   *The Australasian*, 16 September 1905, p. 41; 21 October 1905, p. 41.

22   Nash p 310.

23   *The Age*, 6 September 1905, p. 10; 7 September 1905, p. 10; 9 October 1905, p. 7.

Chapter 21 Big Dog Engineers

1   *Ballarat Star*, 9 February 1906, p. 3; 17 April 1906, p. 2; *Weekly Times* (Melbourne), 5 May 1906, p. 18; *The Tarrengower Times*, 5 May 1906, p. 2.

2   *The Tarrengower Times*, 7 July 1906, p. 3.

3   *Ballarat Star*, 8 October 1906, p. 3; *The Australasian*, 12 January 1906, p. 41; *The Tarrengower Times*, 12 January 1907, p. 2.

4   *The Bulletin*, 28 March 1907, p. 18; *Williamstown Advertiser*, 16 February 1907, p. 2.

5   *Ballarat Star*, 30 January 1907, p. 1; *Kalgoorlie Miner*, 11 February 1907, p. 3.

6   *Leader* (Melbourne), 16 February 1907, p. 36; *The Argus*, 8 February 1907, p. 5; *The Age*, 7 February 1907, p. 7; *The Tarrengower Times*, 16 March 1907, p. 2; *Weekly Times*, 16 February 1907, p. 12.

7   *The Bulletin*, 14 Feb 1907, p19.

8   *The Age*, 24 January 1907, p. 5; Nash p. 315.

9   William Sydney Robinson (1876–1963) by Peter Richardson in the *Australian Dictionary of Biography*, Volume 11, 1988. This also contains information about Joe Baillieu.

10   The story of the visit to Mount Martha comes from *If I Remember Rightly. The Memoirs of W.S. Robinson 1876–1963*. Edited by Geoffrey Blainey, F.W. Cheshire Publishing Pty Ltd, 1967, p. 27.

11   Information about the mansions and guest houses is from Mt Martha – Mornington and District Historical Society (*morningtondistricthistory.org.au*) The Porthos car was French, built in Billancourt, Seine. Robinson recorded the make of car in his memoirs, but his memory was unreliable, and it may have been a French Panhard, the same as Hoover used in Kalgoorlie.

12   *The Argus*, 23 July 1907, p. 6; *Sydney Morning Herald*, 31 July 1907, p. 11; 24 August 1907, p. 15.

13   *The Bulletin* (Sydney), 21 May 1907, p. 13.

14   *The Argus*, 10 September 1907, p. 8.

15   *Ballarat Star*, 29 October 1907, p. 3.

16   *The Bulletin* (Sydney), 26 December 1907, p. 13.

17   *Ballarat Star*, 18 December 1907, p. 3; *The Argus*, 23 March 1908, p. 10; *The Tarrengower Times*, 15 April 1908, p. 2.

18   *The Advertiser* (Adelaide), 31 January 1908, p. 8.

19   Nash p380 provides these two quotes which he found in Hoover's personal papers.

20   *The Argus*, 31 January 1908, p. 8.

Chapter 22 The Junction Dispute

1   *Ballarat Star*, 9 February 1906, p. 1; *The Argus*, 11 May 1906, p. 6; *The Age*, 20 March 1906, p. 6.

2   *Ballarat Star*, 3 April 1906, p. 6; *The Age*, 16 April 1906, p. 7.

3   *The Bendigo Independent*, 11 April 1907, p. 3.

4   *The Age*, 20 June 1906, p. 9.

5   *The Argus*, 1 August 1906, p. 10.

6   *The Argus*, 16 July 1906, p. 10.

7   *Tarrangower Times*, 8 August 1906, p. 4; 14 July 1906, p. 2.

8   *The Age*, 2 August 1906, p. 6.

9   *The Tarrengower Times*, 11 August 1906, p. 3.

10   *The Age*, 10 September 1906, p. 9; *The Tarrengower Times*, 6 October 1906, p. 2; *The West Australian*, 17 September 1906, p. 2.

11   *The Tarrengower Times*, 7 November 1906, p. 3; *The Age*, 11 October 1906, p. 6; 18 October 1906, p. 6; 23 October 1906, p. 6.

12   *The Tarrengower Times*, 13 October 1906, p. 3.

13   *The Tarrengower Times*, 13 October 1906, p. 4; 7 November 1906, p. 3.

14   *The Age*, 15 January 1907, p. 7.

15   *Leader* (Melbourne), 10 November 1906, p. 19; *The Tarrengower Times*, 14 November 1906, p. 2.

16   *The Age*, 13 December 1906, p. 6; *The Argus*, 14 December 1906, p. 8; *Weekly Times* (Melbourne), 16 February 1907, p. 18; *The Argus*, 13 February 1907, p. 6; *The Bendigo Independent*, 13 February 1907, p. 4.

17   *The Age*, 1 January 1907, p. 7.

Chapter 23 A Ghastly Failure

1   *Ballarat Star*, 14 May 1907, p. 6.
2   *Ballarat Star*, 16 February 1907, p. 1.
3   *Bendigo Advertiser*, 17 June 1907, p. 8; *Bendigo Independent*, 13 July 1907, p. 5.
4   *Ballarat Star*, 11 November 1907, p. 6; *The Argus*, 12 November 1907, p. 8.
5   *The Age*, 19 April 1908, p. 8.
6   *Tarrangower Times*, 19 January 1907, p. 2; *The Age*, 22 February 1908, p. 14.
7   *Tarrangower Times*, 16 March 1907, p. 4.
8   *The Argus*, 13 May 1907, p. 5; 17 June 1907, p. 10.
9   Monthly gold production in this period was reported in the *Ballarat Star, Bendigo Advertiser* and the *Tarrangower Times*.
10   *Mount Alexander Mail*, 2 July 1907, p. 3; *The Argus*, 1 June 1908, p. 10; *Tarrangower Times*, 19 February 1908, p. 3.
11   *Leader* (Melbourne), 22 June 1907, p. 2.
12   *Tarrangower Times*, 1 April 1908, p. 2.
13   *Tarrangower Times*, 30 May 1908, p. 3; 22 July 1908, p. 2.
14   *Mount Alexander Mail*, 10 June 1908, p. 2.
15   *Bendigo Advertiser*, 18 June 1908, p. 2; *The Age*, 29 June 1908, p. 6; *Ballarat Star*, 29 June 1908, p. 4; *The Argus*, 6 July 1908, p. 9.
16   *Ballarat Star*, 4 July 1908, p. 9; *Tarrangower Times*, 22 July 1908, p. 2.
17   *Tarrangower Times*, 4 July 1908, p. 3; *Ballarat Star*, 13 July 1908, p. 6; *The Argus*, 22 June 1908, p. 6.
18   *The Argus*, 22 September 1908, p. 8.
19   *Kalgoorlie Miner*, 4 January 1909, p. 3.

Chapter 24 If Collins Street Were a River Bed

1   *Bendigo Advertiser*, 4 August 1908, p. 3; *Ballarat Star*, 14 August 1908, p. 2; 27 October 1908, p. 6; 7 January 1909, p. 3.
2   *Bendigo Independent*, 5 August 1908, p. 3; *The Argus*, 15 July 1908, p. 10; *The Age*, 6 July 1908, p. 7.
3   *Mount Alexander Mail*, 19 August 1908, p. 4; *The Age*, 24 August 1908, p. 11; *The Argus*, 28 September 1908, p. 9; 10 September 1938, p. 7; J Lack, Sir Macpherson Robertson (1859–1945) in *Australian Dictionary of Biography*, Volume 11, 1988.
4   *Tarrangower Times*, 8 August 1908, p. 2.
5   *The Age*, 12 October 1908, p. 7; *The Argus*, 26 October 1908, p. 10; *Ballarat Star*, 9 December 1908, p. 3; 13 November 1908, p. 6; *Tarrangower Times*, 23 December 1908, p. 3; 18 November 1908, p. 3; *Mount Alexander Mail*, 17 November 1908, p. 4.
6   *Punch* (Melbourne), 4 February 1909, p. 7.
7   *The Age*, 20 November 1908, p. 5; *Ovens and Murray Advertiser*, 16 January 1909, p. 2; *Tarrangower Times*, 20 January 1909, p. 3; 3 February 1909, p. 3.
8   *Tarrangower Times*, 26 May 1909, p. 3.
9   *The Argus*, 21 August 1909, p. 20; *The Age*, 10 June 1927, p. 12.

Chapter 25 Liquidation

1   *Government Gazette of the State of NSW*, 20 January 1909, p. 414; *Tarrangower Times*, 31 March 1909, p. 2; *Mount Alexander Mail*, 19 May 1909, p. 3; *Ballarat Star*, 3 July 1909, p. 5; *The Argus*, 30 July 1909, p. 8; *Bendigo Advertiser*, 11 September 1909, p. 7.

2   *Tarrangower Times*, 6 November 1909, p. 3.

3   *Ballarat Star*, 21 October 1909, p. 5.

4   *The Argus*, 26 August 1910, p. 8; *The Age*, 15 February 1911, p. 8; *The Advertiser* (Adelaide), 30 July 1910, p. 8; *Weekly Times* (Melbourne), 28 October 1911, p. 40; *Castlemaine Mail*, 7 February 1918, p. 2.

5   *Bendigo Advertiser*, 24 February 1911, p. 3; 24 October 1910, p. 7; *The Age*, 5 September 1912, p. 11; 18 August 1913, p. 6.

6   *Weekly Times* (Melbourne) 28 May 1910, p. 39; *Ballarat Star*, 11 July 1910, p. 4; *Sydney Morning Herald*, 28 May 1913, p. 11; *Maryborough and Dunolly Advertiser*, 6 February 1914, p. 3; 23 February 1914, p. 2; 22 April 1918, p. 4.

7   *The Australasian*, 10 June 1911, p. 47; *Sheffield Daily Telegraph* (UK), 15 August 1919, p. 7.

8   *The Age*, 10 June 1927, p. 12.

Chapter 26 Afterward

1   I am grateful to John Tully and the Carisbrook Historical Society for information on some of the post-mining history of Moolort.

2   *Punch* (Melbourne), 21 September 1916, p. 7; *Jewish Herald*, 22 September 1916, p. 6; *Daily Telegraph* (Sydney), 7 July 1922, p. 7; *The Argus*, 16 November 1922, p. 12; *The Age*, 12 December 1934, p. 11; *The Sun-News Pictorial* (Melbourne), 14 May 1935, p. 5.

3   James Brown in *parliament.vic.gov.au*; James Drysdale Brown in *Australian Dictionary of Biography*.

4   John Paull 10 October 1916 in the Victoria, Australia, *Wills and Probate Records, 1841–2009*.

5   Henry Gore in *parliament.vic.gov.au*; *Ballarat Star,* 8 February 1909, p. 2.

6   A Gregory, Sir Alexander James Peacock (1861–1933) in *Australian Dictionary of Biography*, Volume 11, 1988.

7   *Western Mail* (Perth), 24 July 1909, p. 43; *Upper Murray and Mitta Herald*, 1 October 1925, p. 2; *The Age*, 6 March 1939, p. 10; D F Branagan and T G Vallance, Reginald Augustus Frederick Murray in *Australian Dictionary of Biography*, Vol 5, 1974.

8   *Kalgoorlie Miner*, 25 April 1911, p. 3; 9 September 1942, p. 2; *The Argus*, 1 July 1938, p. 10.

9   *The Argus*, 23 September 1910, p. 7; *The Age*, 24 December 1910, p. 9.

10 Personal and family Papers of Philip Lyttelton Gell in *The National Archives* UK D3287/114–131; Philip Lyttelton Gell in *Wikipedia*.

11 Waldemar Lindgren in *Wikipedia*.

12 *The Argus*, 6 January 1909, p. 7; *The Capricornian* (Rockhampton), 25 March 1911, p. 31; *The Northern Miner* (Charters Towers), 23 January 1928, p. 3.

BIBLIOGRAPHY

Books

Blainey G, *The Rush that Never Ended*, Melbourne University Press, Melbourne, 1963.

Brough Smyth R, *The Gold Fields and Mineral Districts of Victoria,* published 1869, reprinted by Queensberry Hill Press, Carlton, 1979.

Hoover HC, *The Memoirs of Herbert Hoover. Years of Adventure 1874–1920.* Macmillan, New York, 1951.

Lawrence S and Davies P, *Sludge. Disaster on Victoria's Goldfields*, Latrobe University Press, 2019.

McGeorge JHW, *Buried Rivers of Gold*, Melbourne, Hallcraft Printers, Prahran, 1966.

Nash GH, *The Life of Herbert Hoover. The Engineer 1874–1914.* WW Norton and Co. New York, 1983.

Robinson WS, *If I remember Rightly.* FW Cheshire Publishing, Melbourne, 1967.

Stacpoole HJ, *Gold at Ballarat East Goldfield*, Lowden, Kilmore, 1971.

Weston & Edwards, Maryborough (printers), *Victorian Deep Lead Mining, The Charlotte Plains Consolidated Gold Mines Limited*, Victoria, 1902.

Williams LM, *Diary of Disaster. The New Australasian Mine Tragedy* Creswick, 1882, pub Hedges and Bell, Maryborough, 1982.

Articles, Technical Papers and Pamphlets

Bradford W, *The Creswick Field, Indicator Series No 3*, Ballarat, 1902.

Crozier LA, Victoria's Gold Mines, *Chemical Engineering and Mining Review*, Dec 8, 1936.

Danvers Power F, Deep Alluvial Mining in Victoria, *The Engineering and Mining Journal*, Sept. 29, 1904, p 509.

Davey CJ and McCarthy PL, Deep Lead Mining in Victoria, *Second AusIMM Mineral Heritage Seminar*, Sydney New South Wales, July 1988.

Fitz-Gibbon B and Gizycki M, A History of Last-Resort Lending and Other Support for Troubled Financial Institutions in Australia, *Research Discussion Paper 2001–07,* System Stability Department, Reserve Bank of Australia, October 2001.

Limbaugh RH, 'There is a game against us': W.J. Loring's Troubled Years as Bewick-Moreing Company's General Manager and Partner in Western Australia, 1905–1912, *Australian Mining History Association,* Annual Conference, Kalgoorlie, 2001.

Limbaugh RH, Pragmatic Professional: Herbert Hoover's Formative Years as a Mining Engineer, 1895–1908, *Mining History Journal,* 2004, pp 43–58.

McCarthy PL, The Remarkable Life of John Phillips C.E. Mineral Surveyor, *Journal of Australasian Mining History* Vol 18, October 2021, pp 62–84.

McCarthy PL, The 1853 Canadian Gully Nuggets, Ballarat, Victoria, *Journal of Australasian Mining History* Vol 20, October 2022.

McCarthy PL, The Great Northern Junction Inrush, *The AusIMM Bulletin,* August 2011, pp 86–89.

Mouat J, Looking for Mr. Wright: A Tale of Mining Finance from the Late Nineteenth Century, *Mining History Journal,* 2003, pp 6–17.

O'Malley, GB, Deep Lead Mining in Victoria. *Chemical Engineering and Mining Review,* March 9, 1939.

Stoneman A, *Deep Leads Mines in the Central Goldfields Book 1 Majorca and Craigie,* Carisbrook Historical Society, 2014.

Stoneman A, *Deep Leads Mines in the Central Goldfields Book 2 Carisbrook,* Carisbrook Historical Society, 2014.

Stoneman A, *Deep Leads Mines in the Central Goldfields Book 3 Moolort,* Carisbrook Historical Society, 2014.

White A, The Story of the London and Globe. The Case of Whitaker Wright. *Pearsons Magazine,* June 1904, pp 557–567.

Wilkinson HL, Deep Leads of Victoria. *Trans IMM, London Vol XVII* 1907–08.

Wilkinson HL, Deep Leads of Victoria, *Victorian Institute of Engineers,* 1905.

Victorian Government Publications

Canavan F, Deep Lead Gold Deposits of Victoria, *Bulletin 62, Geological Survey of Victoria*, 1988.

Dept of Mines, Victoria. *Mining and Geological Journal*, various issues July 1937–Sept. 1952.

Annual Report of the Acting Secretary of Mines and Water Supply 1884, Government Printer, Melbourne, 1885 and 1903.

Hunter S, The Deep Leads of Victoria. *Memoirs of the Geological Survey of Victoria*, No 7, 1909.

Lidgey E, Report of Lecture on the Deep leads of Victoria and Some Indications of Ore Deposits, *Special Report of Department of Mines Victoria*, 1898.

Online Resources

Background information on many of the characters was augmented or confirmed using Ancestry.com, a subscription service.

Australian references were searched using Trove, a free archive of Australian newspapers and journals.

UK references were searched using The British Newspaper Archive, a subscription service.

www.ingramcontent.com/pod-product-compliance
Lightning Source LLC
Chambersburg PA
CBHW051433270326
41935CB00018B/1811